DATE DUE

The Green Mantle

The GREEN MANTLE

An Investigation into
Our Lost Knowledge
of Plants

MICHAEL JORDAN

CASSELL&CO

First published in the United Kingdom in 2001 by Cassell & Co
A Member of the Orion Publishing Group

Distributed in the United States of America
by Sterling Publishing Co., Inc.
387 Park Avenue South, New York, NY 10016-8810

A CIP catalogue record for this book is available from the British Library

ISBN 0 304 35589 5

Edited by Stuart Booth and Alison Copland
Picture research by Cecilia Weston-Baker
Designed by Yvonne Dedman
Indexed by Dr Caroline Ely of Indexing Specialists

Printed and bound in Slovenia by Delo Tiskarna,
by arrangement with Korotan Ljubljana d.o.o.

Cassell & Co
Wellington House
125 Strand
London WC2R 0BB

Title page: Wistman's Wood on Dartmoor in Devon is a typical
ancient Oak woodland of the uplands of southern England.

8/02

Contents

Introduction

In the winter of 1998, erosion and extreme tides on the coast of East Anglia in England laid bare an extraordinary monument to a forgotten religious belief, a circle of 56 part-fossilised Oak-hewn posts surrounding a massive tree stump that had been turned upside down and deliberately rammed into the ground. Archaeologists have calculated that the ring is 4,050 years old and therefore roughly contemporary with the early Bronze Age site of Stonehenge in Wiltshire. The tree circle was not always sited on the sea shore but was probably constructed on swampy ground some way inland. The passing centuries have seen considerable changes to the coastline of the British Isles. Over a long period of time, after falling into disuse, the circle would have sunk into the peat bog that served to preserve the wood until, at a later date, the sea rolled in and completed its concealment.

A few years ago the discovery of the circle of posts with their bizarre central focus would have earned a column in the newspaper and visits from occasional day-tripping sightseers. In the summer of 1999, however, it became the object of an impassioned stand-off between archaeologists wanting to dig it up and preserve it in a museum before the sea put paid to it for good, and New Age followers of Druidry who claimed that it represented hallowed ground that should remain untouched. The entire monument was finally moved by English Heritage in order to safeguard it from the ravages of the elements and to ensure that a proper record of the timbers was made.

Left: 'Seahenge' discovered after the tides exposed it on England's east coast at Holme-next-the-Sea in Norfolk in the winter of 1998. Thought to date from the early Bronze Age, some 4000 years ago.

For many people, trees impart an extraordinary mystical power that has not diminished down the millennia. We are drawn to their spiritual strength, and to enter a great forest is to understand that we are melding with a living thing. Our ancestors throughout Europe lived within the confines of forests that probably seemed unfathomable and endless. Within these vast wooded tracts certain trees and lesser plants of the undercanopy and forest margins took on particular spiritual significance. This transition from utilitarian to sentient happened for reasons many and varied. The sacredness of the Oak probably came about because of its enormous resilience and longevity. Whatever the precise reasons may have been, the Oak possessed great mystery and occult significance, and the symbolism of turning the central stump upside down with its roots stretching upward like gnarled and supplicating hands must have been profound. It seems that on the misty edge of history people had worshipped in this mysterious place and, perhaps, had placed bodies of the dead on the altar created by the flat root table of the upturned tree, if that is what indeed it represents. They had exposed the bodies to the elements in order to allow the flesh to decay in the open air and for the bones to be scoured clean by birds and insects thus liberating the dead person's spirit – a practice common to many tribal cultures from much later times.

The ways in which we have related with plants down the millennia since our first conscious awakening have contrasted strikingly. For a multitude of social reasons, many of which are purely utilitarian and functional, we have regularly exploited the plant kingdom. It has played, and continues to play, a fundamental role in agriculture and world economics. Yet undoubtedly in this respect we have also been careless because, for the greater span of our civilised history, we have not understood that our dependence on plants is greater than theirs upon the human race. We have been blind to the fact that plants are the ultimate survivors on which we are obliged to rely for our own existence, but the old adage that 'all flesh is grass' is literally true, and unless the plant kingdom is cared for properly it will not look after us. Life on earth began with plants and without them, if one day some dark cataclysm overruns the planet, the animal kingdom will cease to exist. Rather belatedly, we have begun to reach a new understanding and this explains, to some degree, our more recent concerns about the well-being of the plant kingdom.

We have not understood that our dependence on plants is greater than theirs upon the human race.

Today, however, another side to our relationship with the green world, largely buried in distant traditions, has started coming to the fore again. It is one based on a deeply ingrained interest that is less practical than spiritual. In the beginnings of human experience, in the time of the Ice Age hunters whose practical approach to plants was one of casual foraging, there was probably an almost total blurring of distinction between the utilitarian and mystical aspects of the natural world. Animism, the earliest form of spiritual belief, operated on the principle that each and every object in nature possessed both a tangible and an ethereal dimension and that the one could not be separated from the other, whether the primitive eye was viewing a mammoth, a mountain or a tree. We do not know the extent to which the plant world featured in the spiritual interest of the early hunters because the record that they left behind as a legacy of their beliefs is generally too occult, too esoteric.

There are, however, some clues. Even further back in prehistory, as much as 60,000 years ago, a tribe of Neanderthals left material evidence that suggests that they understood and profited from the medicinal properties of plants. More remarkable is the fact that they also buried their dead surrounded by these medicinal species. Apparently they recognised a spiritual dimension to plants. We can also reach some informed guesses by looking at the known spiritual beliefs of more recent nomadic hunters living in surroundings not dissimilar to those of our Ice Age forebears. The remote and isolated tribes of eastern Siberia, whose culture was protected until about a hundred years ago from the assault of Christian evangelism, probably took an equally casual utilitarian view of plants as a source of nuts, berries and building materials; but the limited amount of research into their customs and beliefs by ethnologists reveals that their spiritual relationship with the plant kingdom was more profound. The mythology of the Siberian tribes is richly coloured with tales of plants and trees inhabited by spirit beings that can change from human to plant form in an instant.

The sense of spirituality residing in plants arose for a number of reasons. Before the advent of agriculture, primitive societies needed a constant source of food and this could only be obtained by hunting or foraging. We tend to imagine that our prehistoric ancestors, first and foremost, were hunters. At face value this may be true, but we also need to remember that they were confronted with an immensely hostile environment, populated by wild beasts frequently larger than themselves and better equipped for defence and attack. Slaying a mammoth, an elk or an auroch with primitive weapons was strictly a hit-and-miss affair and was highly dangerous. More often than not, obtaining the week's groceries involved foraging for leaves, seeds and fruits rather than bringing home a side of meat. Through trial and error it must soon have become apparent that the consumption of some plants resulted in sickness or agonising death while others possessed curative properties. Experimentation led to another discovery with more far-reaching implications. A number of very special plants brought about trance or hallucination, which to a superstitious mind equated with transport to the spirit world.

At least some of the belief in the spiritual power of a plant lies in the earliest concepts about the nature and source of rain, which was recognised to be a far more powerful substance than mere drops of water falling from the sky. Today, we view such quaint ideas with condescension, but we need to remember that primitive people walked the green world without any understanding of the science we take for granted. No technology and no microscopes were at their disposal. The birth of a plant must constantly have been a thing of mystery and wonderment because the act of botanical procreation does not happen visibly. The minute grains of pollen plunging deep into the ovary to ejaculate their life-giving germs were innocent flecks of dust on the breeze. Yet with each spring thaw a new coat of green emerged from the once frozen and dead earth. By what secret and magical intercourse had this mantle germinated and grown in the womb of the soil? The nomadic hunter would look, instinctively, to the gentle spring rains falling from the sky as the heavens darkened with the presence of the creator spirits. The logic followed that since these 'existences' are the source of the rain, the semen of the celestial gods, then every plant is of their creation. The green world, in the eyes of such a person, immediately takes on a special kind of ethos.

As understanding advanced and the development of language allowed us to communicate and preserve our knowledge with a greater degree of elaboration, our early ancestors discovered more about their environment and communities began to cultivate rather than forage for plants. At the same time they also began to distinguish between, and distance one from another, the utilitarian and the sentient. New rationales allowed for a plethora of mystery and magic to arise based on the changing of the seasons, and these advances in awareness spawned entire religions focused on the plant world. Gods and goddesses of the green mantle reached the top of the celestial ladder. Plants now began to exert a profound influence on the evolution of human society in so many ways beyond the provision of food, clothing, weapons, warmth and construction materials. They were poised to take on a vital role in culture, religion, healing and herbalism. They featured as objects of simple vicarious pleasure and also in the magic arts; when they contained powerful hallucinogens, they transported the most elite members of society, the shamans, out of themselves so that they too might climb the stairways of the heavens.

We have little more to go on, as far as the prehistoric eras are concerned, other than snippets of information from archaeology and, perhaps, analogy with modern primitive tribes (though this has its drawbacks and is far from conclusive). Much more information about early civilisation's attitude to plants can be trawled from Mesopotamian and Egyptian records and from the writings of European classical authors. The Greeks and Romans were thoroughly familiar with the sentient aspects of the plant world in ways that, today, we have largely forgotten. This knowledge was transmitted throughout the empires of Greece and Rome and continued to filter down in the writings of classical authors long after political and military influence had waned. Throughout the medieval centuries, plants were relied on as sources of medicine and magical cure and often, in the absence of more sophisticated understanding, the two aspects were inextricably bound together.

The plant kingdom, with all its mysteries and strange powers, has always been the perfect candidate to acquire a rich clothing of superstition. Sometimes evidence of an age-old esoteric view can be detected in the common name of a plant. This is generally descriptive of associations, appearance or properties and such names can often be traced back to ancient times. The Black Henbane (*Hyoscyamus niger*) is a poisonous herb that was well known in northern Europe. Records extend from the era of the Anglo-Saxons but the plant and its powers had probably been recognised for many centuries before, in word-of-mouth traditions. Its first recorded English name, from about 1000 CE, is 'Henbell'. The name was coined in part because of the bell-shaped calyx of the flower and in part because *H. niger* tends to grow on middens and rubbish heaps where hens traditionally enjoy scratching about. The title was destined to change, however, and by 1398 writers were referring to the plant as 'Hennebone'. The epithet 'bone' is not, as one might imagine, a reference to skeletal appearance but an Old English form of the word 'bane' which implies a source of poison or a cause of evil. Chickens were seen to fall sick and die when they ate the seeds, and doubtless in this way society discovered that the plant possessed a dangerously poisonous nature. This knowledge soon stimulated all kinds of lore and superstition, particularly when it was discovered that the plant, used in controlled quantities, also delivered a narcotic effect. The Latin name *Hyoscyamus* is based on a strange, yet not wholly inaccurate, idea that the gods favour certain animals with immunity. In the case of Henbane, the idea was a simple misconception, promoted by a Greek herbalist. *Hyoscyamus* is derived from the Greek *hyoskyamos*, a word resulting from the combination of *hys* meaning a hog, and *knamos*, a bean, hence 'hogbean'. Why? Because it was believed, erroneously, by the 1st-century classical Greek herbalist Dioscorides that pigs could eat the poisonous seeds without harm. In the text of his work *De materia medica*, he also referred to an alternative name *dioskyamos*, which means 'bean of the gods'. This probably stems from an early ritual exploitation of the plant's capacity to render a person delirious or senseless when exposed to the fumes of the burned leaves or seeds. The specific epithet *niger*, meaning black, is also a clue to the dangerous nature of the herb. It relates to a bygone folk belief that the colour black equated with death and that if any part of a dangerously poisonous plant was to touch the skin the flesh would turn black and rot.

We might be tempted to believe that spiritual interest in the green mantle has been swept away by modern science, but such a quick assumption would be an oversight. Notwithstanding our apparent technological sophistication, much of the interest is still with us even if its true origins and meanings are sometimes heavily disguised. The utilitarian, the sentient and the various shades ranging between these two extremes are self-evident and occasionally paradoxical. Plants synthesise the deadliest poisons, yet if there are ever to be effective cures for diseases such as Alzheimer's, AIDS and cancer they will probably come from synthesised copies of natural plant extracts. Some of the most valuable plants on earth are used in the cosmetics industry. The commercial value of the opium poppy industry, worldwide, is probably as great as that of wheat production. Today we still send the dead on their journey to the unknown with flowers heaped over their coffins, much as those distant Neanderthals did 60,000 years ago.

The edges between the mystical and the scientifically proven also remain stubbornly blurred. We willingly accept claims that pills and potions including *Ginkgo biloba* and *ginseng* will prolong our active life; we buy shampoo containing exotic plant extracts of questionable benefit to our hair; and some of us probably still believe that carrots will help us see in the dark. On the other hand, many associations which originated in folklore possess more than a ring of truth. Where would we be today without penicillin or aspirin?

Yet, as the millennium turns, another element, something infinitely more profound, has resurfaced in our human consciousness. Probably for the first time since that distant era when the Bronze Age inhabitants of East Anglia raised their Oak monument to some arcane God, perhaps even since the era of the Palaeolithic hunters, we have begun to retrace our spiritual romance with the green mantle. We are moving back towards merging the utilitarian and the mystical into a seamless whole.

The recent furore over the removal of the East Anglian tree circle reflects a bond that is not merely non-material, religious and esoteric but a primeval instinct that has

survived down an immense passage of time. It is a product of the same enduring sensitivity that has caused so many people to rebel against the spread of genetically modified crops, an adverse reaction that surely goes beyond mere concern about poisoning ourselves or generating some Triffid-like menace. It is not too hard to find other illustrations of this same blurring of the edges. How often do we now see television images of the most conservative members of society sitting down to obstruct the passage of new roads through swathes of ancient greenery?

For a pithy illustration of the ambiguity in our modern attitude to plants we probably need look no further than the Norway Spruce (*Picea abies*). It epitomises much of the diverse relationship between humanity and plants, which not only affects our lives at the start of the 3rd millennium but has done so since the earliest times. This rather unprepossessing evergreen serves two strongly contrasting functions. It is extensively cultivated in forest plantations throughout the cooler regions of the northern hemisphere for timber which is used in a variety of manufacturing industries from paper production to door frames. Yet it enjoys an alternative role that is bereft of utilitarian

Above: A sea of floral tributes laid on the lawn of Kensington Palace, London, as symbols of national mourning after the death of Diana, Princess of Wales in August 1997.

value but possesses an immense mystique. Each year in Europe alone our collective wallet parts with more than £20 million in order to bring into our homes at midwinter an immature stage of a trenchant symbol that life endures when the rest of nature seems dead. We carefully drape it with baubles, tinsel and coloured lights and revere it until the sixth day of the New Year when we abandon it to the rubbish heap and the bonfire.

At the dawn of the 21st century, as we predate with increasing ferocity upon the world's green mantle, there exists an irony in that we are probably more acutely aware of human dependence on plants and of their increasing vulnerability than we have ever been during the span of our conscious awareness. Yet we persist in behaviour towards the plant kingdom that is both alarming and contradictory. On the plus side we have developed such innovative and forward-looking programmes as the Eden Foundation in West Africa. In the more contentious 'grey area' we have begun the exploitation of genetically modified crops. In thoroughly negative vein we pursue our destruction of the green mantle at an ever-increasing rate, from depletion of England's hedgerows to the hewing down of the planet's vital tropical rainforests. We continue to satisfy our selfish demand for needless indulgences such as walnut-veneered offices, teak stereo cabinets and mahogany lavatory seats. We fail to invest funds in promotion of sustainable third-world farming methods less destructive to the environment than slash-and-burn, a practice of convenience, which often causes irreversible damage to natural vegetation and hitherto stable plant habitats.

Through the following chapters we shall explore the largely spiritual, often 'dark', side of our long inter-relationship with the plant world, starting from the first known evidence provided by archaeology and concluding in the present day.

Left: 'The Christmas Tree', a woodcut by the German
artist Karl Girardet (1813–71) and typical of 19th-century
European romanticism.

CHAPTER I

The First Awakening

O ne of the most famous pieces of art from the Ice Age, some 15,000 years old, is the so-called Montgaudier baton from southwest France. Engraved in mammoth ivory, it contains a small scene depicting the coming of spring. The 'baton' includes migrating eels, some young grasses and even a tiny, delicate flower bud. It was found at a time when the world was thrilling to discovery of the great painted caverns in the Dordogne and, beside their grandeur, the baton seems barely significant. The walls of the caverns, memorials at the misty edge of prehistory, served as a canvas that was to record the aspirations of prehistoric man. They stand not only as the world's earliest known art galleries but reflect a reverence for the natural environment that we, in our cocooned, technological world, can scarcely imagine. The enduring 'mother tongue' of primitive awareness is art and, today, much of our knowledge about the beliefs and understanding of our earliest forebears is gained from that remarkable outpouring of scratching, painting, sculpture and engraving which archaeology has only recently brought to light.

The subjective creations of hand and eye that have survived the passage of time from the last Ice Age best reveal the spirituality of people who lived before the advent of the written word and the recording of history. We should, therefore, begin our search for the earliest view of the green mantle among these remarkable and arcane galleries created in the geological periods known as the Aurignacian and Magdalenian.

Left: The lives of ancient peoples were inextricably linked to the natural world, as the 15,000-year-old depictions of extinct aurochs show, in the famous paleolithic wall paintings found in the Lascaux cavern in the Dordogne region of south-west France.

We are not exactly spoilt for choice when we start out at this point in time because, although at the known outset art focused on the natural world and indulged in some subtle copying of twigs and leaves, it reflects, in the main, a passionate interest in drawing animals. First and foremost, the people of the Ice Age were hunters. Their realm was a brutal wilderness without frontiers, where the plough and the field of grain were unknown and the core of existence lay with the reindeer and mammoth, bison and horse. Animals were the preferred choice. They were also imbued with status and therefore their more esoteric importance swelled out of proportion to their practical value. It is the paradox that survival may more often than not have lain with the gathering of leaves, seeds, nuts and berries.

Much Palaeolithic art was engraved not on the walls of caverns but on pebbles and bones, and this 'portable' art, though less dramatic than the canvases of the great caves, reinforces the message of a deep and sensitive awareness of nature. In all of these smaller works, however, only fleeting hints emerge of the plant world. Artists incorporated a limited amount of plant design into their work, perhaps more for decorative purposes than to convey some esoteric message.

Hence, such fragments as the Montgaudier baton are rare treasures. In its depiction of an Ice Age spring, the baton clearly reflects a renaissance of tremendous importance to people who must often have believed that the intense cold of the nine-month winter permafrost, when the natural world seemed dead, would never end. The people of the Ice Age did not benefit from calendars, so they could not predict when the green mantle would return to the world. The spring thaw coincided with migrations of animals, but this very rarely took place at the same time each year. This was a spiritual renaissance and, looking at its unpredictability, one begins to understand how Stone Age people could believe that the life of plants was, literally, 'in the lap of the gods'.

The Montgaudier baton is a simple composition that lacks human presence and appears not to possess deeper meaning. Of greater significance, perhaps, is an engraved bone fragment from the same period found at Les Eyzies in southwest France. It includes the front end of a bison with a procession of nine figures walking between trees that look like leafless Alders. There are somewhat similar winter trees engraved on an Ice Age bone fragment found in a cave at Bruniquel.

What did such things represent to artists who lived in a world separated from our own by such an immense passage of time? We can do little more than guess and make tentative comparison with the customs of Stone Age tribes living today. There is, unfortunately, no argument to be won that because a 21st-century tribe adopts certain attitudes towards plants it is following a tradition going back into prehistory. The passage of time is generally far too great, but also those early tribesmen were part of a progressive society possessing great energy and curiosity in a new and unfamiliar world. Their modern counterparts are generally in a state of active decline and, for this reason, their outlook is totally different. In the absence of any better way forward, however, analogies with the cultures of present-day Aborigines, academically fraught as they may be, are still worth drawing.

During the year of 1900 an American-Swedish ethnologist, Waldemar Jochelson, elected to live in one of the remotest parts of eastern Siberia among a primitive Iron Age tribe. As part of the research, sponsored by the American Society for Natural History, Jochelson was to investigate the culture of this ethnically distinct group of nomadic hunters before it was lost for ever. The clan was to be selected as a social group, in effect, untouched by the outside world and living in an environment similar to that which we know to have been experienced by the prehistoric Stone Age hunters of the Ice Age.

Jochelson discovered a clan with precisely the required qualifications living just beneath the Arctic Circle in the uncompromising wilderness of the Kamchatka Peninsula that stretches out from the northern Asiatic land mass like a knobbly artichoke and continues in an archipelago towards the islands of Japan. These hunter-gatherers were the Koryaks. They roamed through a vast area of mountain, steppe and rocky coast eking out a cold, harsh existence as hunters of seal, white whale and reindeer, and their approach to life seems to epitomise that of many other Siberian tribes.

The Koryaks viewed plants, in one sense, in a utilitarian capacity and in this they shared some common practices with the Ice Age hunter-gatherers. Sometimes they did more than forage casually for nuts and berries, because they dug ice pits into which vegetables such as Rosebay Willow Herb (*Epilobium angustifolium*) were packed and stored for preservation through the long dark winter months. Palaeontologists searching for evidence of domestic activities from 15,000 years ago have found the remains of similar storage pits in areas that would once have been covered with permafrost for most of the year. This utilitarian interest in plants, however, was inextricably bound up with a spiritual one that was probably also shared by the Palaeolithic hunters and their modern counterparts.

The art of the Siberian tribes reveals little interest in artistic drawing of plants, but the mythology, an aspect of prehistoric culture that we will never know very well, tells an altogether different story. In Siberian legend, for example, a tree exists that sprang up initially without branches. The Koryak creator spirit, Tenanto'mwan, caused nine branches to shoot from the trunk and nine men were fashioned at its foot, ancestors of nine races that populated the world. On the tree, five of the branches provided fruit for humankind and the animals; the other four bore fruit that men were not permitted to eat. This aspect of the legend is clearly a tradition that has become adulterated with the Christian mythology of the Paradise garden and its forbidden fruit. Yet it is tempting to ponder whether the leafless tree and its nine human offspring are part of an understanding stretching back over tens of thousands of years and linking with an anonymous Ice Age artist scratching a scene onto a small piece of bone.

Waldemar Jochelson spent much of his time collecting the myths and legends of the Siberian Koryaks and it is these stories that provide the greater insight into how primitive people view the green mantle. They reveal a world in which plants are richly imbued with mystique. In the eye of the hunter-gatherer everything in nature is included in a common frame in which he himself sometimes seems less an integral facet than an outside observer bound by the often claustrophobic prison of his own

An engraving which shows a family of Siberian nomads in 1900
in the northern tundra of Russia.

physical and mental limitations. Every natural object is also 'alive' or animate. Modern sociology has coined the term *animism* to identify this kind of fundamental belief in which the natural world is perceived to include both earthly and spirit form. This is not entirely hard to understand since it is a logical extension of the awareness of a two-fold nature that primitive man already recognises in himself. He sees everything around him as part of a huge and constantly varying chain in which every object, living or inanimate, is a link. The links, however, are fluid and can be changed one into another. The power to make these changes comes from the spirit world. A spirit can turn in an instant into a flower, a deer, a tree, a log of wood or even a wraith of morning mist. Nothing can be presumed from appearances!

In the understanding of the Siberian tribesman, the green world is richly inhabited by spirits, though these ethereal beings are rather vaguely drawn. They are not described in any measure of detail other than earning general names that tally with the trees or herbs with which they are associated. Hence one finds personalities like Grass Woman or Root Man. This vagueness is to be found throughout primitive cultures, though sometimes the physical features of a plant lend to stories about its unseen nature. A story recited to Jochelson in a village on the shores of the Bering Sea, its ending obscure and perhaps muddled, is not untypical. It tells of a powerful shaman, Quikinn.a'qu (Big Raven) in one of his frequent meetings with the spirit people of the trees. The spirits of this particular tale lived in a Stone Pine conifer (*Pinus cembra*), a species that grows extensively in the Alps, the Carpathians and the Siberian ranges. The oily seeds are nutritious and the wood itself possesses a fine, even grain for woodcarving.

> Quikinn.a'qu went to the woods and, finding a stone-pine cone, pounded it with a stone. Out of the stone-pine cone came a girl with a head like a copper tea-pot. Quikinn.a'qu said, 'Oh. What a pretty little girl.' 'Do you say that I am pretty? Mama says, come into the house.' The house was a twisted stone-pine and the sleeping room was in the hollow of the bough. He entered the house. 'I am very hungry – open the old woman's abdomen.' He opened it and looked in. Behold! it was full of the meat of a mountain sheep, all nice and fat. He fell to eating, choked himself and died. That's all.
>
> (After Jochelson)

The story reveals a very ancient ritual associated with trees wherein the tree is decorated and hung or filled with meat and other offerings to its spirit guardian. It also suggests that the shaman, Quikinn.a'qu, was punished by death for taking the sacrifice due to the tree spirit. We know from separate sources that other tribes in earlier times flayed the skins from captives and hung these in the branches of trees overlooking sacred groves.

To us, living in the 21st century, such notions as belief in plants with spirit guardians and magical powers may seem quaint, but we need to remember that the world of the primitive nomadic hunter was, and still is, very far removed from ours. Notions of spirituality also follow wholly different principles but our view of them has too often been coloured by the biased attitudes of the Christian establishment. For many hundreds of years the dogma and doctrine of Christianity denied that any credible spiritual belief existed before that detailed in the Bible, in other words before Abraham 'saw the light' of true faith. Primitive religion should, so conventional under-standing dictated, more properly be described as sympathetic magic. This is defined as a performance purely dictated by certain prescribed formulae. The truth, however, is that we cannot possibly say whether or not the prehistoric hunters had a rationalised faith. In these more enlightened and open-minded times, it is difficult to avoid the conclusion that they may have developed and used a formalised kind of religion in ways not far removed from those that we employ today. Like us, they seem to have felt the urge to hypostatise the spirit world into some kind of form and substance. This is a need that is as true today as it was 30,000 years ago, the only real difference lying in the logic that is employed. To an observer from another planet, reverence to a tree trunk and reverence to an image of Christ fashioned from a tree trunk might seem to bear little more than academic distinction.

Reverence to a tree trunk and reverence to an image of Christ fashioned from a tree trunk might seem to bear little more than academic distinction.

Trees or parts of trees have been turned by many primitive cultures into totems — the outward symbols of an unseen presence. Use of wood to symbolise the presence of spirits was familiar to the Koryaks of Jochelson's acquaintance and other north European tribes at the turn of the last century. Some of the Koryaks who frequented the coasts of the Kamchatka Peninsula earned their livelihood from the sea, hunting seal and whale. These clans erected carved wooden pillars called *kamaks* on the seashore in the belief that the spirits that resided in them would encourage the whales to swim close inshore. A small version of the *kamak*, known as a *kalak*, worked as a personal guardian for children. The *kalak*, carved to represent a watchful face, was tied to the child's back with a piece of string and if the child became dangerously ill, so that its soul wandered off, the face would find the soul, catch it and put it back. The same whaling clans took forked twigs of Alder, which they carved into a vaguely human outline and then placed, as spirit guardians, in the bows of their newly built skin-and-wattle boats. Further west, another Siberian tribe, the Yukaghir, believed that their ancestral spirit guardians resided in the trees. A twin-headed guardian deity of their tents, called the Nganasan, was represented by a carefully selected piece of forked wood in which the forks gave the impression of two stylised heads. The Yukaghir also invoked their ancestor spirits by carving crude images called *can-coro'mo*. Each figure was created from a flat board, about a metre in length, with a notch at the 'neck' to separate head from body, a deep incision for a rudimentary mouth and a split along part of the length to represent legs. These images were hung in trees of the forest, on mountain paths that generally passed through the old tribal hunting grounds.

It is easy to see why trees, because of their size and longevity, became places of the spirits, but what was it about other plants that caused early man to single them out as sacred? We can be reasonably sure that the hunter-gatherers first used leaves and roots for food, as well as timber for tools, weapons and shelter, in a purely practical fashion. Eating greenery must have involved a very prolonged process of observing the types of vegetation browsed on safely by animals and noting the behaviour patterns of wild beasts with different trees, shrubs and herbs. Trial and error among more adventurous members of society added to this knowledge at first hand and no doubt resulted in frequent tragedy before a basic 'checklist' emerged of what was and was not good to put in one's belly. Early man would have discovered during this process of self-education that certain leaves or bark, when chewed, alleviated symptoms of headache and toothache. When he injured himself and reached for leaves or moss to staunch the blood he would have learned, over a period of time, that certain plants gave protection against infection and speeded up the healing process.

Archaeology has provided a fascinating insight into the level of knowledge achieved, tens of thousands of years earlier and in a place far removed from the painted caverns of southwest France. In 1960 the skeletons of a group of Neanderthals were exhumed from what seems to have been a burial chamber in a cave sited deep in the mountains of northern Iraq. The remains were subjected to radiocarbon dating and it was established that they were not less than 60,000 years old. One among them was a man who seems to have been accorded special rites and was perhaps a chieftain. When the dust around the remains of this individual was analysed under the

microscope, large numbers of pollen grains were identified, suggesting that the man had been laid to rest surrounded by flowers. Some of the pollen deposits were in large clumps that could not have blown into the cave on the wind.

Two aspects of the burial are striking. Firstly, it was an organised interment – the body of the man had not been 'dumped' but was carefully arranged in a foetal position with his head resting on his hands and a ring of stones that created a form of niche surrounded him. Secondly, and no less importantly, the identity and nature of the flowers are significant, because they can all still be found listed in the modern herbal *Materia Medica*. They included Ragwort and Groundsel, both of which are plants specified for healing of infected or inflamed wounds. The pollen of Thistle and Grape Hyacinth was also present in the cave, as was that of Hollyhock and Yarrow. The 1st-century CE Greek physician and herbalist, Dioscorides, who compiled one of the best known of the early medical books, rated the juice of Groundsel highly for healing. In his *Complete Herbal*, the 17th-century English physician and astrologer Nicholas Culpeper extolled the juice of Ragwort as being 'singular good to heal green wounds'. Culpeper also described ointment made from Yarrow to be no less effective in the treatment of infected wounds, while Hollyhock has been of value in treating fever.

Above: Flowers of Ragwort (*Senecia jacobea*). Seeds of the species were found associated with the burial of a Neanderthal in a cave at Shanidar, Northern Iraq, and may have been recognized as having medicinal value.

One can surmise that the Neanderthal recipient of the flower burial was a victim of a local attack or that he had succumbed as the prey of the animals that he hunted. His wounds had become infected and gangrenous and this had cost him his life. He had been sent on a journey to the other world equipped with the herbs that would allow his spirit the best chance of recovery.

During our prehistoric ancestors' tentative excursions into pharmacology, certain plants would inevitably have been recognised to possess very special properties. Among the whale-hunting Koryaks who travelled the edges of Penzhinskaya Bay, Waldemar Jochelson recorded a legend concerning such a 'plant' that also reveals one of the key elements in the more occult view of primitive people towards the plant world:

> Quikinn.a'qu caught a whale, but could not send it to its home in the sea. He was unable to lift the grass bag containing travelling provisions for the whale. Quikinn.a'qu called to Tenanto'mwan to help. Tenanto'mwan said, 'Go to a level place near the sea; there you will find soft white stalks with spotted hats. These are spirits, the Wapag. Eat some and they will help thee.' Quikinn.a'qu went to the place that Tenanto'mwan had told him of and meanwhile Tenanto'mwan spat on the Earth. Out of his saliva at the place where it fell, fungus appeared which Quikinn.a'qu found and ate, and began to feel gay. He started to dance and the Wapag spirits of the fungus said to him, 'How is it that though being such a strong man, thou can'st not lift the bag?'
>
> 'That is right,' said Quikinn.a'qu. 'I am a strong man. I shall go and lift the travelling bag.' He went and lifted the bag and sent the whale home. The Wapag showed him the whale going out to sea and how it returned to its brothers and sisters. Quikinn.a'qu said, 'Let the fungus remain on earth and let my children see what it will show them.'
>
> (After Jochelson)

From very early times it seems we have known that certain plants possess the capacity to transport us out of ourselves, to allow us to perform feats of physical strength, to see that which would otherwise be hidden from us. Today we recognise them, more prosaically, as hallucinogens, but to primitive people such plants are governed by immense powers of magic. The white stalks with spotted hats were in fact the fruiting bodies of a fungus species known as Fly Agaric (*Amanita muscaria*) that secretes a range of hallucinogens. The cap of the species displays a striking appearance with pure white patches on a brilliant red background, and Fly Agaric has long been used by shamans to enter a state of trance. Technically fungi are not true plants but the tribesmen of Kamchatka were hardly versed in botanical know-how and in their eyes mushrooms constituted an integral part of the vegetation of the forests. Considerable significance was attached, no doubt, to the fact that these strange and sometimes phallic-shaped growths generally appeared shortly after rain had fallen. In the legend of the whale's travelling bag the rain was not envisaged as celestial semen but as the spittle of the creator spirit, Tenanto'mwan, from which the fungi were spawned. Nonetheless the sentiment expressed remains more or less the same since the breath of gods and goddesses has often been imagined to have a procreative capacity.

To a person with limited understanding the latent energy of the herbs and fungi that secrete these drugs in their tissues would have been as enormous as the power of the atom. They could unlock the door to the heavens and the esoteric knowledge of them could place men of intelligence and vision infinitely higher than their peers. It was an energy that demanded it should be used in a proper way and then only by a privileged group of people. This elite, we can guess, was made up of the tribal shamans, the oldest form of the priest and witch, whose job it was to enter trance-like intercession with the powers of the spirit world. The purpose of the shaman was, and always has been, to stand as the honest broker between the world of the supernatural and temporal earth. These are the men and women of special intelligence and dexterity who see that which ordinary people are unable to see, and who mediate with the spirits and with the birds, animals and trees whose form these invisible and ethereal beings take on. The special and magically empowered herbs that synthesise hallucinogenic drugs in their tissues became the gateways to the unseen spirit world. Not surprisingly, their powers became jealously guarded and the plants took on an esoteric mystique. They became a subject of taboos, which demanded that they were to be left strictly alone by ordinary people lest their powers should become dissipated and commonplace. The taboos, in turn, generated a folklore.

The magic fungus was a basic element of Koryak culture, but there is no evidence that it ever appeared in the art of the Koryaks. For all its importance, had it not been for men like Waldemar Jochelson, all trace of its use would have vanished. It is more or less impossible, on the strength of current archaeological evidence, to know whether the early 'cavemen' discovered hallucinogens in the plants growing around him before other kinds of naturally occurring medicines, but it is probably safe to assume that the two went hand-in-glove. Such plants, or species like them, evolved in Europe soon after the last Ice Age, and it seems unlikely that objects of such striking appearance would go unchallenged by curiosity. It must therefore be a probability that the earliest hunter-gatherers found their own doors to the spirit world through the power of magic plants, but that they too chose not to describe such things in their art.

We can make such assumptions, in part, because it seems that our spiritual attitudes towards plants tend to find parallels the world over when human society is at comparable stages of development, irrespective of the period of history in which this takes place. To a quite remarkable extent primitive cultures share a common awareness of their surroundings, and they discover a similar mystery and magic in the plant world. They interpret the mystique of the green mantle in comparable ways.

Jochelson achieved a limited insight into the spiritual beliefs of modern hunter-gatherers, not possible when we attempt to investigate the beliefs of our Ice Age ancestors, because he was able to obtain privileged access to some of the Koryak folk-lore. Even so it was difficult at times to tell where ancient culture left off and Russianisation began. Myths and legends were becoming muddled and once-respected shamans were increasingly being ousted to the fringes of influential society. Through the work of ethnologists in other parts of the world, however, we now know that the reverence attached to plants made sacred by an accident of their chemistry is not restricted to Siberian tribes. It happens universally and involves many plants other than Fly Agaric to which the Koryak legend of the whale's travelling bag refers. Yet, in spite of their influence, note of such plants hardly finds its way into the records of shamanistic practices. Ethnologists have reported that a plant known as Pitchuri (*Duboisia hopwoodii*) has been used in initiation ceremonies for Aborigine shamans in Australia because it contains hallucinogens that allow the initiate to experience the presence of spirits. Such insights, however, are rare.

The Fly Agaric achieved its magical lore because its tissues happen to produce hallucinogens, but the value of the plant can be more utilitarian. The Aborigines of northern Queensland believed in an ancestor spirit being, known as Mangrove Woman. During the Dreamtime she had taught people how to grind the Mangrove seed into flour before she was attacked by her brother, Wolkolan, the bony bream, who pierced her head with one of his spines. She ran away with the spine embedded in her head and eventually she found a sacred place by the sea where she laid herself down and became a Mangrove plant, its pods sticking out from the flower petals like a spear. A not dissimilar folklore is attached to the ancestor spirit of the Sweet Potato, known as Yam Woman.

Sometimes unusual physical attributes of a plant have led to their own mystery and lore. Aborigines also have a tree called the *kurrajong* or 'water tree'. Its roots retain water better than other trees during periods of drought and, in an emergency, they can be

Overleaf: Chumash cave paintings in the Californian coastal region, created by shamans high on the hallucinogenic plant drug peyote.

used as an emergency water source. The clans living in central Australia created a story to explain this phenomenon:

> Two brothers owned a water carrier made out of a kangaroo skin and when the drought came they prudently filled it. While one brother was away hunting the other was overcome by thirst. In his haste to drink he spilled the water which gushed out to form a great flood in which both brothers drowned. The birds, concerned at the spreading inundation, built a dam using the roots of the Kurrajong, which absorbed all the water and stemmed the flood.

It is the deep-rooted tribal belief that plants are inhabited by unseen spirits that has made the harvesting and eating of plants a somewhat hazardous affair which must be made safe by ritual. Largely for this reason, a number of tribal societies, including several North American Indian tribes, have observed solemn ceremonies before eating the first fruits of the season, irrespective of whether these are wild or cultivated. The body of the plant is believed occupied by an unseen guardian spirit, which must be placated before part of the plant's tangible form is cut down and used.

One of the more obvious potential sources of information to draw on about the mystique of plants is that of the North American Aborigine clans. The records of a tribe that once roamed the northwest of British Columbia, the Thompson Indians, reveal that they treated the root of an edible sunflower-type plant, *Balsamorrhiza sagittata*, with considerable reserve. The plant was thought to be the tangible form of a spirit being and so there was a list of taboos attached to its collection and preparation. The women who dug it up and cooked it were not allowed to engage in sexual intercourse for a period of time before and after collection and men were obliged to keep a distance from the oven where the roots were baked. When the root was to be eaten, an invocation was sent to the guardian spirit of the plant asking permission to include what was regarded as a tangible part of its body with the meal. With similar sentiment, Creek and Seminole Indians once followed a curious ritual that involved swallowing a purgative before eating the first sacred meal of new corn, the intention being to rid the stomach first of any impurities that might be contained in the everyday food.

Many of the Indian tribes have lived as nomadic hunters, following herds of bison (buffalo). While traditions among the clans such as the Sioux, Comanche, Blackfoot, Crow, Apache and others indicate very little by way of interest in plants other than spasmodic growing of tobacco, others recognise a plant mystique associated with hunting. This underlines the view of many Indian tribes that all plants are sacred,

brought to earth by sky spirits and nurtured by the Earth Mother. At the celebration of the winter solstice, when the plant world appears dead and there is a greater reliance on hunting, the Zuni tribesmen tie prayer plumes, made from the feathers of various birds such as eagle and duck, to twigs of the Salt Bush (*Atriplex canescens*). These are offered to the spirit of the Cottontail rabbit in order that the animal may emerge in large numbers.

The tribes who lived, pre-colonisation, in more permanent settlements or pueblos, such as the Zuni and Hopi, once irrigated and farmed parts of the arid landscape of New Mexico and northeastern Arizona. They have more to offer in plant-focused rites. They have also resisted the degradation of their culture by Christian missionaries, although Roman Catholic influence has been directed at them since the early part of the 17th century.

Most of the pueblo-living Indians revere the forces of nature, the rain and in particular the power of the sun, life-giving but also immensely destructive. The Sun Father is the great deity of the Zuni who rules in partnership with the White Shell

Above: The flowers of Balsam (*Balsamorrhiza sagittata*) growing in the foothills of the Bridger Mountains. The plant is revered by the Thompson Indians of British Columbia.

Bead Mother. It is she who commands the Rain God to bring relief from the fierce drought of summer. In order to appease the Sun God and the White Shell Bead Mother, the High Priest conducts rain-making ceremonies, which include the ritual use of certain plants. As an integral part of invocation, the priest presents flowers of the Evening Primrose (*Anogra albicaulis*) to young girls before they perform a ceremonial dance known as the 'Coming of the Corn Maidens'. The petals are chewed and the girls smear the yellow juice over their bodies. During the dance they also carry sprigs of Wild Sage (*Artemisia frigida*), mixed with ears of maize. The significance of these species is not entirely clear, though the colour of the Evening Primrose blooms may represent the sun and, in Europe, *Artemisia* has long been associated with midsummer.

The idea of a partnership between a god and goddess who control the forces of nature and the world of plants and animals probably extends back to prehistoric times. It has to be said here that a degree of misconception clouds our understanding, not least because of the wave of neo-pagan romanticism that began to capture the imaginations of Europeans early in the 19th century. It became fashionable to claim that there had been a universal mother goddess, the so-called 'corn goddess' or 'earth mother', whose son and lover suffered annual death and rebirth to coincide with the harvesting of the corn and springtime germination in the fields. The concept, it has been argued, arose in the ancient Near East and spread across Europe. The ubiquitous goddess was associated with the moon and she was the apotheosis of the earth itself. For a time during the 1950s even some eminent archaeologists in Britain backed the argument. The idea provides a rather romantic antithesis to Christianity with its male-dominated hierarchy and its emphasis on a heaven somewhere up in the sky as distinct from on earth among the greenery (artists have favoured drawing the celestial realms decked with fluffy pink clouds and staffed by winged angels).

The notion is also a gross simplification. Claims of the existence of a single motherly goddess who was all things to all people and merely went under different regional names are thoroughly tenuous and without solid archaeological or historical support. There is widespread evidence of goddess cults existing during prehistory, particularly during the Neolithic period, and there is some support for the argument that the protagonists of these earth mothers were somewhat frenetic male figures possessing inexhaustible reservoirs of libido. Yet it is impossible to establish whether the protagonists were interpreted in the same way from clan to clan.

Dance, too, seems to have formed an integral part of tribal ritual invoking these deities from far back in prehistory. Evidence of a male fertility spirit (or of a shaman impersonating such a spirit) can be seen in images like the so-called 'Sorcerer' drawn in some of the painted caverns in the Dordogne region of southwest France. The best known of these is the half-man/half-beast engraved on a cave wall in the Trois Frères system in the Vezere valley. This figure appears to be engaged in some kind of frenetic dance.

Dancing has also formed a key element of the rites of North American Indians, not only the hunting tribes of the great plains but also those whose religious festivals are tied very closely with the changing seasons and with key points in the farming year. The Creek Indians of Alabama and Georgia, mostly living along rivers and creeks from which they earned their title from white settlers, have traditionally farmed maize and other crops. One of their key religious ceremonies has been the annual husk or greencorn dance to celebrate the ripening of the crop.

Not all dancing invocations of the spirits of nature, however, centre around plants, even though the purpose may be to ensure a good harvest. Both the Zuni and the Hopi grow maize, beans, squash and fruit. Like the Zuni, the Hopi also recognise an all-important Rain God, but their rites to the supernatural powers include a spectacular rite known as the Snake Dance. This is celebrated once every two years, close to the third week in August, and performed after eight days of ceremonies, most of which are still held in secret. The snake is considered to be the brother of the Hopi people and to have special powers of intercession with the spirit world; the Snake Dance represents a plea to the powers of nature to bring much-needed rain after the intense drought of summer.

Hopi traditions notwithstanding, many plants are used directly in Indian tribal ritual, and sympathetic magic (offering a recognisable token of what is asked of the gods) plays a large part in their selection. Thus physical appearances, or signatures, are often significant (see Chapter 8). Among the plants held sacred by pueblo-living Indians in connection with the need for rain, Cotton (*Gossypium hirsutum*) takes a key role, purely on account of the appearance of the cotton balls, which is similar to that of clouds. By similar token and following principles of sympathetic magic to ensure a good maize crop, pueblo Indians have traditionally worn phallic-shaped gourds or squashes as fertility symbols during their harvest rites.

Like their counterparts among the circumpolar tribes in northern Europe and Asia, North American Indian priests use hallucinogenic plants in order to achieve trances in which they communicate with the spirit world. One of the plants used in this way is the Thorn Apple or Jimson Weed (*Datura stramonium*). A member of a small

genus of shrubby plants that extend all over the warmer regions of the world, it produces white trumpet-shaped flowers from midsummer until the first frosts, and these
give rise to the spiny green chestnut-like fruits from which the plant earns one of its
common names. In North America, Jimson or Jamestown Weed has been used by
Indian tribal priests who either chew on the root or place a small amount of root
powder in the eyes, ears and mouth during invocation ceremonies designed to bring
rain. Tradition has it that if the Thorn Apple is ingested the birds will sing for rain
and the weather will change on the following day.

As with so many of the plants with narcotic or hallucinogenic properties, a legend
explains the origins and magical properties of the Thorn Apple. The plant is said to
be the descendant of a boy named A'neglakya and his sister, A'neglakyatsi'tsa, who
once lived beneath the earth but who occasionally made adventurous trips to the upper
world on the surface. One day they wandered by mistake into the sacred council
grounds of the spirits and, on returning home, related to their parents what they had
seen and heard. The spirits were sufficiently enraged about this infringement that they
changed the children into Jimson Weed. In consequence, others who ate the plant were
also able to learn the secrets of the spirit world from the children's tittle-tattle. This
capacity to induce visions has also led to the use of the plant in more prosaic circumstances. If a man has lost property or been robbed, the priest may give him a portion
of root to chew, whereupon he will discover the identity of the thief or envisage the
location.

Trees earn a special place in the mystique of the green mantle that ranks alongside
that of the hallucinogenic plants, and the lore that became associated with them
almost certainly extends back into prehistoric times. Because of their longevity and
great size and strength, they have taken on a particular spiritual quality from which
have arisen all kinds of superstitions and taboos. The Palestinian philosopher and
writer Porphyry, who lived from 233 to 309 CE and who happened also to be a strict
vegetarian, once made a succinct observation:

> They say that primitive men led an unhappy life, for their superstition did not stop at
> animals but extended even to plants. For why should the slaughter of an ox or a sheep
> be a greater wrong than the felling of a fir or an oak, seeing that the soul is implanted
> in these trees also? (*De Absentia*)

It is known from the evidence of archaeology that because it was necessary to fell trees
for a wide range of needs and because they were also places where spirits resided, the

matter of felling was taken very seriously in prehistoric Europe. The axe became a sacred tool long before it was a weapon of war and it played its part in what must have been seen as a paradoxical liaison between death and regenesis. The blade that hewed down the corpse of the tree also conjured a renewal of life, because young saplings soon grew from the soil that had been enriched by the decaying remnants of the old. The symbolic fertility connection has been preserved in the form of huge ritual axes, too mighty for human arms, unearthed from the Neolithic and Bronze Ages in Scandinavia, while contemporary rock carvings depict massive weapons in the hands of sexually charged gods.

Hints about the nature of reverence towards trees can also be gleaned from present-day Aborigine traditions. The most famous symbol of Australian Aborigine culture, the *didgeridoo*, is a long tube fashioned from the hollow bough of a tree. It is regarded across the breadth of the continent as the symbol of a male deity with strongly phallic connotations, whose deep voice is heard when it is blown.

Above: Massive ritual axes, highly decorated and too big to have been used as weapons, were sacred throughout much of the pre-Christian north because of their association with the felling of trees.

One of the most intriguing insights into the possible logic for planting the Bronze Age Oak stump that was discovered on the Norfolk coast of East Anglia, upside down in the centre of a sacred circle, also comes from Australia. Spiritual belief among many groups of Aborigines has included a tree called the *Yaraando*, otherwise known as the 'dreaming tree of life and death'. In the great ceremonies held in their most sacred places, the *boro* circles, a tree has been traditionally planted with its roots pointing upward into the air. This has indicated that it grows in the sky world of the ancestor

Above: An aboriginal tribesman decorated with body paint
plays the most famous instrument of his culture, the didgeridoo,
in the Northern Territory of Australia.

spirits who, during the Dreamtime, first reached the realms above the clouds by way of a giant tree. The mythology surrounding these ceremonies records how shamans would climb the dreaming tree, disappear and then return to tell of marvellous things they had witnessed in the upper world.

Among the Wik Munggan tribes living in the Cape York peninsula of northern Queensland, the Matchwood Tree (*Erythroxylum ellipticum*) has traditionally served as the Dreaming Tree. It has a shallow root system that spreads out flat around a main taproot. In the past, when a member of the tribe died and was taken to the burial ground, a small Matchwood Tree was uprooted and its stem cut off to leave a stump. This was planted upside down on the grave with the taproot pointed towards the west, where it was believed that the entrance to the sky world could be found. The parallel between this and the Bronze Age discovery in England is difficult to ignore and it lends strongly to the argument that the East Anglian Oak stump represented an altar on which bodies of the dead were left in order that they might ascend to the spirit world above.

Decorated poles hewn from tree trunks are revered by various Australian Aborigine tribes and are generally thought to have been given by the ancestor spirits during the Dreamtime, perhaps to serve as a stairway between souls of the living and the dead. A special kind of decorated totem pole which is considered to have a life of its own, called a *tnatantja*, symbolises the 'dreaming tree of life and death'. Mythology tells of a great red and white *tnatantja* pole, tall enough to reach the sky, that was set up during the Dreamtime at a place called Kerenbennga. Aborigines also believe that their traditional bent throwing stick, the boomerang, was first fashioned during the Dreamtime, from the 'dreaming tree'.

In very early times it appears that some Australian Aborigine tribes placed their dead in trees rather as their North American counterparts have used raised wooden platforms. In an intriguing development of this practice, as part of Aborigine funeral ceremonies long decorated and carved wooden totems known as *pukamani* burial poles are planted in the ground and left to rot. These poles seem to represent both sacred trees and ancestor spirits, but sometimes they are hollowed out and fashioned into upright coffins for the dead. Clearly these are symbolic ladders that the soul of the dead person may climb from earth to heaven.

It is with some of the more recent European descendants of the hunter-gatherers, the Celts, that reverence for trees truly evolved and it is to Celtic culture and belief in the spirituality of the green mantle that we must now turn.

CHAPTER 2

The Sacred Groves
of Northern Europe

The Celts are the first civilisation of northern Europe known to history by name and they provide a bridgehead, in terms of evolution of society, between the Palaeolithic hunters and the great agriculturists of the ancient Near East. Although the rise of Mesopotamian culture predated that of the Celts by several thousands of years, the vast area of lands north of the Alps lagged far behind Mesopotamia in terms of civilised development. The establishment of settled European communities based on farming and division of labour came about only when many of the great cities of the Sumerians, Assyrians and Babylonians had long since been abandoned and reduced to rubble. In due course we will come to focus on the great farming civilisations that developed in the fertile lands between the rivers Tigris and Euphrates.

When investigating the distant ancestors of the Celts, we were obliged to rely on archaeological evidence and questionable analogy with present-day tribal customs. In the traditions of the Celts we have a wealth of Irish literature and the observations of Roman writers from which to obtain information. If, however, there is an inherent problem to gaining a true picture of Celtic attitudes to the green mantle, it is that

Left: Conifer forests that once clothed large tracts of northern Europe are dark and moody places where it easy to understand that people once believed spirits roamed. But, as evergreens, the trees were also seen as being immortal when other vegetation died away.

their culture has been the victim of an almost unparalleled level of distortion. The Classical empire-builders were fascinated by the Celts. To a citizen of Rome, however, these people were barbarians. They were to be respected and feared militarily but viewed with cultural disdain. Their cultural legacy found itself in the somewhat cavalier possession of historians like Julius Caesar, Strabo (63 BCE to 21 CE) and the 1st-century writer Tacitus. It also fell into the positively mischievous hands of Christian clerics and monks. The Church was extremely reluctant to extend any credit to what it regarded as unacceptable heathenism, and this has led to some wild notions that are only now being laid to rest.

We still tend to envisage the Celts as 'ancient Britons' whose Druid priests had long white beards, waved golden sickles and bits of Mistletoe and stamped around Stonehenge in white robes. Yet much of this is sheer unsupported romance. Modern Druid revivalists revere the Oak and the Mistletoe only because they have seized on a scant observation made, second-hand, by a solitary classical writer, Pliny. It is known from the writing of early Christian monks in Ireland that the Celtic Druids celebrated a series of annual festivals coinciding with different periods of the agricultural and astronomical year; but what exactly they believed in, and the nature of the rites they performed, boils down to modern inventiveness, because the Druid priesthood was extremely circumspect about divulging the nature of its rites to outsiders, and this clearly included Christian clerics, the only people able to make written records. The records that were created frequently described pagan activities in a distorted and derogatory light.

In reality, the Celts were the guardians of complex and sophisticated beliefs that they were unable to preserve for themselves other than by word of mouth. They began their rise to power in the 7th century BCE. Before the Roman empire swallowed them up, they had become masters of a vast area of land above a line referred to by contemporary writers as 'transalpina', which began roughly at the Pyrenees and followed the Alps and the river Danube to the shores of the Black Sea. At the peak of their power, the Celts also controlled large parts of the Iberian peninsula, the Balkans, Anatolia and even Italy itself, but by the 1st century BCE the only independent Celtic region on the continent was Gaul. The forebears of the Celts evolved from hunter-gatherers when the climate of Europe dried and warmed, and they began an efficient system of mixed farming that has persisted to the present day. Yet they were dominated and surrounded by the great forests. The tundra of the Ice Age had receded thousands of years earlier and been replaced by more temperate vegetation.

Tacitus wrote of 'a land of bristling forests and unhealthy marshes'. If a person stood on a high vantage point in the Jura or Vosges mountains and looked eastwards across the Rhine, a seemingly endless sea of trees rolled to the distant horizons, the virtually impenetrable Hercynian forest. A similar view was obtained by turning and looking westwards where the trees were uninterrupted until they thinned into the marshes of the western seaboard. Similar virgin forests covered a large part of the British Isles and Scandinavia.

Much of Celtic belief reflected their environment and echoed that which we know of hunter-gatherers. Strong animistic links existed between natural features of the landscape and the 'other world'. Everything in nature was seen as a cloak for a spirit being that could also take on human form. The counterparts of the Celts in Scandinavia knew these beings as *landvaettirs*. Not surprisingly, trees were more than tangible living things. They were particularly associated with the spirits and possessed a cryptic power that singled them out over all other objects in nature for a special kind of reverence. The forests became living temples. As Tacitus put it of the Celts, 'They deem it incompatible with the majesty of the heavenly host to confine the gods within walls, or to mould them into any likeness of the human face: they consecrate groves and coppices, and they give the divine names to that mysterious something which is visible only to the eyes of faith.'

The Celts regarded the sacred woodlands as places wherein the trees were sources of oracular utterance and were owned by deities whose names the tribes often adopted. Hence the tribe of Nemetes revered a goddess of the woodlands named Nemetona. When a wood or more precisely a clearing in the wood became dedicated to her worship, as a naturally formed sanctuary or 'grove', it was described as a *nemeton*, and this word subsequently became adopted for all Celtic sacred places. In his *Annales* covering Roman history prior to 68 CE, Tacitus mentions sacred groves on the island of Anglesey that were destroyed

The need to create such sacred places is a time-honoured belief that was probably inherited from the hunter-gatherers.

sometime prior to 61 CE by the Roman commander Suetonius Paulinus. Similar sanctuaries existed across Europe. The need to create such sacred places is a time-honoured belief that was probably inherited from the hunter-gatherers. The sylvan groves allowed the invitation of the unseen spirit forces into a place where men could commune with them readily and at least on a semi-permanent basis. Not all such sanctuaries seem to have been formed in woodland clearings and in Romano-Celtic times the word *nemeton* eventually came to have a wider meaning, which included places for the seasonal gatherings of the tribes. Because water was also believed to be sacred, the semen of the gods, the *nemeton* that served as a shrine was very frequently associated with springs or pools.

Traces of the Celtic names of sanctuaries have sometimes survived. The original name for the spa town of Buxton in England was *Aqua Arnemetiae*, suggesting that, even at that time, its thermal springs were associated with a sacred grove. There was also a place called *Vernemeton* in Nottinghamshire, and one of the major Mediterranean authors, Strabo, described how a conciliatory council meeting between three warring Galatian tribes was held at a place in Asia Minor called *Drunemeton* which means 'sacred oak grove'. This, however, would have required considerable space to accommodate such a gathering and can hardly have been a small clearing in a wood.

An indication of the extent to which the Celts revered trees in general can be drawn from a curious alphabet which forms the basis for the Celtic rune script known as Ogham. This is the so-called Beth-Luis-Nion tree alphabet that was first researched in a book *Ogygia* by Roderick O'Flaherty, and was subsequently brought to a wider audience by Robert Graves in his *White Goddess*. The title Beth-Luis-Nion is drawn from the Irish Celtic names of the first three trees in the alphabet – Birch, Rowan and Ash. The sequence of letters has survived down the centuries, with some variations, and it still constitutes the basis of the modern Irish alphabet where each of the five vowels and 13 consonants is given the name of a tree. Today, the Beth-Luis-Nion alphabet (sometimes called Beth-Luis-Fearn as an alternative when Alder becomes the third tree) is used by neo-pagans almost exclusively for divination purposes. In Celtic times, however, and in its original form, it may also have been used by the Druids more as the basis of a kind of esoteric signalling apparatus, not unlike modern deaf-and-dumb sign language.

For the Celts and their successors in Europe, individual trees became marked out as sacred. Important meetings took place beneath these special trees and they became regarded as symbols of the identity of the individual clans. The records of their existence first emerged during the Christian era among the Irish Celts who coined the term 'bile' (pronounced bee-lah) meaning 'sacred tree'. The 'bile' often stood beside a sacred spring and it was a source of great ancestral wisdom and strength, the interface between temporal and 'other' worlds. The measure in which these trees were regarded not only as sacred but also as a vital and valuable commodity in the Celtic world is

Right: Oak trees were sacred to many ancient cultures. This remarkable specimen, with dead branches standing like deer antlers, grows in England's famous Sherwood Forest, near Nottingham.

difficult for us to comprehend today, but they were, for example, often the focus of vandalism by rival communities. A gruesome insight can be gleaned from an ancient Germanic penalty against deliberate peeling of the bark of a standing tree. Damage of this kind would invariably bring about the death of any tree because the bark includes an essential food-carrying system between roots and leaves. An offender found guilty had his stomach cut open and his gut nailed to the tree that he had fatally wounded. In a symbolic replacement of the bark with living substitute he was then driven around the tree until his gut swathed the trunk like a bandage.

The single most important tree in the minds of the Celts was the Oak. According to the 1st-century Roman historian and naturalist Pliny, the first syllable of the title 'Druid' is derived from the Oak whose name in Greek is *drus*, while the second syllable is believed to come from an Indo-European root, *wid*, meaning 'to know'.

The great strength and longevity of the European Oak (*Quercus robur*) and related species lent it a particular spiritual quality not only in Europe but everywhere in the world that it grows. In their seasonal calendar the Druids chose it as the tree that symbolised all the meaning and purpose of the summer solstice, held on 21 June, the longest day of the year. It was their summer tree and Tree of Life, but this did not mean that it was barred from more utilitarian uses. Hewn with proper ceremony, the Oak bark was employed in tanning leather, the acorns fed pigs and the timber built boats and houses.

When Celtic culture became infused with that of the Romans, the magical aura of the Oak was strengthened since in Greco-Roman lore it was a tree sacred to Zeus on account of the frequency to which it is susceptible to lightning strikes, thunderbolts being the chief weapons of Zeus. The association with thunderstorms extended to the Oak being associated with the old Germanic thunder god, Donar, and his Norse counterpart Thor, a link that also gave the tree a claim to powers of fertility. The storm deities who sent the rain, the semen of the gods, brought fruitfulness to the womb of the earth.

Nor did the Oak lose its spiritual kudos when Christianity took over as the dominant faith. Old German records note that, in the 8th century, the Christian missionary St Boniface ordered the destruction of a sacred Oak in Hesse that went under the name *Donares eih* or 'Donar's Oak'. In *The Golden Bough*, James Frazer describes how, in the Baltic states, Oak fires were kept burning permanently in honour of the local thunder god Perkuns, and there was an outcry when Christians began to cut down his sacred groves. Even in very recent times, an Irish tradition has persisted of

hammering coins into the bark of Oaks or tying ribbons called 'clouties' to the branches as invocations to Mary the Virgin and other Roman Catholic saints.

The great resistance of Oak has also given it a protective aura that extends far beyond Europe. A Japanese legend tells of a Zen Buddhist monk named Shido Muman Zenji who was carrying a large sum of money with which to build a new monastery. While travelling home Muman Zenji spent the night at an inn where a thief attempted to rob him in his sleep. When the robber entered the monk's bedroom, however, he found not a sleeping figure but a vast Oak tree arising from the tatami mat and filling the room.

Among the Nordic and Germanic races, whose zenith was reached with the Vikings in the 8th and 9th centuries CE, tree worship was a fundamental aspect of ritual. It is worth bearing in mind that much of European culture remained stubbornly pagan during the early Christian era and some northern tribes were not destined to embrace Christianity for nearly a thousand years after its foundation. Sweden, for example, became Christian only during the 12th century and parts of central Europe were still officially flying pagan colours as little as 600 years ago. The pervading sense

Above: Clouties, or cloth decoration hangings, on
branches besides what was once a wishing well at Madron,
near Penzance in Cornwall.

is that trees were still intimately linked with life and fertility, not least because of their longevity and their robustness in the face of environmental adversity. Other more esoteric factors were also involved and these became combined in an assortment of spiritual beliefs.

When the medieval traveller and writer Adam of Bremen visited the last real bastion of paganism in Sweden at Uppsala in 1070 CE, he reported on a magnificent temple, said to have been sheeted in gold. The sanctuary was dedicated to various Norse deities including Othin, Thor and the fertility god Freyr, and beside the temple was a grove in which, according to Adam, every tree was sacred. This grove seems to have witnessed sacrificial slaughter. Adam describes talking to an old man who claimed to have seen human corpses hanging in the trees, as well as horses and dogs.

It is a distinct possibility that aged Swedish kings occasionally found themselves sacrificed as the priests of Freyr. It is thought that they were slain at the end of a nine-year term of office, and that the killing took place in the Uppsala grove. Hints of similar practice are known from Greek and Roman times, though in the Mediterranean region trees that witnessed ritual slaying were more frequently the sacred precincts of goddesses rather than gods. A famous grove once existed beside the small sacred lake of Nemi near Aricia in the Alban Hills of Rome, dedicated to the Roman goddess Diana Nemorensis. According to legend, the ruler of the old pre-Roman Italic kingdom, who was also the priest of Diana's sacred grove, only gained his high office after slaying his predecessor. Thus each generation of Diana's hapless royal servants patrolled the grove in the sober knowledge that he would, sooner or later, meet with the same violent death that he had administered. During their term of office, however, the priests of the grove not only watched their backs but engaged in a ritual. Part of their duty was to masturbate and ejaculate semen against the trunk of the sacred tree in a symbolic act of donating their life-giving seed to the goddess whose presence was implicit in the tree. Evidence from the grove at Uppsala suggests similar sentiment. The victims, king and commoner alike, were stabbed to death before hanging and their blood was spilled on the hallowed ground so that the sacred trees might be revitalised.

The sacred trees of the Celts were the preserves of the Druid priesthood whose mysterious rites conducted in remote forest clearings were of particular fascination among the Greco-Roman historians. Druid and sacred trees were inseparable. This close spiritual association, involving human sacrifice and divination from human remains, led to all kinds of lurid reports when the Celtic lands in continental Gaul were occupied by the Romans. The 1st-century CE poet Lucan composed a work called *Pharsalia* in which he described a Celtic *nemeton* sanctuary that Julius Caesar ordered his legion to destroy near Marseilles. The demolition, it has to be said, was not out of religious objection but because Caesar needed timber for siege works. Lucan's prose indicates the same kind of sacrificial slaughter that was reported among the Celtic Druids of later times by Adam of Bremen:

> A grove there was, untouched by men's hands from ancient times whose interlacing boughs enclosed a space of darkness and cold shade, and banished the sunlight from above. No rural Pan dwelt there, nor Silvanus, ruler of the woods, no nymphs; but gods were worshipped there with savage rites, the altars were heaped with hideous offerings, and every tree was sprinkled with human gore. Of these boughs, if antiquity, reverential of the gods, deserves any credit, birds feared to perch; in those coverts wild beasts would not lie down; no wind ever bore down upon that wood, nor thunderbolt hurled from black clouds; the trees, even when they spread their leaves to no breeze, rustled among themselves. Water also fell there in abundance from dark springs. The images of the gods, grim and rude, were uncouth blocks formed of felled tree trunks. Legend also told that often the subterranean hollows quaked and bellowed, the yew trees fell down and rose again, that the glare of conflagration came from trees that were not on fire, and that serpents twined and glided round the stems.
>
> (*Pharsalia I*, Loeb Classcl. Libr. Edn.)

One of the more interesting aspects of Lucan's commentary, apart from confirming archaeological evidence that the Celts worshipped deep in the forests and carried out human sacrifice, is the admission that the Romans also believed that spirits were present in trees, albeit trading under Roman names. Silvanus is the archaic name for the Italian god of woodlands!

One of the best known human sacrificial discoveries from the Celtic era is that of a remarkably well-preserved corpse found at Lindow Moss near Wilmslow in Cheshire, England. More than 2,000 years ago, what has now become a massive and commercially worked peat bed would have comprised marshes, scattered woodland and small lakes. Lindow Man appears to have been thrown into a sacred pool in about 300 BCE. We can be fairly certain that he did not fall into the water and drown accidentally because he had been stripped more or less naked, bludgeoned about the head and garrotted with a rope fashioned from ox sinews. His throat had then been cut and he had been placed face down in the pool which, over hundreds of years, filled to become a peat bog, thus preserving the evidence of his violent demise.

When forensic scientists conducted a post-mortem it was discovered that Lindow Man had eaten a somewhat unusual meal shortly before his death, consisting of an assortment of what seems to have been carefully selected plant material. A question that the evidence prompts is whether the man was forced, or agreed voluntarily, to eat a ritual meal, perhaps containing magically imbued herbs, before being sacrificed to some arcane deity of the bog. Lindow Man's stomach content included not only Mistletoe, among an assortment of seeds and berries, but also charred bread, and it is known that charcoal or charred grain had a significant place in Celtic ritual. Traditionally, the Celts broke up or distorted their offerings to the deities, a change of material and earthly form that was also extended to funerary goods. A famous and exquisitely crafted cauldron known as the Gundestrup Bowl was unearthed in 1891 from a small bog called Raevemosen, near the village of Borremose in Denmark, where it had lain undisturbed since the turn of the Christian era. Clearly a precious offering to some unknown deity, it was left behind only after its solid silver sections

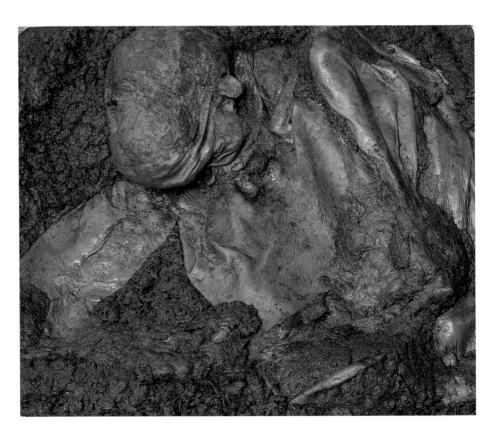

The preserved remains of Lindow Man, found in a peat bog
in Cheshire and believed to have been sacrificed to a Celtic deity
during the Iron Age.

had been carefully separated into individual plates. Weapons deposited as offerings were often smashed to pieces, and perhaps the grain was destroyed by fire, applying similar logic. The same logic, pursued in more recent times by North American Indians, argued that anything destined for the otherworld had to be changed from its normal earthly state before it could be of any future use.

The style of sacrificial death endured by Lindow Man was copied in other parts of Europe. In Denmark various Iron Age bog corpses have come to light, such as those of Tollund Man, discovered during peat digging in 1950, and most seem to have met their deaths in similar manner after having consumed plants that would not normally have comprised Celtic luncheon fare.

It is reasonably certain that Lindow Man was sacrificed to the god of a pool sited in a wood – but which god? For the Celts, ritualised human sacrifice by drowning (as distinct from methods of sacrifice such as hanging or burning that were employed for other deities) was linked with Teutates, the Gaulish tribal god. During the time of Roman occupation Teutates was revered as the Celtic vegetation deity and guardian of the harvest but also, surprisingly, he was their god of war. The need to protect the green world meant that in mythology the vegetation god not infrequently took this parallel role, an aspect of the strong bond understood by early peoples to exist between death and regenesis. It was also a reflection of the violence of natural forces (see also Chapter 4). Hence the Roman war god Mars was revered as a protector of the fields and their produce. The logical conclusion to be drawn from the evidence is that Teutates' victims were drowned in sacrificial lakes. Such archaeological discoveries as Lindow Man, whose stomach contained an assortment of seeds that possibly constituted a final ritual meal, may have been killed as an appeasement to a vegetation deity.

The ritual link between water, trees and death was highlighted on the Gundestrup Bowl. It is engraved with detailed ritual scenes including a man being drowned head-first in a tub. A study on Lucan's poem *Pharsalia* written by an early grammarian and known as the *Berne scholia* contains, in the margin, a note that sacrifice to Teutates was conventionally carried out by putting a man head-first into a full tub so that he was suffocated.

In Europe, it seems that there was another male deity, concerned not with war and the green world but with hunting and vegetation. We know very little about him aside from the fact that he was worshipped until about 1000 CE and that he seems to have been concerned chiefly with animals. Celtic carving and inscription, largely found in

Gaul (central France), reveals a male figure wearing the antlers of a stag and bearing the name Cernunnos. Images of this kind first appeared in Western Europe from about the 4th century BCE and the horned god is depicted on the Gundestrup Bowl where he is drawn squatting and surrounded by wild beasts including deer, a snake, a lion and a wild boar. On his head he wears antlers, which have been interpreted as symbols of virility.

The gods of summer and winter, the Oak and Holly Lords, recognised by today's pagans, are allegedly based on Cernunnos but are largely an invention, as is the character of his female counterpart, the Irish Celtic mother goddess Medb or Maeve. Predominantly herders and breeders of horses and cattle, it is clear from the evidence of art (although little is revealed on the subject in the writings of the Greco-Roman historians) that the European Celts revered a great mother goddess, but little is known of her. She was linked with the moon and fertility and the Roman writer Tacitus claimed that her contemporary among the Teutonic tribes went under the name Nerthus. The benevolent and calm earth mother dreamed up by modern romantics and emulated by millennium witches in suitably decorated robes, waving swords and chalices, however, is a figment of wishful thinking.

Above: The Gundestrup Bowl, discovered in pieces in a bog near
the village of Raevemosen in Denmark, depicts scenes engraved on the
silver, including an antler-headed Celtic god, probably Cernunnos.

Considerable caution needs to be exercised about so-called authentic evidence of Celtic belief in the green mantle. Library shelves responding to the 'Mind, Body and Spirit' vogue are currently stacked with books claiming to provide an authentic insight into pagan belief and practice but most, unfortunately, draw more on romantic nonsense than anything of real historical substance. The 'facts' provided in such works are delivered with great conviction but tend not be supported by primary sources of evidence, and traditions claimed as authentic all too often turn out to be no more than antiquarian fancy dressed up falsely as genuine folklore.

It has been argued by eminent writer on neo-paganism Ronald Hutton that modern witchcraft or Wicca has gained in popularity because it offers an attractive middle-class alternative to orthodox religion. It takes people back to the magical fantasy world of childhood where they may reject modernity and take refuge in a tranquil ideal of nature. It is also probably true, although pagans are reluctant to make such an admission, that the sexual element inherent in their cult also draws men and women for whom the prospect of skipping naked round a bonfire together, for the greater good of the environment, has its appeal.

The Gundestrup Bowl features another intriguing scene among its engravings. Walking towards the victim of drowning is a file of soldiers who appear to be bearing a slender tree trunk on the tips of their spears. There is no direct explanation of their intention but clues can be found elsewhere. In the vicinity of a number of Celtic sanctuaries archaeologists have discovered shafts or pits, some as much as 30 metres (100 feet) in depth, and these seem to have been used for ritual purposes since they often contain votive offerings and animal and human bones. When a shaft sited at Le Bernard in the Vendée region of France was excavated it was found to include a 4-metre (12-foot) high Cypress trunk, which may have provided a symbolic ladder to and from the underworld. This particular tree was dropped into the pit 'right way up', but one fascinating question must be whether such an object relates in any way, albeit from a later period, to the upturned Oak stump discovered on the beach in East Anglia and to modern Aborigine ritual in Australia (see Chapter 1). The evidence of the East Anglian tree circle suggests that tree-stump rituals among the European hunter-gatherers took place as far back as the early part of the European Bronze Age about 4,000 years ago. Such dramatic finds still do not give us incontrovertible evidence of events but they seem to point in that direction. Many primitive cultures have recognised that trees not only provided a stairway from earth to the heavens but also a link between the upper living world and other nether world below.

The Vendée pit discovery provided a tantalising clue to the more detailed links between the Druids and trees. Other archaeological discoveries have come to light from time to time and brought us little nearer to a more complete story. At Pfalzfeld in the Hunsruck region of the Rhineland, a Celtic stone pillar has been found, sculpted with detailed relief carvings and dated to the 4th or 5th century BCE. In the middle of each tapering side a carved face is surmounted by a 'leaf crown'. The face is believed to symbolise a superhuman ability to look in four directions at once and is therefore that of a deity. A fragment of a stone head with a similar leafy crown was also found elsewhere in Germany at Heidelberg. From a later period, when the Celts were under Roman domination, we also have monuments popularly tagged 'Jupiter Columns' because they are largely dedicated to Jupiter, the Roman equivalent of the Greek god Zeus. These pillars are not of a typical Roman design, however, and may have been copied from wooden Celtic totems. An argument put forward by one eminent Celtic historian, T.G.E. Powell, is that all these pillars represent a sacred tree that is either the home or the symbolic embodiment of a tribal deity. The totem probably originated as a living tree that formed the central focus of a cult sanctuary. The phenomenon of the Sacred Tree is explored in more detail later, but we know from Celtic literature and from dedications inscribed in the Romano-Celtic period that named holy or *bile* trees in Ireland were set apart for the worship of various gods. Irish mythological names include *Mac Cuilinn*, meaning Son of Holly, and *Mac Ibar*, Son of Yew. In the beliefs of many primitive cultures whose understanding of the supernatural is based on animism, the soul of a person can be bound up irrevocably with the life of a plant, usually a tree, and one can also find proper names from Celtic Gaul with similar links. The name *Guidgen* means Son of Wood and *Guerngen* is Son of Alder. The tribal name *Eburones* derives from the Celtic word for Yew.

In the margin of his Uppsala report of 1070 CE, Adam of Bremen noted a very special element of the sacred grove, a tree that stood beside the temple yet was separate from and above the rest. He described it as 'an enormous tree, spreading its branches far and wide. It is evergreen in winter and summer. No one knows what kind of tree it is . . .' From the limited description Adam of Bremen gave, the tree must have been a conifer and it probably reflected something that lies within the heart of Norse and Germanic belief – the concept of the World Tree. Germanic lore, popularised more recently in the Wagnerian operatic *Ring Cycle*, describes the tree as an Ash, but it may well have been a massive Yew, an evergreen which possesses a great longevity and tenacity for life and whose wood is exceptionally tough. In the more northerly latitudes of Scandinavia, it may equally have been a Spruce or Fir, but perhaps its botanical identity does not really matter. Whatever the species, it is almost certainly from the World Tree tradition that the Yew trees standing in English churchyards and the Spruce tree that we decorate with baubles and coloured lights in our homes at Christmas derive.

Much of the mythology of the far north of Europe was destroyed under the advance of Christianity, but a few precious fragments were salvaged and preserved in a collection of poems in Skaldic verse that became known as the *Poetic Edda*. The meaning of these poems was amplified by a 12th-century Icelandic scholar, Snorri Sturluson. He was an intellectual politician who took it upon himself to assemble the only comprehensive precis of northern mythology to come out of the Middle Ages in a prose narrative called the *Prose Edda* to distinguish it from the collection of Eddaic poems or lays.

One of the Norse myths from the Eddaic literature implies, indirectly, that the great Norse god Othin or Odin was born from a tree that may well have been envisaged as a Yew. In the *Havamal* of the poetic *Edda*, his mother is described as being Bestla, a daughter of the giant Bolthorn. According to the prose *Edda* of Snorri Sturluson, Bestla married Bur and bore three of the Aesir gods, Othin, Vili and Ve. Bestla's name is conjectured by Skaldic scholars to be derived from words meaning 'giver of bast' where 'bast' means Yew.

The World Tree provided a reason for killing that was quite distinct from sacrifice to a fertility god. Human offerings in its shade were slaughtered for more complex reasons. We have established that the Celts regarded sacred trees as a source of divine revelation and the Germanic and Norse races echoed this view. Certain answers about the mystical and oracular nature of the World Tree lie in its more correct Norse title, the *Yggdrasil*. The name results from combination of two words: *Ygg* is one of the many synonyms of Othin, while *drasil* translates as horse. Thus we have 'Othin's horse'. The name, however, is not entirely as it seems because it bears no relation to Othin's well-documented and winged steed, Sleipnir. *Yggdrasil* is an old colloquialism for gallows and the name arose because Othin elected to hang himself from the World Ash in pursuit of eternal and infinite knowledge.

Celtic stone obelisk found at Pfalzfeld in the Rhineland and dated to the 4th or 5th century BCE. On each side is a face surmounted by a leafy crown.

Much of Nordic mythology reflects strict rules of trust and honour known as *frith*. The story of Othin's sacrifice is closely linked with the fate of the northern world arising from the breaking of *frith* by the gods themselves. Richard Wagner called it *Götterdammerung*, the Twilight of the Gods. Othin knew that his world of brief cool summers and long icy winters was plunging towards a terrible moment of attrition called Ragnarok. It was a day when the sun would be swallowed up by phantom

Above: An engraving of the *Yggdrasil*, the sacred Ash tree of Germanic and Norse mythology, from which the god Othin is said to have hung himself in pursuit of eternal knowledge.

wolves, unleashed by forces of evil to chase it around the sky, and the world would be plunged into eternal darkness and cold. Othin became obsessed with gaining ultimate knowledge not so much out of any vain hope of stemming the tide of impending disaster but of understanding the ancient runes that decreed the destiny that would befall gods and mortals alike.

The extraordinary occult powers of the *Yggdrasil* are explained in a narrative about world origins, forming the first part of Snorri Sturluson's *Edda*. Like the Celtic 'bile' trees, Othin's World Tree stood beside a magical source of water, described as being fed by three springs from the well of a sage called Mimir. Three eternal seeresses, the Norns who spun the rope of destiny, watered the tree each day from the well.

> But under the root that reaches towards the frost giants, there is where Mimir's well is, which has wisdom and intelligence contained in it, and the master of the well is called Mimir. He is full of learning because he drinks of the well.
>
> (*Prose Edda – Gylfaginning*)

Before hanging himself from the World Tree, it was into Mimir's well that Othin had once thrown his right eye, having plucked it out in the quest for knowledge. He had frequently sat beneath the tree to commune with the slain and to learn their wisdom. Norse belief included understanding, however, that only in death was eternal knowledge to be fully revealed. The dead took on the wisdom of the ages by communing with those who had gone before and it was this occult knowledge that Othin, the immortal god, had sought by symbolically taking his own life on the Tree:

> I wot that I hung on the wind tossed tree
> Of all nights nine
> Wounded by spear, bespoken to Othin
> Bespoken myself to myself
> Upon that tree of which none telleth
> From what roots it doth rise ...
> ... then began I to grow and gain in insight
> To wax eke in wisdom.
>
> (From the *Havamal, Poetic Edda*, translated by Lee Hollander)

Men were sacrificed on the World Ash Tree, partly in recognition of the suffering of Othin, but also because their death was a means of accessing and expanding the eternal store of wisdom.

In north European tradition, the most important of the 'bile' trees after the Oak and Ash, were the Yew and Hawthorn. Rudyard Kipling linked three of the quartet in his poem *A Tree Song*:

> Of all the trees that grow so fair,
> Old England to adorn,
> Greater are none beneath the Sun,
> Than Oak and Ash and Thorn.

The fourth member of this eclectic group of trees, the Yew (*Taxus baccata*), is one that has held an extraordinary place in the hearts and minds of our ancestors from at least the time of the Celts. In the wild, the Yew grows locally throughout much of Europe on wooded chalk and limestone slopes, generally among other trees. The sexes are separate, which means that only the female trees bear berries. In the spring the male trees can be identified readily from a distance by the golden effect created by masses of tiny male cones. All parts of the plant are intensely poisonous and the *taxine* it secretes acts as a cardiac depressant slowing the heart rate drastically, the greatest concentration of toxin being found in the leaves and seeds. Cattle seem perversely attracted to browse on the foliage and British law recognises the careless disposal of Yew clippings as a basis for award of damages when stock has been lost through Yew poisoning.

Like the Oak, the Yew tree has a tremendous potential life span. In Surrey, England, in the town of Crowhurst, an aged Yew is claimed to be at least 1,600 years old. This longevity is attributable in part to the extreme hardness of its wood but also to the curious form of growth of the tree. Where the lowest branches touch the ground they are able to root and give rise to new stems. These grow to become the trunks of trees that are separate yet linked organically. Eventually when the original trunk dies a new tree may grow within the decaying mass of the old.

Yew was of great significance to the Celts. The Irish law tracts known as *Fenechas* (the law of the Feine or Freemen), commonly known as the Brehon Law, are probably the oldest known European regulations. First committed to memory by specially trained Druids known as Brehons, they were written down in later ages and preserved in books of law including the *Senchus Mor*, the *Book of Acaill* and the *Uraiccecht Becc*. These early texts originated in the 7th and 8th centuries CE and have come down to us in mostly corrupt forms from manuscripts written in the 14th to 16th centuries. Brehon law gave trees three distinct rankings – Chieftains, Peasants and Shrubs – to some extent based on their symbolic importance to the Druids. Yew was classed as one of

🌿 *In Breton legend the tree that grows in the graveyard is believed to send a new root into the open mouth of each corpse in order to provide a means of escape for the soul of the deceased.*

An ancient Yew tree growing in Wales near the churchyard
of Pennant Melangell, Llangynog, in Powys,

seven great 'Chieftain Trees' that brought prosperity to the kingdom and heavy penalties were imposed on anyone caught felling a Yew without permission.

The Brehon ruling on Yew trees did not, however, possess quite the mystical connotations that one might assume because the tree was protected more for 'its timber, used for household vessels, breast plates and other products' than out of any respect for its sanctity. In a purely practical sense Yew wood was greatly valued in the making of weapons on account of its extreme hardness and imperviousness to water. Irish warriors are also said to have used a lethal cocktail of the juices of Yew, Hellebore (*Helleborus* spp.) and Devil's Bit Scabious (*Succisa pratensis*) on their weapons. The Yew longbow, of course, went on to ensure military dominance during much of English medieval history.

Nevertheless the Yew was also regarded in a strongly mystical light. The name of the tree provides the fifth vowel, *idho,* in the Celtic Ogham tree alphabet because the Old English version of the word was originally spelt *iw* or *iow* (in Old German, *izwo* or *ixwo*). There have been claims that the island of Iona off the west coast of Scotland, the isle sacred to St Columba, was inadvertently misnamed in a 10th-century manuscript and should correctly have been Ioha (a local variation on *iow*). The allegation is made because, since before the arrival of Christianity, the place had possessed magical links with the Yew and with reincarnation. The Druid priests used the wood to carve magical wands and rune staves inscribed with Ogham symbols and they undoubtedly relied on Yew for divination. In the Irish Celtic tale of the *Wooing of Etain* the eponymous heroine was abducted from her husband Echu by a rival faery king named Mider. After vainly searching for his beloved spouse for a year and a day, Echu called on the services of his personal Druid to find her and the priest used three magical wands of Yew in order to trace Etain to Mider's palace.

In addition to being classed as a Chieftain Tree in Ireland, the Yew was one of five magical trees, the so-called Tree of Ros Roigne. It also carried a more sinister title as the 'renown of Badb Catha', a name which represented the aspect of the triple goddess known as the Morrigan who brought death and who confronted the Irish hero Cu Chulainn before battle.

Among its traditional roles down the centuries, the Yew tree has overseen the separation of the spirit from the body. In Breton legend the tree that grows in the graveyard is believed to send a new root into the open mouth of each corpse in order to provide a means of escape for the soul of the deceased. This sentiment is echoed in a tragic tale of love and death, that of Baile and Ailinn, from the ancient Irish text, the

Cycles of Kings or *Historical Cycle*. Baile pined away out of grief for the loss of Ailinn and, after his burial, a Yew tree sprouted from the grave.

In the Classical eras of Greece and Rome, the plant became sacred to Hecate, the chthonic goddess who controlled the pathways of the night accompanied by a spectral retinue of infernal howling dogs. Hecate was also a deity of the moon and so the Romans sacrificed black bulls to her on the eve of the full moon, adorning the animals' necks with wreaths of Yew. Because of its properties, Yew was perceived throughout much of the ancient European world as one of the plants of reincarnation and rebirth but also, paradoxically, as a symbol of death. The latter association was undoubtedly helped along by its lethally poisonous nature. It is thought that the soldiers of Greece and Rome first discovered the deadly efficiency of its juices when rubbed into the tips of their arrows.

The association of Yew in folklore and romance has been as a sombre and forbidding plant that stands in groves and forms gloomy canopies through which the sunlight rarely penetrates. The dense green foliage of glossy dark needles and gnarled stems, with an overall rather squat, spreading outline are a familiar sight in many English churchyards. These trees or their ancestors probably pre-date Christianity, however, because their strongest association is as pagan symbols of immortality and protection of the spirit against evil influences.

Shakespeare was taken up with its more morbid aspects. Hamlet's uncle used the juice of Yew, which the dramatist calls 'hebanon', to poison the king by pouring it into his ear, and it also forms one of the ingredients added to the witches' cauldron in *Macbeth* as 'slips of Yew, sliver'd in the moon's eclipse'. In Act Two of *Twelfth Night*, there arises a moody cry:

> Come away, come away, death
> And in sad Cypress let me be laid;
> Fly away, fly away breath;
> I am slain by a fair cruel maid;
> My shroud of white stuck all with Yew,
> O! prepare it.
> My part of death no one so true
> Did share it.

As recently as the 19th century, poets and writers were keen to draw on the morbid nature of Yew. Gilbert White, the English naturalist, once wrote 'it is an emblem of mortality by its funereal appearance', and Matthew Arnold took a similar line, though in his poem *Requiescat* the sentiment is more one of abhorrence:

> Strew on her roses, roses,
> And never a spray of Yew.
> In quiet she reposes:
> Ah! Would that I did too.

Yet the Yew was not always rewarded with such a dark accolade. It also possessed more gentle and even romantic connotations. During the Middle Ages, boughs of Yew were sometimes carried in procession on Palm Sunday as a convenient replacement for the olive branch, while the Yew tree that overhung a church door was considered to sprinkle its red berries on a bride returning from the altar as a wedding dowry. This tradition is revealed in a group of 13th-century Welsh poems, called *Cad Goddeu* or 'Battle of the Trees', that tells of 'the dower scattering Yew' that 'stood glum at the fight's fringe'. Yew also became recognised as the symbolic 'lucky' tree of the Scottish Fraser clan.

The Celts also revered the Rowan, the Beech and the Elm, each of which was either associated with tribal names or has been identified as sacred in the dedications which were left at various places carved in stone. In the minds of early cultures trees often took on attributes that arose from their physical appearance. A rugged, durable tree such as an Oak or an Ash was associated with masculinity and so, not surprisingly, it became identified with male deities, one reason why the Oak became linked with Zeus, the father of the Olympian gods. On the other hand, a graceful tree like the Birch, with its delicate tracery of leaves and its trembling habit, took on feminine attributes, and during the English Middle Ages the Birch was known as the 'Lady of the Woods'. In Russia, in springtime, time-honoured folk traditions that allude to the gender of the tree still persist. Villagers go into the woods on the Thursday before Whitsun and cut down a birch sapling, which is then decked in woman's clothes and ribbons to honour an unquestionably female tree spirit. Bundles of birch twigs have also been beloved of witches because of the association of the tree with the goddess worship. A tree, particularly when bereft of its soft foliage in winter, can take on a spectral appearance. This is true of some trees more than others. The Ash, with its characteristically gnarled and distorted limbs, has generally earned a sinister reputation as a gallows tree and a haunt of witches, while the Yew, perennially dark and gloomy, has long been associated with death.

Occasionally the old attitudes of reverence towards trees can still be found. In modern Lithuania, there survives a quaint and ancient prayer:

> That I may not fell a single tree without holy need;
> that I may not step upon a blooming field;
> that I may always plant trees.
> The gods look with grace
> upon those who plant trees along roads,
> in homesteads, at holy places,
> at cross roads, and by houses.
> If you wed, plant a wedding tree,
> If a child is born, plant a tree.
> If someone dies plant a tree for their soul.
> At all festivals, during important events,
> Visit trees.
> Prayers will attain holiness through trees of thanks.
> So may it be!

Why did rings of trees or circular spaces within woodlands become sacred? Since very early times, perhaps as far back as humankind's first conscious awakening to the spiritual world, we have found magic in certain shapes and signs. Foremost among these is the circle, the purest shape in nature, that of the outline of the celestial orbs in the sky and, although we did not know it, the shape of our own world. Even today we speak of 'the magic circle' as a club for magicians. The circle is also the strongest shape in nature with no weak points like a square or rectangle. Try crushing a ball! Prehistoric man viewed rings and circles in a special light. It explains why many ancient monuments from the European Bronze Age like Stonehenge and Avebury in Wiltshire, England, and indeed the Sea Henge in Norfolk, were created in the round. North American Indians generate a similar pattern, dancing around its periphery. Modern occultists also believe in the power of the sacred circle. Known to Wiccan witches as the Circle of Being, it delineates a consecrated space in which to concentrate magical powers and invoke the earth goddess. The witches' circle is contrasted slightly from a magician's circle in its meaning, since the latter is drawn in order to protect him from powers outside its circumference.

Not surprisingly, therefore, circles of trees are probably the oldest sacred spaces known to man. Unfortunately, the 'groves' that became the sanctuaries of the Celtic Druids were romanticised virtually out of recognition during the 18th century.

Overleaf: A swathe of Oak and Birch trees growing densely in Birklands Wood, part of Sherwood Forest near Nottingham. Birch was once known as Lady of the Woods', whilst Oak had masculine attributes.

Etchings and other drawings of the period frequently reveal benign-looking men garbed in classical drapes and carrying armfuls of Mistletoe freshly hewn in sylvan glades associated with rings of stones looking suspiciously like Stonehenge. The 18th-century writer William Stukely was keen to compare Gothic architecture with the forest glade. He noted in his *Itinerarium Curiosum* of 1724 that it was 'the best manner of building, because the idea is taken from a walk of trees, whose touching heads are curiously imitated by the roof'. His contemporary Bishop Warburton linked the design of the earliest Christian churches with these pagan groves. He recalled that in northern Europe the Goths had 'been accustomed, during the gloom of paganism, to worship the Deity in groves'.

Whether the clearing was man-made or merely arose naturally is uncertain, but the grove was probably delimited by a ring of stones or felled trunks and generally is reputed to have contained a large sacred tree at its centre. Archaeological exploration has tended to dispute this idea and there is a strong body of opinion that pre-Roman culture in Europe worshipped in sanctuaries built in rings of stone.

Rings or circles of trees growing on hilltops may appear to have religious significance, but this is not always the case. Such celebrated landmarks as Chanctonbury Ring near Findon on the south coast of England bear no relation to spirituality. Originally called Chankbury, the ring was the site of a circular Iron Age fort and was treeless until the year 1760. A local landowner, Charles Goring, decided to plant a ring of Beech trees amid considerable dissent among those who believed he was destroying a natural landmark and disrupting the clean profile of the South Downs. Nonetheless Goring persevered, arranging for regular supplies of water to be hauled up the hill until the saplings had become established. Much of the ring was destroyed in the hurricane of October 1987, but some effort has been made to replant those trees that were lost.

> *Bishop Warburton linked the design of the earliest Christian churches with these pagan groves.*

Thus far we have searched for evidence of the mystical nature of trees largely in northern Europe where the true details of how such plants were viewed in respect of their sanctity are often obscure. In reality, beyond scattered archaeological evidence that occasionally broadens our understanding, more or less all our information about pagan rites in pre-Christian Europe comes from Greek and Roman writers of the Romano-Celtic period. Their comments may, or may not, have been distorted for political reasons. Commentaries are often notoriously subjective when addressing the spirituality of 'barbarians' like the Celtic and Germanic tribes. At best we can glean clues from their contemporary observations and archaeology will occasionally lend support or fill in gaps in our understanding. It must always be borne in mind, however, that nowhere is there a coherent account of the religious beliefs of the European tribes that lived north of the Alps.

Although literate and living many thousands of years after the ice that had governed the lives of the prehistoric hunters had thawed and retreated north, the Celtic priesthood probably fell into line with the traditions of its more distant forebears. The Druids were notoriously secretive and, in short, we do not know precisely the manner in which our European ancestors sanctified plants. To some extent the dearth of information is explained by the fact that cult – Christian, pagan or otherwise – makes a timeless demand for secrecy. Esoteric cult and ritual are reliant to a large extent on fear of the unknown. Fear has always been, and continues to be, the 'muscle' of religion that persuades its congregation to maintain the letter of the faith. Fear, therefore, amounted to the 'powerhouse' of the earliest priests and shamans and the secrecy that generated the fear was the instrument through which the few held sway over the rest. Bringing cult into the public eye put the power at risk of being dispelled in the presence of familiarity. The desire for secrecy generated its own process of selection because those who aspired to become shamans, by whatever name, tended to be of high intelligence and strong character.

Much nonsense has been written about so-called ancient traditions associated with the Celts. A Canadian source on the Internet suggests, for example, that the traditions of Halloween including decorating with turnips and cornstalks originates with the Druid festival of Samhain and that Celtic priestesses travelled the countryside, chanting to frighten away evil spirits thought to be roaming the earth on Halloween night. In short, we have no idea of the kind of festival traditions adopted by the Druid priesthood because its ritual activities were maintained with great secrecy. Such ideas are the stuff of Gothic romance.

In order to gain the real, dramatic evidence of plant rituals in the ancient world, we must turn to another part of the globe altogether. The evidence is to be found in the hot dry soil of the Near East. In many respects cult followed the same principles of secrecy but enough evidence of priestly ritual, mythology and legend was committed to posterity by the scribes of Mesopotamia in the form of the written word for us to establish a clearer view.

CHAPTER 3

The Mesopotamian Tree of Life

D uring the year of 1845, a chance meeting took place in the town of Mosul in Iraq that was to trigger one of the great archaeological finds of the century. The discovery was set to expand our knowledge of the extent to which the first civilisations understood the mystery and magic of trees and yet, paradoxically, it was to provide an enigma that has never been entirely deciphered. Mosul is now acclaimed as Iraq's second city on the northernmost tributary of the river Tigris, but 150 years ago it was a dusty provincial town favoured largely by archaeologists. Mosul was a convenient stepping-off point for a number of major Mesopotamian ruins. Most of these sites date from the period of the Assyrian and Babylonian empires that reached the height of their powers between two and three thousand years ago.

The meeting was between the local French consul, Paul Emile Botta, and an English archaeologist, Austen Henry Layard. Botta, himself a keen amateur archaeologist, related to Layard how three years earlier he had discovered an old imperial city of the Assyrian Empire, Dur Sharrukin, at Khorsabad. He had also come across historical documents suggesting that the fabled city of Nineveh was somewhere close by.

Left: The enigmatic Tree of Life was once at the centre of a cult
led by the all-powerful King Ashurnasirpal II in the 9th century BCE
Assyrian city of Kalakh, the Calah mentioned in Genesis.

Layard was excited by the prospect of discovering the whereabouts of Nineveh and, in the following year, he began to dig into a *tell* or archaeological mound in the sands some 32 kilometres (20 miles) south of Mosul at the village of Nimrud. Through an odd twist of fate, the ruins that he came upon were not those of Nineveh but an even older city, Kalakh, named in the Book of Genesis as Calah. Its architect during the 9th century BCE had been a tyrannical Assyrian despot named Ashurnasirpal II, and at its heart he had built a vast and fabulous palace. It was in the artwork that had fallen from the walls of the collapsed staterooms that Layard discovered an enigma that was to become recognised as the Assyrian sacred tree. Much of what he discovered now rests in the British Museum in London.

The art of Ashurnasirpal's palace is, in itself, a paradox because the emphasis in its stone iconography is warlike. It was clearly designed to subdue and probably terrify the visitor. Lions with human heads, fabulous winged bulls and other awesome hybrids loomed in colossal proportions beside doors and gates. The state rooms, however, exuded a singularly different atmosphere. Carvings of Ashurnasirpal's personal and very non-warlike reverence towards a small but distorted plant dominated them. On dozens of panels the same theme was repeated, with variations. The king, often accompanied by a bizarre hybrid creature with the hallmarks of an Assyrian *genie* but who was probably a role-playing priest or vizir, faces a tree that has no equal in nature. It rises in a central trunk from which springs a weird cat's cradle of branches reminiscent of the contorted stems of a lotus. Yet the branches are clothed in bands of metal or some other substance and each ends in a stubby seven-lobed leaf design known as a *palmette*. This neither relates to the lotus nor is recognisable botanically so, clearly, it is symbolic and carries a deeper, esoteric meaning.

Sometimes the king, but more often the attendant, carries two objects – a bucket and pine cone. The cone, held in the right hand, pointed end forwards, is usually directed at the tree, while the bucket is held in the left hand. The king and his hybrid attendant are clearly in the act of some ritual that, apparently, takes the form of reverential devotion towards the tree.

Kalakh is by no means the only ancient city in Mesopotamia where archaeological evidence reveals that this same sacred tree was worshipped. Layard eventually went on to discover the ruins of Nineveh and found similar scenes of devotion, albeit in a miniaturised form, among stone carvings that had been authorised by the last of the Assyrian rulers, Ashurbanipal, whose reign witnessed the collapse of the empire in 612 BCE. No direct explanation exists of the ritual, but Ashurnasirpal's tree at Kalakh probably represents the earliest moment in history when we can definitely say that people viewed trees in a sacred capacity. We have no concrete evidence that the pre-historic hunter-gatherers did so. All we can say for certain is that scattered archaeological clues from prehistory suggest that people of the Palaeolithic era had gained a reverence for trees.

Ashurnasirpal II ruled the world of the ancient Near East and his reign, in the 9th century BCE, was one of conquest marked by considerable brutality, which makes his tree worship all the more striking. One can imagine that Ashurnasirpal worshipped a bull god or some similar macho deity, but his was also an era of pioneer farming. Mesopotamia, the 'land between the rivers', has come to be known as the Cradle of Civilisation because it was there that the dawn of agriculture took place some five or six thousand years ago. Scattered hunting tribes were lured to the fertile river valleys of the Tigris and Euphrates and began experimenting with the growing of crops. The change of lifestyle from the nomadic wanderings of the hunter-gatherers brought about settlement into permanent communities.

The first agricultural civilisation was that of the Sumerians who lived in Meso-potamia before the Assyrians and it was among these early farming communities that sacred trees began to find a serious place in spiritual belief and ritual. The Sumerians invented the art of writing and, with the advent of historical records, the search for early culture no longer relies solely on evidence from archaeology and art. In this respect it is a cruel irony that none of the inscriptions accompanying the carvings at Kalakh shed any light either on the nature of the tree or what is taking place. They refer only to the magnificence and otherwise bloodthirsty nature of Ashurnasirpal. Yet answers do exist.

Cylinder seals used as personal markers by Sumerians, the rough equivalent of rub-ber stamps, were sometimes engraved with scenes including stylised trees. In early versions of these seals the trees were depicted with animals in attendance, usually goats or deer and occasionally lions, and this probably represents a vestige of hunter-gatherer belief. Only on those from later dates are human ministers present. To add to this record of tree worship on art in miniature we also have sparse fragments of pottery revealing a similar emphasis. A decorated potsherd at least 5,000 years old, taken from an archaeological site at Mari in Syria, may be among the first from anywhere in the world to show human devotion to a sacred tree. It is crudely engraved but its artist has drawn a garden setting at the centre of which is a small tree apparently being tended by a goddess. Several goat-like animals are browsing on foliage in the background. The same scene is described in the *Gilgamesh Epic*, a vast Mesopotamian heroic tale written down in the 3rd millennium BCE concerning the life and exploits of the eponymous half-invented, half-genuine king of Sumer, Gilgamesh. In a part of the saga that explains the creation of the world, the tree is named only as the *halub*, which cannot be identified botanically though it may have been a willow growing on the river bank. However, the goddess figure with the tree is Inana, the earliest of the Mesopotamian mother goddesses:

> A tree, a *halub* tree
> On the banks of the pure Euphrates grew
> The river was its drinking water
> The mighty south wind wrenched at its base, tore at its crown;
> The waters of the Euphrates carried it away.
> A lady walking in fear at the word of An, in fear at the word of Enlil
> Took the tree in her hand and brought it to Unug
> To pure Inana's holy garden she brought it.
> She tended the tree with her hand, let it stand at her foot.

The story supports the notion that the sacred tree was a symbol of the fertility goddess. After Inana had taken the sapling uprooted by the floodwaters of the Euphrates back to her sanctuary, she nurtured the tree so that its wood might be used to create her bed and her throne, in other words her symbolic presence:

> When at last shall I have a holy throne that I may sit on it? concerning it she said;
> When at last shall I have a holy bed that I may lie on it? concerning it she said.

The story goes on to relate how the *halub* tree was usurped by a demoness until Gilgamesh won it back for the goddess, felled it and fashioned it for her personal use. Unsophisticated imagery of this kind may have formed the basic liturgy of sacred tree worship.

Other written evidence of sacred trees from ancient Mesopotamia has also come to light. One of the major cities of the southern marshes at the head of the Arabian Gulf, Eridu, was the centre of a tree-worshipping cult for more than a thousand years from the 3rd millennium BCE or even earlier, as its poetry reveals (unfortunately, as with the *halub*, the name given to the sacred tree, *kiskanu*, cannot be translated botanically):

> In Eridu there is a black kiskanu-tree
> Growing in a pure place,
> Its appearance is lapis lazuli, erected on the Apsu.

> Enki, when walking there, fills Eridu with abundance,
> In the foundation of it is the place of the underworld,
> In the resting place is the chamber of Nammu.
> In its holy temple there is a kiskanu tree, casting its shadow.
> Therein no man can enter.

The description suggests that, in its earliest form, the sacred tree of the ancient Near East was a living plant, decorated in honour of the deity it represented. The tradition of decorating the tree probably developed from another mythical episode included in the *Epic of Gilgamesh*. While he was searching for Utnapishtim, the only person to have been given the secret of immortality, the eponymous hero came across a land where trees belonging to the Sun God, Shamash, were growing in a jewel garden, adorned with precious and semi-precious stones:

> [… he] came out in front of the sun.
> […] brightness was everywhere.
> All kinds of [thorny] spiky bushes were
> Visible, blossoming with gemstones.
> Carnelian bore fruit, hanging in clusters, lovely to look at,
> Lapis lazuli bore foliage, bore fruit and was delightful to view.

The *Gilgamesh Epic* began as a collection of word-of-mouth stories centuries before it came to be written down and, clearly, it represents traditions and beliefs that stretch back into prehistory when spiritual ideas were typically promoted in simple ways. From adorning a living tree it was an easy step to create a stylised totem. The indications are that by the time of the Third Dynasty at Ur, late in the 2nd millennium BCE, the tree was taking the form of a hewn trunk or pole decorated with metal bands and ribbons and studded with precious stones.

Where the *Gilgamesh Epic* touches on trees, the pictures drawn are suggestive of sacred groves and gardens. Babylonian texts suggest that these were areas set aside in the grounds of the royal palaces, which became the responsibility of the god king who was also known as the *nukarribu* – the 'Gardener'. He alone took the responsibility of guarding and tending the sacred grove. A fragment of text dating from the reign of the Akkadian king Sargon the Great, who reigned in the 24th century BCE, includes the line 'Akki (Enki), the waterscooper, placed me as his gardener. When I was a gardener Ishtar was in love with me.' Ishtar is the name given to the mother goddess Inana by the Akkadian successors to the early Sumerian rulers.

Sumerian culture soon spread to other nations of the ancient Near East and the rites of tree worship were copied widely. Early in the 3rd millennium BCE in what is now Anatolia, a region of Turkey, the Hittite people shared a conviction about the great spiritual power of trees. One of their documents, inscribed in cuneiform on a tablet, most of which has been obliterated by the passage of time, contains tantalising reference to a ritual that took place in a sacred grove. An image or symbol of an unnamed deity was brought from the temple, seated in a decorated chariot and hauled to a sacred wood in a night-time procession that included temple harlots carrying torches. There it appears that the image underwent ritual washing. Once more we have evidence of trees and water being joined in symbolic partnership:

> The women go in front, also the dancers and the temple harlots go in front and they hold lighted torches . . . and the god comes behind and they take the god down through the Tarnawi gate to the wood. And where the god comes to the bath house in the wood, the priest takes muttis and water and goes around the house and the god enters the house.

Another important clue to the riddle of the obscure tree carvings discovered at Kalakh is to be found in an unlikely source, the texts of the Biblical Old Testament. The Hebrew chroniclers and prophets were constantly critical of an object which, in the original language of the Old Testament, is called an *asherah*, but which the translators working on the King James Bible in the 17th century described as 'the grove'. The *asherah* was a stylised tree named after, and symbolising the presence of, the most important fertility goddess of Canaan, a country that also borrowed heavily from Sumerian culture. The *asherah* is, therefore, the earliest example of a sacred tree that written evidence links with a named deity. Biblical evidence indicates that the Assyrians and Babylonians also revered an object similar in style and purpose to the Canaanite model because during the time that the Assyrian hegemony dominated the nations of Israel and Judah, the Israelites were oblige to maintain an Assyrian *asherah* in the Temple of Jerusalem. The prophetic Book of Jeremiah contains an astonishingly detailed description of this object that stood beside the altar of Yahweh, probably during the reign of Jehoiakim at the turn of the 7th century BCE. A wooden pole or trunk was hung with woven cloth and decorated with precious metals and, although its home was in the Temple, it was sometimes carried about in procession:

> For the customs of the people are vain: for one cutteth a tree out of the forest, the work of the hands of the workman, with the axe.

They deck it with silver and with gold; they fasten it with nails and with gold, that it move not.

They are upright as the palm tree, but speak not: they must needs be borne, because they cannot go. Be not afraid of them; for they cannot do evil, neither also is it in them to do good.

For as much as there is none like unto thee, O Lord ...

but they are altogether brutish and foolish: the stock is a doctrine of vanities.

Silver spread into plates is brought from Tarshish, and gold from Uphaz, the work of the workman, and of the hands of the founder; blue and purple is their clothing: they are all the work of cunning men.   (*Jeremiah* 10. 3ff.)

It becomes clear that the *asherah* was worshipped not only by overtly pagan societies in the ancient Near East but also, rather more discreetly, by sections of the Hebrew tribes, and that their behaviour was resisted by many of the Israelite prophets and elders. *Asherah* worship went on for many hundreds of years and even extended into the Christian era. Such was the antagonism among sections of orthodox Jews that the *Mishnah*, a book of Jewish law compiled in the 2nd Christian century, lists a whole catalogue of prohibitions associated with the illicit worship of the *asherah*. These restraints were clearly directed towards people who were still being lured from Jewish orthodoxy into idolatry of pagan deities. The *Mishnah* confirms that the *asherah* was wooden and could take the form of either a consecrated living tree or a man-made object resembling a tree. It lists a miscellany of *asherah*-related items that was strictly 'off limits' if put to ritual use. It included vines, palm branches, myrtle and willow branches. Any of these things could, technically, have been misused to construct or decorate an *asherah* or were already associated with *asherah* worship.

Among the prohibitions contained in the *Mishnah*, however, was a specific ban on the sale of fir cones to pagans. This ruling might seem innocuous enough, aimed at protecting a vital economic interest since, in Biblical times, the products of Palestine's extensive cedar forests were something of a rare commodity in the Near East. The emphasis on cones, however, suggests other motives since any commercially driven prohibition would have been against the sale of seeds. It sounds an echo of the Assyrian rite drawn so obscurely in the Kalakh carvings.

A logical explanation of the Mesopotamian ritual begins to emerge. The strangely stylised tree of Kalakh represents the paramount fertility goddess, Inana or Ishtar, the counterpart of the Canaanite goddess Asherah. A number of additional clues point towards this. In the intricate detail of the carvings from Kalakh and Nineveh, many of the human and hybrid figures wear a wristband bearing a rose symbol. Other archaeological evidence confirms that the rose was identified not only with the Assyrian Ishtar but also of such powerful fertility divas as the Phrygian mother goddess Kybele and the Greek Aphrodite.

The unusual design of the leaves on the Kalakh tree is puzzling but details from ancient medical texts may place the *palmette* in context. The art of several ancient Near East cultures including Egypt reveals that a regularly favoured symbol of fertility goddess was the uterus. Most frequently this was drawn as a bag, open at the bottom, and shaped like a Greek omega, but the *palmette* offered a variation on the theme. Its seven lobes symbolised the seven chambers of which it was widely believed that the human uterus was constructed, before dissection of human cadavers became freed from religious taboos.

Taking the logic a stage further, the sacred tree came to represent the fertility goddess and when the cone, phallic in shape, was directed at the tree the ritual represented a symbolic impregnation of her womb. The bucket depicted in the carvings from Kalakh probably held water, and Mesopotamian poetry of the period reveals that water was seen as the semen of the gods by the people of the ancient Near East much as it was for the nomadic European hunters. A hymn from late in the 3rd millennium BCE includes a vivid description of the activities of the god of fresh water, Enki:

> After father Enki has lifted his eye over the Euphrates
> He stands up proudly like a rampant bull.
> He lifts his penis, ejaculates,
> Fills the Tigris with sparkling water.

Trees were revered by the peoples of the ancient Near East for at least one reason common to other early cultures. Human life tended to be precarious and short and it deferred to the principle of the survival of the fittest and strongest. Unless felled by men or brought down through the actions of the gods in storm and tempest, trees generally outlived human beings and this extended life span made them seem immortal. Yet the Mesopotamians also worshipped trees for reasons peculiar to their environment and probably subtly different to those existing elsewhere in the world. On the alluvial plains of the Mesopotamian river valleys trees were, and still are, uncommon, but those that survive – date palms, willows and a few other species – are undeniably tough. They represent some of the few plants capable of withstanding the periods of intense drought that result in all other greenery withering. Thus, in

Mesopotamian eyes, the trees stood out as lone and tenacious survivors. The mystique of trees would also have been fuelled for the people living on the alluvial floodplains with the tales brought back by travellers from distant parts. To the west, north and east Mesopotamia is ringed by mountains where forests of great trees grew, far more majestic in stature than those on the alluvial plains, and the mountains, according to Mesopotamian mythology, were the preserve of the gods! The trees stretched out their arms to heaven. They were the largest and tallest living things in the natural world and they provided the closest animate link between gods and mortals.

Often myths seem to have been created in order to deter ordinary people from entering the great woodlands. In the lands of the ancient Near East, society held the forests and their spirituality in deep respect and fear. They became places of taboo. *The Epic of Gilgamesh* tells of a terrifying ogre of the forests named Humbaba:

> Enlil (the Sumerian national god) has destined him to guard the Pine Forest,
> To be the terror of the people:
> Great infirmity would seize all those who penetrated his forest.

It is understandable that the deity responsible for life and fertility in nature, the great mother goddess and Queen of Heaven, should be represented by a sacred tree. The

Above: Palm trees growing beside the River Euphrates at Hadditha in Iran. Ancient people saw such trees as tenacious survivors in a hostile landscape, where all other vegetation perished.

Mesopotamian fertility god, however, also seems to have earned tree symbolism in common with his more recent counterparts in northern Europe and with such early contemporaries as the Hittites. According to the mythology that ancient peoples learned by way of explanation of the 'death' of nature during the winter months and during extensive periods of drought, this deity was ill-fated, destined to be lost to the underworld for a part of each year (see Chapter 4). In Mesopotamia it was the god Dumuzi, the dying-and-rising son and incestuous lover of Inana. He became Tammuz in Babylonian times and is mentioned in the Old Testament book of the prophet Ezekiel, which describes women sitting by the temple 'weeping for Tammuz'. A cedar wood pole is thought to have represented Tammuz.

The Mesopotamian sacred tree, along with the later traditions that derived from it, did not stand alone but merely came to prominence a great deal earlier than some others. It had its counterparts elsewhere in Asia. Further to the northwest from Mesopotamia, in what is now the Anatolian region of Turkey, the presence of the Hittite god, Telepinu, who 'went missing' for a part of each year, was symbolised by a pine tree. In Phrygia, where the great mother goddess was known as Kybele, her son and lover was Attis who became Adonis in Greek myth. Attis was cast as a typical dying and rising god. Like his counterparts he needed to die in order to be reborn as the agricultural season turned from dearth to plenty. He did not, however, merely get himself lost like the Canaanite god Baal or descend into the underworld for part of the year. He castrated himself beneath the sacred tree of the goddess and bled to death from his terrible wounds.

Wherever the idea of sacred trees has been adopted, the association with both genesis and death is never far removed. In Egypt the cow goddess, Hathor, enjoyed a tree cult in ancient times with epithets that describe her as 'Lady of the Date Palm' and 'Lady of the Southern Sycamore' (another name for the Fig tree). Yet she was also revered as a funerary goddess who meted out food and drink to the dead. The Papyrus plant was also, incidentally, sacred to her and in pharaonic times a ritual of gathering Papyrus stalks was performed in her honour.

Trade routes were established in prehistory between Mesopotamia and India and resulted in a considerable amount of cultural exchange. Images of sacred trees can be found on seals fashioned by the earliest known peoples of the subcontinent, the Indus Valley civilisation. The Indus Valley people lived about 4,000 years ago before the Aryan migrations took place from the north and stamped an alien culture, irrevocably, on the indigenous population of prehistoric India. From very early times in India, as in Mesopotamia, trees have also been worshipped as symbols of fertility. The general term for these trees is *vrksa* (*rukkha* in Pali) meaning 'Tree of Life' (see Chapter 14).

In Classical European tradition, sacred trees also played their part. During the 8th century BCE in Sparta, the goddess Helen became identified with the Plane tree. The heroine made famous in the Homeric legend of the sack of Troy was not a mortal woman but the daughter of Zeus by Leda and a sister of the heavenly twins Castor and Polydeuces. Although her best known aspect lies in her rape away from king Menelaus by Paris, an abduction that provided the trigger for the Trojan Wars, shrines at various ancient places in Greece indicate that she originated in pre-Homeric times as a tree goddess known as Dendritis.

The Romans, obsessed with the myth accounting for the death of Attis, imported the cult from Phrygia and, under Roman influence, offerings to the sacred tree became particularly savage. Kybele and Attis were honoured each year on 22 March in a festival known as the Day of Blood. A Pine tree, a model of Attis hung in its branches, was carried with great pomp and ceremony by a Guild of Tree Bearers to the Temple of the goddess. It was draped with coloured cloth and decked with the violets that, in classical tradition, are flowers of death. When the tree had been positioned, the noviciate priests of Kybele ran through the streets dressed in gowns that were, at first, pure white but soon changed to a bloody crimson. As they went they seized knives placed conveniently in scabbards by the roadside and, in a dreadful re-enactment of the Attis myth, emasculated themselves before depositing their testicles on the altar of the goddess.

By the advent of the Christian era the symbolism of the Mesopotamian sacred tree had become so popular that it had even entered into orthodox Jewish worship. In the remains of a 1st-century synagogue at Hammath by Tiberias, archaeologists unearthed a massive block of limestone engraved with the outline of a *menorah*, the familiar seven-branched Jewish candlestick. Grooves designed to hold the lamps are carved into the stone and the tips of the candlestick branches are worked with pomegranates and flowers suggesting a link with trees. More convincing evidence of the interest in crafting the *menorah* as a sacred tree has come from a comparatively modern synagogue at Al-Buqai close to the Lebanese border that was built, in part, with stones salvaged from an earlier ruined building. Under a layer of plaster hacked off during refurbishment, an aged carving was discovered, in the centre of which is the clear outline of a *menorah*. This object is carved unmistakably in the form of a tree.

Tree worship in pagan Mesopotamia is perhaps to be expected. More surprising is the extensive evidence of holy plants to be found in Biblical tradition.

CHAPTER 4

Divine Death
and Genesis

In some parts of the world, mainly in tropical and subtropical regions, there is little visible transformation of seasons. The leaves on the trees are constantly replaced and there are always flowers to admire and fruits to pick – evidence that the spirits of greenery are alive and well. In other regions, however, a change takes place that, in times past, has mystified and frightened humankind – the seasonal death of the green mantle. In hotter, dryer parts of the world this demise takes place during the summer months when temperatures can soar to more than 55°C (130°F) in the shade, and for many months the land bakes, rainclouds do not appear and rivers and lakes dwindle and dry up. In more extreme northerly and southerly latitudes, the same dearth of greenery is associated with the cold months of winter when many trees shed their leaves and herbs shrivel away to nothing.

It has been necessary to create myths to explain the alarming changes in the green world and, by and large, such stories have centred on a divinity that, for one reason or another, is seasonally indisposed. The deity who goes absent from duty is usually cast as a somewhat unpredictable and frenetic male god and there is often an interplay, in the myth, between himself and his consort the mother goddess. Frequently the 'miss-

Left: A Rowan tree growing from a cleft in rocks beside an upland stream in Snowdonia, North Wales. To ancient people winters were times of death in the green world.

ing' deities are linked with the growing of corn or other cereal, an association that is not entirely surprising since cereals were among the earliest crops to be cultivated and have always provided a staple and vital source of nourishment. The invocation in the Christian prayer 'Give us this day our daily bread' is a universal sentiment.

The story of divine death and genesis probably began with the Neolithic hunters, but the first recorded evidence comes from the ancient Near East some 5,000 years ago. It centres around the tribulations of a vegetation god named Dumuzi, the son and incestuous lover of the Sumerian mother goddess, Inana, the apotheosis of the earth that the pioneering peasant farmers tilled. The earth was her temporal womb, and all that grew from it her progeny. The womb of the goddess had to be sexually impregnated to bring new life to the fields and orchards and, at each New Year, Inana was ritually married to Dumuzi. In an ancient hymn that celebrates the occasion, Inana cries out her need:

> As for me, my vulva. For me the piled-high hillock,
> Me, the maid, who will plough it for me?
> My vulva, the watered ground – for me,
> Me, the Queen, who will station the ox there?

A great exuberant roar of response follows from the congregation attending the rite:

> O Lordly Lady, the king will plough it for you,
> Dumuzi the king will plough it for you.

It is alleged that Dumuzi was once a living king, the son of a great warrior named Lugalbanda. For how long the legend of the sacred marriage had existed, no one knows. The belief that the male and female elements of nature, through their divine intercourse, brought new life to the world lay within the core of Mesopotamian creed and must have travelled from deep in prehistory. Yet the logic of the belief was impaired, because for half the year the genesis failed. Life withered in spite of the celestial union and death announced herself, for the goddess of death and nemesis was also a woman, in the desolation of the harsh Mesopotamian summer. In order to account for this there had to be an antithesis to the explanation of new life. It came in the shape of another myth, a disturbing tale of Inana's confrontation with the powers of desolation; a meeting that went tragically wrong.

Inana, the goddess of life, had a sibling, an *alter ego* named Ereshkigal, the goddess of death. Inana descended to the underworld to challenge her sister's power but, in a telling foretaste of the Christian Passion story, she was overwhelmed and slain.

Stripped of her regal finery, she was beaten, placed naked on a throne in a parody of queenship and finally sentenced to death, to be hanged from a post by a nail until life departed. All was not lost, however. Through the mediation of the gods, concerned at what would befall the living world without Inana, she was restored to life (see also Chapter 3). Nonetheless a condition was applied to her rescue. Ereshkigal insisted that a hostage must be sent in her place. Inana returned to the upper world but, in a fit of pique at having found her lover, Dumuzi, lording it on her throne in her absence, she ordered him to the underworld as her substitute. Realising the implication for the natural world that lay in this impetuous decision, however, she was persuaded to adopt a measure of pragmatism. Dumuzi, who became the Tammuz mentioned in the Old Testament Book of Ezekiel, was to remain in the underworld for half of every year, and his sister, a minor goddess named Geshtinana, was to take his place for the other half. Dumuzi's absence coincided with the period after the harvest in the Near East when, under the relentless heat of the summer sun, the alluvial plains of Iraq and Iran bake into an iron-hard pan and become an arid desert in which little may grow. Thus the Mesopotamians accounted for the death of the natural world under the blistering heat of the summer sun. They had neatly invented a myth to explain the endless alternating cycle of life and death and, in some respects, the saga mirrored what took place in the real life of their farms. During the dry summer months, seed corn, the embodiment of Dumuzi, was stored in underground silos.

The early historical records of the ancient Near East make clear that, while the underlying concept of a sexual partnership between goddess and god was widespread, probably having arisen in Mesopotamia at some time during prehistory, the individual personalities developed separately in different cultures. The Sumerian goddess Inana possesses an altogether distinct character from her counterparts, the Canaanite goddess Anat and Hannahannas, the celestial diva of the Hittite kingdom of Hatti. Moving forward in time, in Europe the Greek classical goddess Demeter bears little similarity to the Germanic and Scandinavian fertility deity Freyja. In the myths associated with Demeter, it was her daughter Persephone who descended to the underworld for the winter season and who ruled over the kingdom of death. Freyja, by contrast, had a twin brother, Freyr, who was also at times her sexual partner, but he was not a vegetation deity. Freyr was chiefly concerned with peace and prosperity in the world.

Among the consorts of the goddess, the dying-and-rising vegetation god of Sumer, Dumuzi, was an accountably different personality from his counterparts elsewhere in the ancient Near East. In Canaan, Baal fought a tremendous battle with the forces of adversity in the shape of the god Mot, was killed and then restored by his sister Anat with whom he enjoyed the all-important sexual partnership. In the mountainous Hittite kingdom, frequently beset by unpredictable storms, the vegetation god Telepinu was not slain but departed suddenly in a characteristic rage and went missing until his anger was soothed and he was persuaded to return to his duties. The ill-fated dying-and-rising god of Norse myth was Balder. However, there is – incidentally – little suggestion that he was recognised as a vegetation deity or that he enjoyed a sexual liaison with any fertility goddess such as Freyja or Idunn, who was the keeper of the apples of immortality.

In the ancient Near East the conventional thinking seems to have been that the vegetation god was masculine, unpredictable and destined for periods of absence in some form of netherworld where he was incapable of looking after the green world. Not all cultures, however, have made the vegetation god male. In Hinduism the god of agriculture is Balarama but in some of the more primitive forms of worship in India the responsibility was placed with a goddess named Bhumi. The second wife of Vishnu, she is a Hindu fertility diva, but agricultural tribes such as the Bhils still reveal her original purpose when they invoke her, as Zami Mata or 'earth mother', to ensure the well-being of vegetation. By similar token, not all traditions have made the dying-and-rising god responsible for vegetation.

Bearing in mind that early societies envisaged celestial impregnation taking the form of rain penetrating the earth, in various parts of the world the vegetation deity was not infrequently a god of storms and thunder. In Hittite mythology, the storm god Teshub was also regarded as a vegetation god whose role at times seems to have paralleled that of Telepinu. The supreme deity in ancient China, Yu Huang Shang Ti, was generally considered to be out of touch with the ordinary events on earth but, nonetheless, he became recognised as the god of agriculture in Taoist belief because he also controlled the natural forces of rain, wind, thunder and lightning. Turning to Central America, the Mayan deity responsible for agriculture in pre-Columbian Mexico, Ah Bolom Tzacab, otherwise known as the 'leaf-nosed god' since he wears a leaf ornament through his nose, took on the responsibility for growth of produce in the fields and for bringing the necessary rain.

The early agriculturist appreciated the violence of nature, and the understanding that life in the fields was inextricably linked with death and destruction was never far from the minds of people. The chthonic deities, those concerned with matters of the earth, were generally engaged in conflict as often as they were in love-making. The Sumerian goddess Inana, and her successor among the Babylonians, Ishtar, were often depicted bristling with weapons of war. The Canaanite goddess Anat who rescued Baal's body from the underworld had decidedly sanguinary tastes:

> Much she fights and looks, battles and views.
> Anat gluts her liver with laughter
> Her heart is filled with joy.
> Anat's liver exults,
> Her knees she plunges in the blood of soldiery
> Thighs in the gore of troops.

Modern pagans, believing that they are revitalising some old pan-European religion based on a mother goddess, make the mistaken assumption that she was a benign and motherly personality, ruling a kind of rusticated utopia while occasionally commuting backwards and forwards to the moon. The only downside to her green and glorious world, and a serious interest in looking after animals and plants, comes when she is grieving her absent son and lover during the 'dark' season. The reality is somewhat different. Most of the goddesses in the ancient Near East were as much concerned with waging war and acting as tutelary heads of rival kingdoms as they were in ensuring that animals bred and plants grew successfully. In northern Europe, a similar trend emerged. Freyja was directly associated with death, and legend has it that she received half of those mortals slain in battle. In summary different partnerships of deities responsible for the natural world behaved quite distinctly in different cultures, and the way in which they were perceived depended to no small extent on the environmental conditions under which people lived.

One of the most elaborate and fascinating tales of death and genesis in the green world comes from ancient Egypt. The Egyptians, dominated by a hostile desert environment, were acutely aware of the implications that lay in the seasonal loss of their world's green mantle followed by its mysterious reappearance. Egypt developed a remarkable and unique cult that brought together death and regenesis in a way not found in western Asia. In common with their contemporaries further north, two of the most important deities in the pantheon of the early Egyptians were the vegetation god Osiris and his sister, the fertility goddess Isis. Osiris, however, was to become associated with a cult so elaborate that those of his counterparts, Baal in Syrio-Palestine and Dumuzi or Tammuz in Mesopotamia, pale into comparative insignificance. To appreciate why this took place we need to delve back further into Egyptian prehistory.

North Africa did not always have the harsh and arid climate we know today. In prehistoric times, when the Egyptians were nomadic and tribal, the Nile valley was lush, watered with frequent rains and grazed by hippopotamus, antelope and giraffe. Among several theories of the origins of Osiris is that he first emerged among the early herdsmen and agricultural pioneers of North Africa as a tree spirit. The climate changed, however, and the desert began to encroach ever more severely. By the time of the great civilisation epitomised by the Pharaohs, which began in about the mid-3rd century BCE, the only saving grace that stood between survival in Egypt and the disastrous necessity of abandoning the country to the desert was the periodic flooding of the Nile valley. This permitted irrigation, the spread of fertile alluvial soil and the ability to grow all-important crops. By the Middle Kingdom period, from 2133 to 1786 BCE, Osiris, symbolised by a phallic pillar, was being hailed as the spirit of the corn, the progenitor of crops. Examples of this pillar, known as the Djed Column, have been dated to as early as 2600 BCE at the close of the Early Dynastic Period and, before it came to represent Osiris, the Djed Column was closely associated with granaries, presumably as a fertility totem.

There might seem, on the face of it, to be little to choose between the climate of Mesopotamia and Egypt. Both lands are subject to extremes of heat and drought, crossed by major river systems that flood periodically, and heavily dependent on water. There are, however, significant differences. The Nile does not rise in the haphazard way of the Tigris and Euphrates and the agricultural season runs in a very precise manner. From late April until July the lands around the Nile are cracked and blasted by hot relentless winds off the desert. They await the surge of waters from the Ethiopian highlands and the great equatorial lakes. These come towards August and, provided that the river level reaches a critical height, the banks overflow and the plains are covered. Crops are traditionally sown as the waters recede sometime in November and are harvested between March and April.

From long ago, the Egyptian farmers celebrated these moments, which they believed to be in the hands of Osiris and Isis. The regularity of the seasons invited the development of a mythology the like of which is not found elsewhere. We also need to bear in mind that Egypt's cultural origins are quite distinct from those of western Asia. They derive from the African south and from the Libyan desert to the west. Osiris may have represented the implacable and universal belief that the green

mantle of the world can only bloom, phoenix-like, out of the decay of the old, but in him the concept took a radical shift. Osiris rose from the corruption of nothingness to reign forever over the paradise kingdom of the dead.

In order to explain the 'death' of the green world, Osiris, like Baal and Tammuz, had to die. His demise was a particularly violent one and its story has been assembled from fragments inscribed onto the walls of pyramids and the inner linings of coffins and sarcophagi. In the minds of the ancient Egyptians, Isis and Osiris – the fertility goddess and her consort – were once living people, an incestuous royal brother and sister who travelled the world teaching the newly found techniques of cultivation, and then returned to Egypt to be hailed as a god-king and his queen. There were, however, jealous rivals, among whom Seth, the brother of Osiris, had murder in mind. Seth represented the old Egypt, a land of lion and elephant, to be hunted over and pillaged while Osiris guarded and nurtured its bounty. Seth slew Osiris by entombing him in a coffin that he threw into the Nile. For years afterwards Isis searched for her husband and brother until she discovered the coffin, opened it and used her magic to restore Osiris' corpse to a state of virility from which she was able to conceive a son, Horus.

Above: The Egyptian goddess Isis, in the form of a falcon,
restored to life her dead brother and husband Osiris, so that
he might reign over the Kingdom of the Dead.

Enraged by Isis' action, Seth located the body of Osiris and tore it into 14 pieces, which he hurled all over the land of Egypt so that Osiris might never again father a child. Osiris is mentioned in this context, in the *Dramatic Ramesseum Papyrus*, an instructional manual concerning Egyptian ritual techniques. The papyrus depicts the dismemberment of Osiris carried out by Seth who is drawn as an ass and who is described as 'hacking the god to pieces', and the text draws on the analogy of barley-threshing. The dismemberment and scattering of Osiris' body thus carries echoes of a part of the Canaanite saga of Baal and Anat, when Anat allegedly took her revenge on the underworld god, Mot:

> She seized divine Mot,
> With a blade she split him,
> With a sieve she winnowed him,
> With fire she burnt him,
> With mill-stones she ground him,
> In a field she scattered him.

There is a reasonable argument, however, that this incident in the story has been misplaced at some time in history and that the dismemberment was not carried out by Anat on Mot but by Mot on Baal, a scenario that would make far more sense.

In the mythology of the Osirian saga, the gods of Egypt joined the broken pieces of corpse that Isis had, once more, searched out and painstakingly collected together. The body was swathed in linen bandages. Isis fanned life into it and Osiris was revived to reign as god of the dead. The logic proceeded that each Pharaoh reigning over the temporal world of the living was the embodiment of Horus, the son, during his earthly existence and Osiris, the father, Lord of the Underworld or Duat, the place of the setting sun, after death.

Osiris was commemorated in a confusing assortment of yearly rites that trace back to his various responsibilities as a god of trees, crops, fertility and death. The old Egyptian calendar was based not on the solar cycle of 356 days but on the first sighting of the star Sirius in the dawn sky. This resulted in an irregular calendar of only 360 days before it was changed in 30 BCE to the proper Alexandrian solar year. Based on the latter the Egyptians celebrated the restoration of Osiris in a festival that took place from 13 to 16 November. This occurred after the inundation of the Nile valley in August, a flood that was believed to be caused by the tears of Isis mourning her lost lover and brother. At the festival's climax, the priests of Osiris went to the Nile carrying a gold casket representing the coffin in which the god had first been entombed. Into it they poured the sacred water of the river and gave a great cry that Osiris had been found. Inside the casket the dead god was represented by a model made of earth and grain or by a small boy who perhaps embodied Horus. The model, once wetted, would quickly sprout with new greenery.

The November festival honoured the first restoration of Osiris by Isis. It was followed shortly afterwards by a rite of mourning that effectively linked the sowing of the corn with the dismemberment and scattering of Osiris' corpse by Seth. It began with the ploughing of a field using two black cows symbolising death. The small boy playing the part of Horus then sowed the ground with various types of grain, an essential dispersal of seed that lay at the heart of the legendary breaking and scattering of Osiris' corpse. The germination of the seed was further encouraged through the spilling of sacrificial blood. Victims were slaughtered and cremated in the fields and their ashes were scattered with the implements normally used for winnowing of grain, the separating of seed from chaff. Towards the end of these rites the image made from cloth packed with earth and seed was removed from the casket and replaced by a fresh one. The original was by then in the process of sprouting to symbolise the resurrection of the god.

According to myth, Seth hurled Osiris' penis into the Nile where it was eaten by a crocodile, but Isis fashioned an artificial organ and it was made clear in a specific cult of the Osirian phallus that he had lost none of his sexual ability in Paradise! The processions that took place in his honour across the length and breadth of Egypt included women carrying wooden articulated models of the dead god. By operating strings attached to the penis of the puppet, these Egyptian ladies no doubt stimulated a degree of merriment among the crowds.

By the time of the New Kingdom, which commenced in about 1567 BCE, the burial chamber of some royal tombs included what has been described as an 'Osiris bed'. This was a model of the god placed on a wooden frame and filled with silt in which barley had been sown. When the crop sprouted, it was seen to symbolise the resurrection of the dead person in the Osirian underworld. Osiris statues were often painted green to represent the vibrant living vegetation in the fields.

The connection between life, death and trees was also strong in Egyptian mysticism. The Roman writer Firmicus Maternus described a ceremony in which a felled pine was hollowed out, and from the cut wood an image of Osiris was fashioned. The image was then returned to the trunk cavity and sealed inside. Among the ruins of

Dendera which included a temple dedicated to Osiris, a coffin was discovered in which, typical of many others, the mummy of the god was depicted closely associated with a female tree figure.

The best known of the corn deities from the European Classical period is Demeter, the great mother goddess of the Greeks whose responsibilities were transferred in Roman culture to Ceres, the old Italic goddess of agriculture. Although she is described as an Earth Mother, her real focus of interest and power is in the corn, and her attribute is an ear of grain. Demeter is often depicted holding a bunch of grain stalks. At sowing time she was invoked by the Greek peasant farmer and she was also honoured in a harvest festival that took place on the sacred threshing floor (see also Chapter 13). Her association with harvest rites is commemorated in Homer's *Iliad* epic:

> See in the mind's eye wind blowing chaff on ancient threshing floors when men with fans toss up the trodden sheaves and yellow-haired Demeter, puff by puff, divides the chaff and grain.
> (*Iliad* v. 500)

Although Demeter herself was cast in the typical role of a mother goddess, it was not an incestuous male consort who provided the element of instability in nature but her daughter, Kore or Persephone. She became identified not only as the Corn Maiden but also as Queen of the Underworld. Even with the change of sex, life and death remained inextricably entwined in the symbolism of the corn deity who descended underground. The myth of Demeter and Persephone has always been interpreted as an allegory on the vegetation spirit going down into the earth and remaining dormant through the winter until the spring, but this does not equate with what happens during the Mediterranean season. The corn sprouts almost immediately after the autumn sowing and then grows continuously. The story of Demeter and Kore, however, has her roots in the Mycenaean Bronze Age civilisation that shaped more or less all of what was later to become Greece. In Mycenae, the ancient citadel in the Greek south that reached its zenith between 1600 and 1200 BCE, Demeter was described as the *sitopotinija* or Grain Mistress. If anything, the myth of Demeter and Persephone is either borrowed from Mesopotamia, through the Minoans, or is a throwback to much earlier times in Europe when the climate was different and there was indeed a long period of winter dormancy. Regardless of origins, many local north European corn deities were subsequently modelled on Demeter, including Gabjauja in Lithuania, Pellonpekko and Kondos in Finland.

The theme of the corn mother and her child persisted throughout the medieval period in Europe. A host of traditions and rituals arose surrounding the harvesting of the corn and the pacifying of the corn mother, many of which are detailed in Sir James Frazer's *The Golden Bough*. More or less at the same stage of development of any given culture, regardless of time or place in history, similar types of deity gain prominence, and very often the notion of winnowing and scattering also emerges somewhere in their biographies. Maize is known to have been cultivated in Meso-America as early as 5000 BCE, but for thousands of years the evidence of this is purely archaeological. We can only guess that the Neolithic people of the region recognised spirits of the corn in a manner similar to that which developed in Europe and elsewhere. In Aztec Mexico, during the Classical period from about 150 to 900 CE, the Maize God emerges as a notable figure among the ranks of deities. According to an old dictionary of names, he was called Pitao Cozobi; but in Aztec times, he was better known as Cinteotl and was believed to represent an aspect of the heroic god Quetzalcoatl, the Feathered Serpent. The theme of violence and dismemberment attached to the vegetation deity appears to have been universal in parts of the world where there are clear seasons of dearth in nature. In Mexico, far removed from ancient Egypt in both time and place,

Above: The underworld goddess Persephone confronting Hecate, goddess of pathways, from the 5th century BCE site of Eleusis in Greece.

the god actually responsible for the annual renewal of vegetation in the spring was not Cinteotl but Xipe Totec, whose name means 'the flayed one'. He was often represented by a priest wearing the flayed skin of a human sacrifice, seen to be the new vegetation of the earth that emerges after the rains. The skin was worn for 21 days, approximately the time needed for seed to germinate and appear as green shoots.

Where the dearth is less pronounced, the counterparts of Osiris and Xipe Totec are given more benign personalities and circumstances. In Polynesia, for example, the god of agriculture responsible for the growth of food plants is Rongo. He is also a rain god, but he abhors violence, including any form of blood sacrifice, and is a god of peace.

Myths of great antiquity describe the origin of the Maize plant and one of these stories is preserved in the Nahuatl colonial work *Leyenda de los Soles*. While roaming the earth looking for suitable sustenance for the newly created human race, Quetzalcoatl noticed an ant dragging along a single grain. After some discussion, and a degree of intimidation on the part of Quetzalcoatl, the ant was persuaded to show the god where it had found the grain. Having transformed himself into another ant, Quetzalcoatl was taken into the heart of mount Tonacatepetl, where he was shown a vast pile of the grains that the ants had been hoarding. In order to scatter the grain it was necessary for the god Nanahuatzin, with a little help from fellow deities, including the rain god Tlaloc, to split the mountain open. Tlaloc then scattered the Maize seeds far and wide.

In the Classical art of Mexico, the grain god was drawn with an elongated head like a cob of Maize, his hair sprouting to emulate the tuft of silk at the crown of the cob. As with most grain deities the world over, he was destined to die violently, and

An Aztec painting from the Fejervary-Mayer Codex,
depicting the changing fortunes of the Maize plant during
the first two years of a four-year period.

each year at harvest time the Aztec priests enacted a ritual decapitation when they removed the cob from the Maize stalk. The rain god Tlaloc was closely linked with the Maize crop – for obvious reasons in a country often parched by drought – and his consort Chalchihuitlicue, although a goddess of flowing waters, was also invoked to encourage the Maize crop to grow. So highly regarded was Chalchihuitlicue that she was the subject of a huge statue, more than 3 metres (10 feet) high, at Teotihuacan (now Mexico City), and an even larger unfinished image, weighing about 200 tonnes, was found on the slopes of the Tlaloc mountain.

In Far Eastern countries, where rice is the staple cereal crop, the harvest festivities are geared to celebrate the safe harvesting of the *padi* fields. In Sarawak, the Gawai Festival is celebrated at the end of May or early in June by various clans including the Bidayuhs and Ibans. A considerable amount of drinking and dancing takes place and the alcohol is, predictably, produced from fermented rice. One of the key features is a dance known as the Ngajat Lesong, in which individual participants attempt to lift the heavy mortar or *lesong* used for pounding the *padi* using only their teeth. During May in Sabah, another region of Malaysia, clans including the Dusuns and Kadazans celebrate a similar harvest festival known as the Kaamatan. This is more of a religious event and at its climax a rite of thanksgiving is led by a high priestess known as the Bobohizan.

The traditions of the dying-and-rising god survived well into the Christian era, particularly in country districts. In Britain, the successor to Dumuzi and Tammuz, Baal and Osiris was a character called John Barleycorn. A traditional English song goes:

> There were three men come out of the west
> Their victory to try
> And those three men took a solemn vow
> John Barleycorn must die
> They plowed, they sowed, they harrowed him in
> Throwed clods upon his head
> And those three men made a solemn vow
> John Barleycorn was dead.

In some parts of Europe, traditions have persisted that reveal the strong links between the harvest and the midwinter celebrations performed in pre-Christian times. Both possessed a magico-religious element designed to protect crops and animals and to ensure a good harvest in the following year, and they are largely the origin of the

Christmas feast. We load our kitchens with indulgences to eat and these are really a celebration of nature's bounty. In some parts of the western Ukraine, where Christmas is celebrated on 7 January (based on the Gregorian calendar), the Christmas table includes a sheaf of Oats woven into a special shape with four legs and various small bundles. This is designed to symbolise prosperity for the coming year.

Some of the Christmas traditions in Poland have a similarly rustic flavour and are designed to invoke the old pagan gods of nature into providing a good harvest during the next season. Straw has also been relied on for fortune-telling, as it has the world over when one 'pulls the short straw' to find out who is to be the unlucky member of a group. The Polish variation involves concealing wheat straws under the tablecloth at the Christmas Eve supper. Each guest who volunteers for the challenge pulls out the straw at his or her place. Green ones presage marriage within the year, one that is withered foretells a longer wait. A yellow straw betokens spinsterhood and a short one premature death.

The forthcoming harvest element of the Christmas festivity was strong in rural parts of Poland until very recently, and it was made to symbolise the ubiquitous partnership of death and rebirth in nature. After the Christmas Eve supper, the senior member of the family would go outside carrying dried fruit, which he would throw on the trees with a cry of 'Apples, pears, plums and cherries' to ensure a good crop of fruit. The host would wield an axe and a small straw figure, similar to a harvest dolly, was tied to a tree trunk. The tree was then issued with the warning that it would be cut down unless it bore fruit.

Many of the mythical characters whose personalities were shaped on the model of the dying-and-rising god of the harvest have come and gone, often perhaps lost without trace. Others are immortalised as part of our familiar architectural heritage. Look up into the roof of some of the oldest churches and cathedrals in Europe and you may see a gargoyle-like face staring down, framed by leaves or with greenery sprouting from the head. They first appear from about the 2nd century CE when they were sometimes carved on memorial stones. About 200 years later they were influencing Christian stone-carvers who worked a similar design into the decoration of tombs, and the fashion of using them to decorate Christian places of worship began in the 6th century. Yet the origin of these figures, which became known as the Green Man, lies in paganism. Among the earliest and best known are those which were installed in the cathedral of Trier, France, by the 6th-century bishop Nicetius, but these had originally been removed from a Roman pagan temple.

Who exactly the Green Man is, or was, is uncertain, but it would probably be a mistake to link him with the English Jack-in-the-Green character associated with celebrations on May Day. The Green Man seems to have more ancient pre-Christian origins. Since some of the earliest appearances of the leafy head are on memorial stones and tombs, it is more likely that he represents a character in the mould of the dying-and-rising vegetation god.

Does the Arthurian Green Knight fit into this mould, and is he based on a dying-and-rising nature deity? Morgan le Fay, the half-sister of King Arthur, persuaded the Green Knight, a man of gigantic stature, to challenge the Arthurian knights into striking a blow against him. There was, however, a condition attached, namely that the Green Knight could then return the blow a year to the day later. Sir Gawain rose to the challenge for the honour of Camelot and the Knights of the Round Table and when he decapitated the Green Knight it was in the belief that he would then never be liable for the forfeit; but the Green Knight picked up his severed head and rode away.

Above: The Green Man was a popular figure in German
morality plays during the Middle Ages. Almost certainly he
possess pre-Christian credentials as a pagan fertility god.

The character of Sir Gawain seems to have been associated with some of the old Celtic fertility traditions, including the imagery of a partner who was the maiden, mother and hag, symbolising the spring, summer and winter of the green mantle. Gawain was coerced into marriage to a repulsive crone who advised him that he must choose whether he wished her to appear repulsive by day, in which case she would become beautiful as darkness fell, or vice versa. In a spirit of chivalry Sir Gawain left the decision to the woman and she rewarded hum by becoming permanently beautiful. Although the story has become distorted, it is a reminder of the Irish Celtic legend of the hero who agreed to marry an ugly old woman, when no one else would woo her, and in return she became beautiful.

To a large extent we have abandoned the rites of the seasons concerned with the corn and its harvest. The modern gods of the supermarket and the sliced packaged loaf have distanced our daily bread from the plants of its source. Yet there is at least one modern experience that belies the notion that we are wholly uninterested. The crop circle is a curious phenomenon associated with corn that attracts much speculation and blends two ancient principles associated with the green mantle – the sacred grove and the spirit of the corn. Crop circles appear mysteriously, generally over the span of one night and without apparent human intervention, in fields of grain. The patterns occur most frequently during the spring and summer growing seasons in wheat and corn, but they have also been recorded in fields which are growing oats, barley, rape and other crops.

We tend to imagine that the crop circle is a modern phenomenon created as a hoax of some extra-terrestrial visitation and, indeed, in September 1991, two men, Douglas Bower and David Chorley, claimed to be responsible for all the modern incidents, using a wood plank and a rope. It comes as something of a surprise, therefore, to discover that the first recorded crop circle was encountered in England either in 1647 or 1678, although there is some dispute about the chronology. It became the subject of considerable speculation, much of which centred on devilish intervention. This explanation is clearly revealed in a woodcut of the period revealing a demonic creature with goat-like legs and a curly tail wielding a scythe. Elsewhere in the world crop circles have also been attributed to divine activity. Tibetan Buddhists,

It comes as something of a surprise ... to discover that the first recorded crop circle was encountered in England either in 1647 or 1678.

for example, recognise them and believe that they are the marks left after the psychic manifestation of *avatars* or incarnations of the Buddha.

The first modern instance of a crop circle was in Tully, England, in 1966. It was not, however, until the 1970s that crop circles began to receive serious attention. At that time they were being detected mainly in southern England, in the cereal-growing regions of Hampshire and Wiltshire, but they were also reported from the Australian outback and, in an isolated occurrence, from Switzerland. The first crop circle reports from Canada date from 1976 when a Saskatchewan farmer announced that several had been left in his fields after a close encounter with alien spacecraft.

Cut either clockwise or anti-clockwise, doubtless a high percentage were created by hoaxers, but when Bower and Chorley were persuaded to demonstrate their technique the results they obtained were surprisingly crude and inconclusive. Many circles remain unexplained despite intensive attention and theorising. From the 1970s onwards it was noted that in most cases the stalks of the cereal grasses were not severed but bent flat and, subsequently, the crop continued to grow, retaining the swirled patterns. From about 1990 designs evolved into more complicated patterns and one massive arrangement discovered on 7 November 1990 at Alton Barnes in Wiltshire ensured ongoing newsworthiness because of its sheer size and complexity. Circles started to appear within circles. Others were found to be grouped together with smaller satellite circles around a central ring. The patterns were also developed with straight lines, angles and spirals, though almost invariably these were elaborated on the basic circular design. Crop-circle devotees invented a jargon to accompany their interest and the informed members began to distinguish between the *mandala* (a petal-like arrangement), the *scorpion* (long chains of decreasing circles), the *galaxy* (stars and planets), and the *asteroid* (circles within circles or circles orbiting main rings). The most dramatic arrangement to date, clearly man-made, is the DNA Double Helix extending to nearly 200 metres and created on 17 June 1996 at Alton Barnes. The biggest recorded pattern is that found at Etchilhampton in Wiltshire in June of the same year extending to approximately 1.25 kilometres (¾ mile).

Circles appear throughout various regions of the world including the rest of Europe, the United States, Canada, South America, Asia and Australia. The only regions where, to date, they have not been recorded are China and South Africa, but it has to be appreciated that for every one that is reported many more go unnoticed. England remains the most popular destination for researchers into the phenomenon and it is in the UK that the most complicated patterns have been found.

CHAPTER 5

Holy Plants of the Old Testament

Across a large part of the world, lore and superstition about plants has arisen because they are to be found in the works of the Holy Bible. They have not necessarily been a direct part of Jewish or Christian ritual but have often taken on spiritual colours by association.

The Israelite tribes that migrated from Mesopotamia, via Egypt, sometime before 1500 BCE to their 'Promised Land' in Syrio-Palestine, maintained their own tradition of a Tree of Life. The founding fathers of Judaism, the Patriarchs, probably brought the idea from Mesopotamia or emulated the local Canaanite population who themselves had borrowed it. More or less all the culture of the ancient Near East stems from roots in Mesopotamia. The writers of the Book of Genesis, doubtless describing a centuries-old word-of-mouth tradition, gave the tree growing in the Garden of Eden a peculiarly Hebrew character. Romantic lore has identified the plant variously as an Apple, a Fig and a Pear, though there is nothing in the Old Testament texts to support the idea and, if anything, the evidence suggests that the Tree of Life in Genesis was definitely not an Apple. Where the Biblical author referred in Hebrew or Aramaic to the Tree of Life, his original description has been translated in the Greek from

Left: Adam and Eve in the Garden of Eden painted by the German artists Lucas Cranach the Elder (1472–1553).

which most modern renderings are taken as Sycamore. Classical Greek scribes incidentally describe the Egyptian Tree of Life using the same term. This results in a measure of confusion because 'Sycamore' in the Western sense bears no botanical relationship to the Biblical tree. It describes the species *Acer pseudoplatanus*, which is indigenous neither to the Nile valley nor to the Bible lands of Syrio-Palestine. It is generally recognised that 'Sycamore' in the Biblical context means a species of Fig tree, *Ficus sycamorus*. This is distinct from the Holy Fig of India, *F. religiosus* (see Chapter 14), and it bears a leaf very similar to that of the Mulberry. It is the likeness of foliage that probably gives rise to the term 'Sycamore', derived from combination of two Greek words: *sycos* (Fig) and *moros* (Mulberry).

We have already discovered how in the ancient world certain trees became recognised as the embodiments of mother goddesses, and the fertility context was probably the earliest in which the pastoralists and agriculturists viewed sacred trees. In Mesopotamia Ashurnasirpal II's enigmatic Tree of Life dominated the artwork of his palace in Kalakh, symbolic of the presence of Inana or Ishtar, the first paramount mother goddess in the Cradle of Civilisation. Trees subsequently took on another distinct characteristic and became recognised as founts of wisdom. For the Celts they provided a source of oracular utterance as they did for the later Vikings whose World Ash Tree *Yggdrasil* formed Othin's gallows. He hanged himself from its branches so that he might commune with the dead and absorb eternal knowledge. Wisdom, life and death became inseparable. Some of the strongest evidence for this intellectual expansion, however, is to be found in Judaic tradition.

Sunday sermons and synagogue rhetoric speak of Eve taking fruit from 'The Tree' in the Genesis myth, and many people brought up in the Jewish and Christian faiths maintain a casual belief that the Garden of Eden contained one single tree of significance. According to Genesis, however, the garden contained two sacred trees: a Tree of Life and a Tree of Knowledge.

> And the Lord God planted a garden eastward in Eden; and there he put the man whom he had formed.
>
> And out of the ground made the Lord God to grow every tree that is pleasant to the sight, and good for food; the tree of life also in the midst of the garden, and the tree of knowledge of good and evil. (*Genesis* 2. 8, 9)

In the Biblical context, the Tree of Knowledge conferred mortality and the Tree of Life immortality. According to the interpretation given by the Genesis writer, Adam was warned that he would eat from the Tree of the Knowledge on pain of death.

> And the Lord God commanded the man, saying, Of every tree of the garden thou mayest freely eat:
> But of the tree of the knowledge of good and evil, thou shalt not eat of it: for in the day that thou eatest thereof thou shalt surely die. (*Genesis* 2. 16, 17)

Several verses on, in the next chapter, Adam's newly created partner, Eve, was seduced by the serpent into eating the fruit of the tree:

> And the serpent said unto the woman, Ye shall not surely die:
> For God doth know that in the day ye eat thereof, then your eyes shall be opened, and ye shall be as gods, knowing good and evil. (*Genesis* 3. 4, 5)

This may seem a confusing contradiction with the previous passage. In reality it draws on two quite distinct traditions that have become merged with a resultant loss of sense. It is generally recognised that when the Genesis writer put pen to parchment, many centuries after the birth of traditions about the mythical events he described, he drew on a variety of sources. The lore had arisen and been transmitted by word of mouth over a long period of time to account for the beginnings of the people of Israel. On the one hand the writer took a peculiarly Hebraic and Jewish idea that, in the beginning, 'God's People' were given perfection and innocence but through their own sin it was taken away from them. When the ancestral woman ate from the Tree of Knowledge she was not punished because she had gained awareness about good and evil but because she had fallen foul of the serpent's suggestion that she could cheat death. It would have been illogical for a quest for knowledge to be censured since the Israelites recognised that their God was the source of all wisdom and that one who searched for wisdom would ultimately find God. In truth the banishment of Adam and Eve from Paradise had less to do with wisdom than the matter of mortality.

Merging with the wisdom ideology, the writer also introduced a much older concept. This too was deeply ingrained in Hebrew traditions, but it was one that they had brought with them from their cultural birthplace in Mesopotamia and it concerned a fundamental difference between gods and men. It delivered the same cruel lesson learned, albeit in different circumstances, by the Mesopotamian hero Gilgamesh when he tried to secure the Plant of Life. It reflected the uncomfortable reality that the immortality owned by the gods is something which flesh-and-blood human beings may never achieve.

What the Genesis writer does not make entirely clear is that the Fall came about not strictly as a result of Eve having eaten from the Tree of Knowledge but because she transgressed the laws made by the Israelite God Yahweh. These rules had been put in place to keep humankind separate from the divine. Adam and Eve were expelled from Paradise because further disobedience over Apple (Mulberry or Fig) 'scrumping' might have resulted in taking and eating fruit from the Tree of Life. Had they eaten from this tree they would, in effect, have tasted the ambrosia of heaven and gained immortality, thus raising human beings forever to the status of gods. The power of heaven could never have allowed such a situation and the Israelite leaders knew this. The Paradise couple became established as the first parents of the human race and human beings were destined not to live forever, as the serpent would have it, like gods. So the Genesis story of the two special trees in Paradise was created in order to explain to the Israelite people, in simple picturesque terms, why it was that human beings could not be immortal. It was made obscure by the merging of two traditions that actually have little in common.

The distinction between the trees, and the real cause of expulsion, is made much clearer in the Gnostic creation account *On the Origin of the World*, a work that was influenced by Greek thinking when it was written by an unknown author in about the 4th century CE. The author's vision of heaven includes an extra tier of celestial beings known as the Authorities:

> It was the deep chagrin and envy of the Authorities which brought about the Fall: 'Behold Adam! He has come to be like one of us, so that he knows the difference between the light and the darkness. Now perhaps he will be deceived as in the case of the Tree of Acquaintance and also will come to the Tree of Life ands eat from it and become immortal and become lord and despise us and disdain us and all our glory. Then he will denounce us along with our universe. Come let us expel him from Paradise down to the land from which he was taken . . .'
>
> (*Origin II*. 5 (120) 25 N.H. Library)

The combination of tree and snake was also adopted from Mesopotamian tradition by the peoples of Syrio-Palestine and it then became entrenched in Judaic lore. The snake provides a common link between the Tree of Life and the Tree of Knowledge. Because of its habit of sloughing its skin, it has been seen by most cultures as the eternal symbol of immortality, but its beady fixed stare has also made it an embodiment of wisdom. Under the banner of the Christian movement, however, the identity of the serpent was changed. It was deemed necessary to depict women as the sinful sex that had earned the curse of Eve and so, in Christian rhetoric, the serpent became the root of evil (even the phrase has botanical connotations), the embodiment of Satan. Christians later came up with the romantic image of the Virgin Mary 'trampling the serpent beneath her heel'.

One wonders where the link between trees and wisdom, apparently taken up by many different cultures, came from? Was it first dreamed up and put into picturesque words by the writer of the Biblical Genesis, a purely Hebraic and Jewish concept, or was it dredged from deeper and more ancient levels of cult? Did a traveller in distant times learn it from some arcane tribal lore, or was it an innate thing that arose as part of the basic human psyche all over the world? It is a question worth asking because the Wisdom Tree in the ancient Near East seems to be quite independent of its counter-part in northern Europe.

Irrespective of origins for their source of inspiration, artists have indulged in an assortment of licences when depicting the Tree of Knowledge. Not infrequently the snake coiled around its stem is depicted as being female, but one of the more bizarre interpretations combines two otherwise unrelated traditions in folklore and mythol-ogy, the Tree of Knowledge and the hallucinogenic mushroom *Amanita muscaria* (see Chapter 13). These themes have become merged in a fresco that survives from the 13th century in the French cathedral of Indres. Eve is confronted by a serpent whose form coils around a tree that is drawn unmistakably in the guise of the mushroom. This suggests that, at some time or other, Christianity has involved the use of hallucino-genic drugs derived from plants. The possibility formed the main platform of a highly contentious and much publicised book of the 1960s (since discredited) by the philol-ogist and historian John Allegro, entitled *The Sacred Mushroom and the Cross*.

The Fig achieves its greatest Biblical prominence in the Garden of Eden, if indeed that is the botanical identity of 'The Tree', but it is mentioned elsewhere in the Old Testament. It stands as the embodiment of happiness, prosperity, safety and security while also displaying a salutary degree of modesty in spite of its fame:

> And Judah and Israel dwelt safely, every man under his vine and under his fig tree.
>
> (*I Kings* 4. 25)

> And the trees said to the fig tree, Come thou and reign over us. But the fig tree said unto them, Should I forsake my sweetness, and my good fruit, and go to be promoted over the trees?
>
> (*Judges* 9. 10, 11)

Many kinds of tree have been targeted at one time or another during Jewish and Christian history as the Tree of Life in the Garden of Eden. Among these is *Aloe*, known since ancient times for its healing powers and generally called Aloe Vera. The genus *Aloe*, belonging to the family Liliaceae, includes more than 200 species indigenous to Africa from Egypt to the extreme south. Most of these are succulent herbaceous plants but the genus also contains a limited number of larger forms known as Tree Aloes, mainly in Namibia in southwest Africa. Aloes have been highly regarded since the time of the Pharaohs, and Queen Cleopatra allegedly used Aloe Vera on her skin as an aid to beauty. There are also some suggestions that Alexander the Great relied on the extract of the plant to heal battle wounds. The Aloes are now grown throughout the Mediterranean region and various warmer parts of the New World where they are cultivated to supply an extensive Aloe Vera industry. This has developed mainly since the 1950s when Aloe Vera became popular in the manufacture of cosmetic and anti-bacterial preparations. Today, the most therapeutic species is considered to be *A. barbadensis*, native to the Caribbean region.

Other trees that, according to some traditions, once grew in the Garden of Eden are actually not to be found in the Near East but belong to the New World genus *Anadenathera*. Folklore suggests that they once grew in Mesopotamia but were uprooted and planted afresh in the more peaceful setting of South American rainforests! These are leguminous plants that have become popularly known as the Trees of the Knowledge of Good and Evil. Two species are included, both of which bear spreading branches with delicate fern-like traceries of leaves, similar to those of Mimosa, and white pompom balls of flowers that mature into pods. *A. columbrina* grows in the Andean foothills, while *A. peregrina* is found in the tropical savannahs of northern South America.

Certain trees of Biblical fame became sacred on account of their longevity and resistance to decay. The Oak provides the obvious example in European pagan lore but in the lands of the Old Testament it was the Cedars, belonging to the genus *Cedrus*, that earned distinction. The Cedar of Lebanon, *C. libani*, seems truly indestructible and once grew in extensive forests covering much of the Lebanese mountains, though today it is restricted largely to the Besharre region of north Lebanon. Of magnificent stature, individual trees can grow to a height of 30 metres (100 feet) with branches forming horizontal layers with the appearance of a ladder reaching up from the earth towards the sky. The Old Testament contains more than 70 references to *erez*, the Hebrew word for Cedar, and, according to the Psalms, the tree was planted by God:

> The trees of the Lord are full of sap; the cedars of Lebanon, which he hath planted;
> where the birds make their nests; as for the stork, the fir trees are her house.
>
> *(Psalms* 104. 16ff.*)*

Among the Hebrews, the Cedar became the symbol of Israel's special relationship to God:

> The righteous shall flourish like the palm tree; he shall grow like a cedar in Lebanon.
> Those that be planted in the house of the Lord shall flourish in the courts of our God.
>
> *(Psalms* 92. 12ff.*)*

The Israelite tribes also exploited the Cedar forests of Syrio-Palestine commercially. They exported Cedar wood, earning considerable revenue, and the timber was much sought after by other nations, including the Egyptians, because of its considerable resistance to decay. For the Egyptians, the Cedar of Lebanon also earned its own special mystique. Its durability, coupled with the pleasantly aromatic resins in the timber, encouraged the Pharoahs to use the timber in the construction of their sarcophagi and the mystical barques by means of which the Sun God, Ra, travelled across the heavens by day and through the underworld by night.

The second tree revealed in the passage from the Psalms, the Date Palm (*Phoenix dactylifera*), also gained religious significance in both Judaism and Christianity. The tree is among the oldest in cultivation, grown in North Africa for at least 8,000 years, and was probably carried by the Moorish invaders to the Iberian peninsula during the 13th century CE from where it was exported to South and Central America. Date Palms were introduced into the United States in the late 1800s, and are now cultivated on a large scale in California.

In common with the Cedar of Lebanon, the Date Palm possesses tremendous resilience and has always been regarded as a life-saver in the desert. It survives in extremely arid conditions when other plants wither and die, and so for some, including the ancient Egyptians, its leaves became a natural symbol of longevity. The Hebrews used virtually every part of the plant. Its trunk provided timber, its fruits a source of food and a strong alcoholic beverage. The Date Palm evolved into a symbol of prosperity, beauty and victory for the Israelite tribes. Palm leaves also provided a common motif in the art of the ancient world, including Solomon's temple. In his vision of the new Jerusalem, the prophet Ezekiel envisaged a city decorated extensively with Palm trees. Tradition also has it that the Palm leaves were used to build the booths for the Feast of the Tabernacles:

And ye shall take you on the first day the boughs of goodly trees, branches of palm trees and the branches of thick trees, and willows of the brook; and ye shall rejoice before the Lord your God seven days. *(Leviticus* 23. 40)

In Christian tradition, the Date Palm is one of several claimed to be the Tree of Life referred to in the Book of Genesis, and the tree also gained religious significance in Islamic tradition. The pillars of the mosque in Medina are said to have been built from Palm trunks by the prophet Muhammad. Arab tradition maintains that the Date Palm has 360 possible uses and the Moslem holy book, the Koran, includes at least 20 references to the Tree. One of the most widely quoted is that contained in the *Surat Maryam*, describing the labour of Mary, the mother of Jesus:

The pains of childbirth drove her to the trunk of the palm tree; she cried 'Ah! Would that I had died before this! Would that I had been a thing forgotten and out of sight. But a voice cried to her from beneath the palm tree: Grieve not! For thy Lord hath provided a spring of water beneath thee: and shake towards thyself the trunk of the palm tree; it will let fall fresh ripe dates upon thee. So eat and drink and cool thine eye. *(Surat Maryam* 19. 23ff.)

Biblical writers attached quite the opposite connotations to the tree *Salix babylonica* that became known as the Weeping Willow. According to tradition the Israelite exiles languishing in Babylon used to hang their lyres from Willow trees along the banks of the Euphrates, the 'Waters of Babylon', while they shed tears of sorrow for their lost homeland:

By the rivers of Babylon, where we sat down, yea, we wept, when we remembered Zion. We hanged our harps upon the willows in the midst thereof. *(Psalms* 137. 1ff)

In the fervour of 19th-century romanticism, the Italian composer Giuseppe Verdi incorporated the theme of the Weeping Willow in the last act of his opera *Othello*, as the tragically fated heroine Desdemona contemplated her future.

A thorough scrutiny of the Biblical texts reveals that several other trees gained spiritual significance. The attitude of the Hebrews towards Tamarisks (*Tamarix* spp.) is somewhat vaguely defined in the Old Testament, but the plant is provided with a mystical aura on more than one occasion. In the area of the Middle East bounded by the Nile and the Euphrates several species of Tamarisk grow as small shrubs or trees, both as desert plants and on seashores and riverbanks. Like the Date Palms, they are extremely robust and can withstand considerable periods of drought. Typical xerophytes (plants adapted for growth in arid regions), they bear long slender branches clothed with scale-like bluish green leaves. The common Tamarisk (*T. aphylla*) is often planted as a windbreak and the Salt Cedar (*T. pentandra*) has been used to combat the salinity in the desert soil.

Tamarisk's strongest claim to fame lies in that it is the indirect source of *manna*, the so-called 'bread from heaven' that allegedly sustained the Israelites on their long trek through the wilderness of the Negeb desert from Egypt until they reached the land of Canaan. The tribes of the Exodus were told by God that they would find food each morning in the dew and that they were to take only enough of this divine providence to last them through each single day:

> And when the dew that lay was gone up, behold, on the face of the wilderness there lay
> a small round thing, as small as the hoar frost on the ground. And when the children
> of Israel saw it, they said one to another, It is manna, for they wist not what it was.
> And Moses said unto them, This is the bread which the Lord hath given you to eat.
>
> (*Exodus* 16. 14ff.)

In reality, *manna* comes less from celestial sources than from a small sap-sucking insect that feeds on the Tamarisk juices and converts them into a sweet honey-like substance that falls to the ground in small particles. *Manna* is still collected and sold in the markets in the Middle East. In the eyes of the Hebrew patriarchs, however, *manna* was a miracle from God and a jar of *manna* was kept henceforth on the Ark of the Covenant as a reminder of their bounty from heaven.

In traditions associated with the Hebrew patriarchs, Abraham planted a Tamarisk at Beersheba as an invocation to his God and to mark the place of a shrine. In the King James Version of the Bible in English, this becomes translated euphemistically as a 'grove', a word that possesses strongly pagan connotations because it came, as we have seen in the last chapter, to represent the symbolic presence of the Canaanite mother goddess Asherah:

> And Abraham planted a grove in Beer-sheba and called there on the name of the Lord,
> the everlasting God.   (*Genesis* 21. 33)

This was the holy grove familiar to many pagan societies but also to the Hebrew tribes of the Biblical Old Testament. The worship of deities in such sanctuaries by some of the rank-and-file Israelites caused considerable consternation among the tribal elders hence the familiar warnings that pepper the Old Testament narratives:

> Thou shalt not plant thee a grove of any trees near unto the altar of the Lord thy God,
> which thou shalt make thee.
>
> *(Deuteronomy* 16. 21)

Such was the extent of interest in sacred trees in the Old Testament, but plants of lesser stature also earned their place in the writings. In the Bible lands, spices were considered to carry a price that went well beyond their high commercial value. Although the Hebrews, for whom the concept of eternity did not really exist beyond an empty nothingness called *sheol*, did not associate them with the afterlife, they recognised the sentient worth of spices in other ways. Because aromatic oils prepared from plant extracts and spices had become an indispensable aspect of physical beauty, they also took on a distinct air of eroticism, and their use was much criticised by the writers of the prophetic books who regarded such adornment as tantamount to prostitution. The early Christian fathers, whose misogynist views did not equate with use of womanly cosmetics, took up the same theme with even greater vigour.

The Queen of Sheba, destined for a glorious and passionate affair with King Solomon, seems pointedly to have presented him with tributes including gold and precious gems but with spices at the top of her gift list:

> And she came to Jerusalem with a very great train, with camels that bare spices and
> very much gold, and precious stones: and when she was come to Solomon, she com-
> muned with him of all that was in her heart.
>
> *(I Kings* 10. 2)

In the Song of Solomon, spices are no less loaded with sexual meaning when included in the physical description of the mysterious Shulamite woman of the love tryst that makes up the main theme of the Song:

> Thy plants are an orchard of pomegranates. With pleasant fruits; camphire with spike-
> nard. Spikenard and saffron, calamus and cinnamon; with all trees of frankincense;
> myrrh and aloes, with all the chief spices.
>
> *(Canticum canticorum* 4. 13, 14)

> My beloved is gone down into his garden, to the beds of spices, to feed in the gardens,
> and to gather lilies.
>
> *(Canticum canticorum* 6. 2)

Spices had also gained purely ritual distinctions for the Israelite tribes. With other aromatics they had become popular in the preparation of anointing oils used in fertility rituals and in the consecration of sacred kings. Expertise in their use became essential to worship in the Jewish temple. Furthermore they were used in the embalming

process. The burial of the Israelite king King Asa is described in the Book of Chronicles:

> And they buried him (Asa) in his own sepulchres, which he had made for himself in the city of David, and laid him in the bed which was filled with sweet odours and divers kinds of spices prepared by the apothecaries art; and they made a very great burning for him. (*II Chronicles* 16. 14)

Frankincense and myrrh, both substances which are extracted from plants, were among the most prized plant extracts in the view of the Hebrew tribes. The aromatic resin

Above: A local tribesman collects the highly prized resin frankincense from a desert tree.

frankincense, or *olibanum*, has been used extensively in ritual throughout the ancient Near East including Egypt and Mesopotamia. Later, its value was recognised by the Greeks and Romans, and during medieval times it was sought after to such a degree that it was often paid for in gold. Trees of the genus *Boswellia* in the Burseraceae family secrete the resin and the Biblical frankincense is a particularly pure form that takes the form of a transparent, almost white gum. It was probably obtained from *B. carteri*, a species that grows in southern Arabia (the kingdom of Sheba) and East Africa. The tree is indigenous to southern Oman, the Wadi Hadhramaut in the Yemen and parts of Somalia and Eritrea. That frankincense was a prized commodity among the Biblical Hebrews is made apparent in the Book of Isaiah:

> The multitude of camels shall cover thee (Zion), the dromedaries of Midian and Ephah; all they from Sheba shall come; they shall bring gold and incense; and they shall shew forth the praises of the Lord.
> (*Isaiah* 60. 6)

Frankincense is a major ceremonial ingredient that was once used in the Israelite Temple. Egyptian records indicate that it was employed in ritual, was an important ingredient in the process of embalming and was used as a fumigant. It has also long been prized for alleged medicinal qualities. Frankincense is derived from a related species, *B. thurifera*, was also imported through Babylon from the eastern coastal regions of the Indian subcontinent, and the Book of Revelation includes this as a high priority among a list of goods that, in the age of the new Jerusalem, will come from Babylon no more:

> And cinnamon, and odours, and ointments and frankincense, and wine, and oil and fine flour, and wheat, and beasts and sheep and horses, and chariots and slaves, and souls of men. And the fruits that thy soul lusted after are departed from thee.
> (*Revelation* 18. 13ff.)

Today the value of frankincense has not lessened. A vial containing a mere 10 millilitres of the resin sells for about US$400, a slightly higher price than one would be required to pay for 28 grams (1 ounce) of gold.

Frequently mentioned in association with frankincense, myrrh is a comparable aromatic resin. Scarcely less costly, it is obtained from the bark of trees and shrubs belonging to the genus *Commiphora*, a related member of the Burseraceae family. Myrrh has been a staple ingredient in perfumes for many thousands of years and principal sources in Biblical times included Arabia, Ethiopia and India.

Frankincense and myrrh were sometimes Biblical euphemisms for a woman's breasts. The terms are used in this way in the Song of Songs when the lover of the Shulamite woman comes to his mistress:

> Until the day break, and the shadows flee away, I will get me to the mountain of myrrh
> and to the hill of frankincense. *(Canticum canticorum 4. 6)*

The writers of the Old Testament revealed that the Hebrews kept a mystical interest in corn, as did many societies that became involved in agriculture. Corn (the general name for cereal crops) developed its own special quality as a life-sustaining essential, an aspect of the green mantle investigated in wider detail in Chapter 4. In the Old Testament, the Corn God Dagan (Dagon in Hebrew) is mentioned as the god of the Philistines:

> Then the Lords of the Philistines gathered them together for to offer a great sacrifice
> unto Dagon their god. *(Judges 16. 23)*

The name Dagan actually means corn but, in Hebrew, the root 'dag' describes a fish and he is often pictured as a fish-tailed god. His counterpart in the Hittite Empire to the north (modern Turkey) was Halki, whose name means 'barley'.

For the Israelite clans, the threshing floors, the places where grain was separated from the chaff, sometimes took on ritual significance of their own because of association with the processing of the corn. The floors were often located on the tops of hills where the wind would more readily blow away the chaff, and since the hilltops were also popular sites of pagan sanctuaries it is not surprising that the threshing floor assumed its own sanctity:

> And Gad came that day to David and said unto him, Go up, rear an altar unto the
> Lord in the threshing floor of Araunah the Jebusite. *(II Samuel 24. 18)*

The aura of sanctity and ritual activity attached to the threshing floor is rarely expressed in the Old Testament, but in other ancient Near Eastern societies this included divination and, probably, the rite of the Sacred Marriage, the sexual drama enacted to invoke the fertility deities. The eponymous Moabite woman of the Book of Ruth, possibly a sacred prostitute, had intercourse with Boaz on a threshing floor and bore him Obed, the grandfather of David:

> And she went down unto the floor, and did according to all that her mother in law
> bade her. And when Boaz had eaten and drunk, and his heart was merry, he went to

lie down at the end of the heap of corn; and she came softly and uncovered his feet
[genitals], and laid her down. (*Ruth* 3. 6, 7)

King David, in his turn, chose the threshing floor of Araunah as the site for a shrine
to avert the threat of plague from Israel. It was also the place chosen for the future
Temple, eventually to be built by Solomon.

A more specific plant that finds its place in the Old Testament is the Mandrake
(see page 157). One of the earliest references to the plant is found in the Book of
Genesis. Here the interest of the writer lies in the reputation of the Mandrake as an
aphrodisiac. In the Hebrew the plant is described as *dudaim*, thought to be a corruption of *dudim* meaning 'the pleasures of love'. Rachel, the wife of the patriarch Jacob,
was apparently barren and increasingly envious of her sister Leah (also one of Jacob's
wives) who had borne two sons. Reuben, one of the sons of Leah, went into the harvest fields and brought home Mandrake roots for his mother, which Rachel craved,
vainly believing that they would make her fertile:

> Then Rachel said to Leah, Give me, I pray thee, of thy son's mandrakes. And she said
> unto her, Is it a small matter that thou has taken my husband? And wouldest thou take
> away my son's mandrakes also? And Rachel said, Therefore he (Jacob) shall lie with
> thee tonight for thy son's mandrakes. And Jacob came out of the field in the evening,
> and Leah went out to meet him, and said, Thou must come in unto me; for surely I
> have hired thee with my son's mandrakes. And he lay with her that night. And God
> harkened unto Leah, and she conceived and bare Jacob the fifth son.
>
> (*Genesis* 30. 14ff.)

The name *dudaim* is also introduced in a sexual context in the *Canticum canticorum* or
Song of Solomon when the Shulamite woman of the impassioned duet is enticed into
the vineyards for love:

> Let us see if the vine flourish, whether the tender grape appear, and the pomegranate
> bud forth; there will I give thee my loves. The mandrake give a smell, and at our gates
> are all manner of pleasant fruits. (*Canticum canticorum* 7. 12ff.)

Traditions associated with plants have often clung tenaciously in the rituals of
Judaism and Christianity. They survive, in part, as reminders of bygone dependence
on the agricultural seasons but also as vestiges of paganism. Modern Israelis celebrate
Shavuot on the sixth day of Sivan (varying from mid-May to early June). Marking the
beginning of the wheat harvest, it is the second of three agricultural festivals. It lies

between Pesach, celebrating the end of winter and the commencement of spring (timed to coincide with the start of harvesting the barley that ripens earlier than wheat), and Sukkot, the Feast of Gathering In when all the harvest has been collected safely.

Savuot is named in the Torah as a festival of nature, an occasion to deck homes and synagogues with greenery, when branches of trees, flowers (including Roses) and various spices are used as decoration. These symbolise the first fruits of the Seven Species with which the land of Israel had been blessed by God and which, traditionally, each person was commanded to bring to the Temple. Seven species do not appear as such in the Old Testament but seven is a mystical number in Judaism and the first fruits celebration is a very ancient one:

> Thou shalt take of the first of all the fruit of the earth, which thou shalt bring of thy land that the Lord thy God giveth thee, and shalt put it in a basket, and shalt go unto the place which the Lord thy God shall choose to place his name there . . . and the priest shall take the basket out of thine hand, and set it down before the altar of the Lord thy God.
>
> (*Deuteronomy* 26. 2, 4)

Today Jewish children carry baskets of fruit to the synagogue as a reminder of this instruction. Yet the origins of the Shavuot celebration do not lie strictly with bringing the harvest home. It is a reminder of the giving of the Torah to the Hebrews, the momentous occasion during the migration from Egypt when Moses received the commandments of God on the mountain. The association of the Torah with greenery is somewhat obtuse but it arises from a passage in the Book of Exodus:

> Be ready in the morning and come up in the morning unto mount Sinai, and present thyself there to me in the top of the mount. And no man shall come up with thee, neither let any man be seen throughout all the mount; neither let the flocks nor herds feed before that mount.
>
> (*Exodus* 34. 2, 3)

This has been interpreted to mean that Mount Sinai was permanently clothed with lush green vegetation and the synagogue decoration provides a symbolic reminder of the event.

The mystique attached to plants, and superstitions concerning trees, have also been taken up in Christian tradition. Some are mentioned in the books of the New Testament, while others, at various times during the last two millennia, have gained an apocryphal reputation.

CHAPTER 6

Plants of the
New Testament

The suggestion that the Christian faith incorporates elements of tree worship may sound foreign to many people's ears, but it should be remembered that Christianity borrowed and adapted many pagan customs. The proper Mass for the Feast of the Immaculate Conception is a rite that celebrates the immaculate birth and perpetual virginity of the Madonna. It includes some revealing words drawn from the oldest book of the Apocrypha, probably written in about 180 BCE, the *Wisdom of Ben Sirach* (known from the 3rd Christian century as Ecclesiasticus). The words demonstrate the extent to which pagan tree worship as the embodiment of the mother goddess had invaded Christian tradition:

> I was exalted like a cedar in Libanus,
> and as a cypress tree in Mount Sion.
> I was exalted like a palm tree in Cades,
> and as a rose plant in Jericho;
> as a fair olive tree in the plains
> and as a plane tree by the water in the streets
> was I exalted.

Left: Based upon the Tree of Life, the Great Cross of Lateran,
as depicted by an unknown artist early in the 4th century CE.

It is clear that some Christian sects were caught up in the romance of the sacred tree from early in their history. A question that has often been asked is whether the Christian crucifix symbol be regarded as such an object and if the Tree of Life became replaced by the Cross in early Christian Europe? In many respects the symbolism possesses logic because, through his death on the cross, Jesus Christ is believed to have given humanity the prospect of life eternal.

What is beyond question is that tree symbolism was being worked into art associated with the crucifixion from no later than the time of Constantine the Great. A mosaic known as the great Cross of Lateran, created early in the 4th century CE, is based on the Tree of Life and has been the model for many later studies of the Crucifixion. One of the clearest examples from more recent times is a crucifix carved for Rennes Cathedral in the early 1800s. The outline of the cross is wholly perfunctory. It has become a tree with a bird, the dove of the Holy Spirit, perched in its branches and a snake, the persistent symbol of knowledge and evil, coiled around its roots. Winged cherubim face inwards towards the tree, much as animals represented on early Mesopotamian cylinder seals and as the Assyrian king, Ashurnasirpal II, and attendant, served the Tree in the artwork of his palace at Kalakh. In the Rennes Cathedral design the Tree is even ringed by rosettes, ancient symbols of the fertility goddess!

The theme of the crucifix being identified with a sacred tree is furthered in one of the oldest services of the Catholic Church, the Mass of the Pre-Sanctified. Taking place on Good Friday, it includes a hymn known as the Adoration of the Wood of the Cross. Part of the Latin reads thus:

> Crux fidelis, inter omnes arbor una nobilis:
> Bulla silva tamen profert fronde, flore, germine ...
> *(Faithful cross, the one tree noble above all:*
> *no forest affords the like of this is leaf, or flower, or seed ...)*

Of all the trees and other plants that have acquired a mystique in the Christian world because of their religious association, it is undoubtedly the Christmas tree, in botanical terms the Norway Spruce (*Picea abies*), that captures the strongest attention. Yet the link is a comparatively recent innovation and, as with the Hawthorn, the traditions that have arisen around the Christmas tree result from the blending of Christian and pagan lore or rather, in this instance, the Christianisation of purely pagan traditions.

Several kinds of conifer have been used in Christmas festivities, all following in the tradition of the very ancient pre-Christian rite of invoking the mother goddess at around the time of the Winter Solstice by decorating a tree, symbolising her presence, with gifts. The popularity of the Norway Spruce, however, only came about in the nineteenth century. In Christian lore, the rite is said to stem from the inspiration of the 8th-century missionary St Boniface. According to this tradition, one Christmas Eve in a pagan sanctuary in Germany, Boniface cut down a sacred Oak. Miraculously, a Fir sapling sprang up at the place where the Oak fell and he adopted it as an emblem of the Christian faith.

The legend of St Boniface and his lumberjacking activities by no means stands alone in the Christian folk repertoire. Another tale relates how the 16th-century German Protestant reformer Martin Luther was strolling homewards beneath the stars at Christmas and was prompted to dig up a Fir tree on which to anchor candles that would remind his children of the star followed by the Three Wise Men. In 18th-century England, court records detail that Charlotte, the wife of George III, had a Christmas tree erected at Windsor. Yet it was the responsibility of Queen Victoria's consort, Prince Albert, that the Spruce was imported seasonally from his native Coburg. Albert also encouraged the English to decorate their Christmas Trees with presents, ribbons, baubles and candles. The evergreen conifer, by whatever name, thus took on deep Christian meaning but its symbolic roots, as a source of life in the dearth of winter when the rest of nature seems dead, have always rested in much older pagan ritual.

Away from tree mysticism, frankincense and myrrh possessed special meaning for Christians as well as for the Israelite tribes. These costly extracts entered the traditions of the Christian Nativity, bringing reminders of the gifts presented to the Virgin Mary by the Three Wise Men from the Orient.

> And when they had opened their treasures, they presented unto him gifts; gold, frankincense and myrrh.   (*Matthew 2. 11*)

Some plants gained their Christian mystique for reasons other than appearance in the Biblical texts, and these even included fungi. The edible toadstool *Calocybe gambosa*, popularly known as St George's Mushroom, is so called because, traditionally, its fruit bodies emerge in rings in pastures and woodlands on or about 23 April, St George's Day. From this calendar coincidence, the mushroom became sacred to the saint. In the 1960s the writer John Allegro made serious claims that a close study of Biblical language and choice of words revealed that the early Christian movement had been nothing more than a fertility cult. Allegro's thesis was at first widely acclaimed in academic circles and in becoming a best-seller, argued that the phallic shape of some fungi, coupled with the hallucinogenic properties of the Fly Agaric (*Amanita muscaria*) and others, had resulted in a mushroom becoming the esoteric focus of worship.

Of more certain provenance is the origin of the name Angelica. The species sold commercially and used in cake decoration is *Angelica archangelica*. It grows naturally throughout northern Europe but was introduced into the British Isles where it was once grown in cultivation. A member of the family Umbelliferae, it is said to bloom on 8 May, coincidental with the memorial feast of the Apparition of St Michael, a miraculous visitation said to have taken place on Mount Gargano in Apulia, Italy. Because of the calendar association, Angelica was assumed to possess attributes similar to those of St Michael, a guardian saint and pillar of righteousness. Possession of the plant was considered a protection against witchcraft and malevolent spirits and, in common with many other holy plants, Angelica was eaten during medieval times supposedly to provide a defence against the plague.

Among other herbs that have gained an apocryphal Christian significance, one of the most celebrated is the Shamrock, although the name does not refer to any single species but is applied to several that bear trifoliate leaves. These include the Wood Sorrel (*Oxalis acetosella*), belonging to the family Oxalidaceae, the White Clover (*Trifolium repens*) and others belonging to the pea family of Leguminosae. The list may also include the Shamrock Pea (*Parochetus communis*), grown today as a creeeping ornamental.

Wood Sorrel is found growing abundantly in woodlands throughout Europe, the British Isles, North America and much of western and central Asia. A low-growing herb with a basal rosette of leaves arising from a slender rootstock, in the spring it bears small attractive white flowers on long slender stalks. Wood Sorrel is probably the original 'Shamrock' or 'Seamroy' of the legend associated with St Patrick, the patron saint of Ireland, though the word Shamrock may also come from the Arabic term *shamrakh*. This was coined to identify triads of deities once held sacred throughout parts of the Ancient Near East.

Prior to the coming of Christianity the Trefoils in general were considered sacred by the Celtic Druids, for whom the number three held mystical and religious connotations. According to Irish tradition, St Patrick is said to have plucked a leaf of the Shamrock while preaching to an open-air congregation on the meaning of the Trinity – Father, Son and Holy Spirit. Presumably knowing of the religious significance of the plant to his new converts from paganism, he used the three heart-shaped leaflets,

Right: 'Adoration of the Magi' by Hieronymus Bosch (1450–1516) and presentation to the infant Jesus of gold, frankincense and myrrh.

joined at their base into a single stalk, to explain the concept of 'three in one'. Another curious legend about the plant alludes to the fact that there are no snakes, poisonous or otherwise, in Ireland. While St Patrick allegedly drove the snakes from the land personally, it is also claimed that snakes would not slither over the Shamrock and that it provided a remedy against the bite of vipers and the sting of scorpions. During the Middle Ages, physicians often prescribed Wood Sorrel for treatment of various disorders including fever and inflammation. The heart-shaped appearance of the leaflets also made the herb a suitable quack remedy for cardiac complaints. Because of its religious associations, Wood Sorrel gained the name Hallelujah Plant among the monastic orders, and its familiar leaf shape is sometimes to be found among old church carvings.

Some largely mythical plants found their place in the Bible. Among them is the so-called Apple of Sodom. Biblical reference according to some authorities is to be found

Above: The 'three-in-one' trefoil leaves and flowers
of Wood Sorrel (*Oxalis acetosella*).

in some obscure verses from the Book of Micah, one of the minor prophets of Israel at the peak of Assyrian supremacy, where the Hebrew word *hedeq.* is rendered as 'brier':

> Woe is me! For I am as when they have gathered the summer fruits . . . that they may do evil with both hands earnestly, the prince asketh, and the judge asketh for a reward; and the great man, he uttereth his mischievous desire so they wrap it up. The best of them is the brier: the most upright is sharper than a thorn hedge.
>
> (*Micah* 7. 1–4)

The Apple of Sodom is, however, largely a medieval Christian invention, a mythical plant mentioned by early writers that grew on the shores of the Dead Sea marking the site of the doomed cities of Sodom and Gomorrah. Seductive to the eye, when the fruit was picked it turned to dust in the hand, or filled the mouth with ashes if one attempted to eat it. The legend probably arose as a timely reminder of the displeasure of God over the slide into debauchery that had taken place in Sodom and a warning of what would befall those who succumbed to physical temptation. The Biblical plant is not to be confused, incidentally, with a North American member of the Solanaceae family, *Solanum carolinense*, also known as the Apple of Sodom, which grows as a coarse perennial bearing orange yellow berries in sandy waste places throughout the United States north of Florida.

If the Apple of Sodom was ever based on a real plant, its identity would be difficult to establish. Based on Biblical inference that any plant associated with wickedness or suffering is generally equipped with thorns, here have been some claims that this mysterious species is a member of the Solanaceae family, for which *Solanum sanctum* may qualify. It is a thorny shrub found growing prolifically in the Jordan valley, bearing fruit not unlike that of the Thorn Apple (*Datura stramonium*). One reasonably certain aspect is that the Apple of Sodom was not a real Apple, in Hebrew *tappuah* meaning 'fragrance', any more than the chance that the Tree in the Garden of Eden produced apples. Although Apples are known to have grown in isolated areas of ancient Palestine, the region is too hot and those that survive produce poor fruit. The Song of Solomon, on the other hand, describes the Apple as a beautiful tree with fine fruit:

> As the apple tree among trees of the wood, so is my beloved among the sons. I sat down under his shadow with great delight, and his fruit was sweet to my taste. . . . stay me with flagons, comfort me with apples; for I am sick of love.
>
> (*Canticum cantorum* 2. 3ff.)

Several Old Testament place names are derived from the 'fragrant' fruit, including Tappuah (in the lowlands), Beth-tappuah (in the hill country) and En-tappuah (to the west of Manasseh). The 'Apple' of the Old Testament may well have been an Apricot because Apricot trees were imported to the Ancient Near East from China as early as the 1st century BCE. Other contenders include Quince and the citrus fruits Lemon and Orange.

The word 'thorn' provides few clues to the identity of the Apple of Sodom because a large number of thorny plants grow in Syrio-Palestine, and an equal number of Hebrew words is used in the Old Testament to describe them. 'Thorn' tends to have become used euphemistically for the undesirability of a land or a situation and even for the wrath of God. This is not surprising. In practice thorn trees provide little or no benefit to mankind, are painful to handle and provide no protection from the heat of the sun.

In Christian tradition the thorns are plants with considerable mystique attached to them. They feature strongly and one of the most tantalising questions, but without any conclusive answer, is the botanical identity of the thorns used to make the crown placed on the head of Jesus prior to his death on the cross. Two species that, by tradition, are popular contenders can probably be discounted. The so-called Christ Thorn (*Zizyphus spina-christi*) is not found in Judean uplands and occurs naturally only in the lower parts of Palestine. The Paliuris Thorn (*Paliurus spina-christi*) is not found anywhere in central or southern Palestine. Most authorities today believe that the crown of thorns was fashioned from stems of the Thorny Burnet (*Poterium spinosum*), which has numerous thorns, bears small red flowers and is common in Palestine. Another possible contender is the common Camel Thorn (*Alhagi camelorum*).

Irrespective of the identity of the plant from which it was made, the crown of thorns has attracted its own mystique. Various contenders claim to possess this sacred relic, among them Sainte Chapelle on the Ile de la Cité, Paris, built by Louis IX in the mid-13th century to house relics brought back from the Holy Land during the Crusades.

In the English Middle Ages a considerable romantic fiction was loaded onto the Hawthorn (*Crataegus monogyna*), also known as May, when in bloom. This small thorny tree occurs throughout much of Europe and Asia except in the far north and develops white or pink flowers in large, strongly scented umbels. Its branches are armed with stout, sharp thorns. One particular tree of the genus, whose fame arose from a wholly different apocryphal tradition to that of the Crown of Thorns, is the Holy Thorn at

Glastonbury in Somerset. Growing in the grounds of Glastonbury Abbey and the nearby St John's Church, it comprises several Hawthorns said to be derived from an original plant carried from Palestine by Joseph of Arimathea, the affluent member of the Jewish Sanhedrin who provided Jesus' tomb.

According to legend Joseph travelled to England during the time of Jesus' childhood, possibly with Jesus, in his capacity as a merchant buying tin. After the crucifixion, he returned to England on a pilgrimage and came ashore near Glastonbury. At the time, the place took the form of an island surrounded by marshland or sea. Carrying strong Arthurian as well as Christian connections, it is known romantically as the Isle of Avalon and is supposed by some to have been the location of King Arthur's capital. Joseph rested at the foot of Worral Hill, a name derived from 'weary-all'. He thrust his staff into the ground, where it took root and the original Glastonbury Thorn grew from it. In purely horticultural terms this is not especially miraculous. There is a well-known technique known as truncheoning for regenerating or reviving a tree by removing the crown and branches. A length of young stem can also be made to put down roots and sprout under suitable conditions. In the

Above: Blossom of Hawthorn (*Cratageus monogyna*) stimulated much romantic fiction in the English Middle Ages. The tree became associated with Joseph of Arimathea and the legends of Glastonbury.

Old Testament Book of Exodus, the miracle of Aaron's rod sprouting and bearing Almond blossoms is probably attributable to the same phenomenon.

What has drawn attention particularly to the Glastonbury Thorn is the unusual nature of its flowering. The trees blossom twice a year, in springtime and at the old date of Christmas (before the reform of the Julian calendar) on 6 January. They are also said occasionally to show simultaneous evidence of buds, flowers, berries and dead leaves. Not surprisingly, legends have arisen embellishing the original tale that related to Joseph of Arimathea. As is so often the case with matters of folklore, much of it is contradictory in nature and can be traced to more than one cultural origin. In the case of the Glastonbury Thorn, Christian folklore has become interwoven with old Celtic belief and the relics of ancient tree worship. Among the latter, the Hawthorn has earned strong sexual connotations, chiefly though the traditions of the Maypole, long regarded as a phallic symbol. In the revival of Wicca, the witch's *stang* or stave (also imbued with phallic symbolism) is sometimes garlanded with May for the spring *sabbat* of Beltane with its keen emphasis on fertility. Notwithstanding these links, the Hawthorn has occasionally stood as a barrier to passion. In the German fairy tale of *Sleeping Beauty*, the heroic prince was impeded initially from reaching the object of his amorous attentions by a thorn forest.

In Christian terms, the Glastonbury Thorn became a natural contender for the tree that provided the crown of thorns at the Crucifixion. From this the belief arose that to bring any part of the plant into the home, particularly the blossoms in springtime, would result in the 'death' of the house. Sleeping in a room containing May was considered especially risky. In the *White Goddess*, Robert Graves notes that the tree possesses a negative influence. The notion stems not from Christian tradition but directly from Welsh Celtic mythology where the Hawthorn appears as the malevolent Chief of the Giants, Yspaddaden Penkawr. The Hawthorn also become associated with witchcraft. In Norfolk, England, a tree that stands beside the church in the village of Hethel near Norwich is known as the Witch of Hethel. Allegedly the plant has survived for many centuries and is now protected. There is said to be a deed dating to the early part of the 13th century stating that this Hawthorn was 'old' even at that time.

Other traditions of the Hawthorn have argued conversely that, being a holy plant, it would dispel evil influences. In bygone days in Suffolk a farm labourer who carried in blossoms of May on May Day earned a reward. The branches were hung over doorways as a protective device and in many parts of England were thought to guard against witchcraft. In *The Golden Bough*, James Frazer quoted an old rhyme:

We've been rambling all the night and sometime of this day
And now returning back again we bring a garland gay
A garland gay we bring you here and at your door we stand
It is a sprout well budded out, the work of our Lord's hand.

The blossoms of the Holy Thorn at Glastonbury were once exported around the world and, to this day, the Queen and the Queen Mother both receive a spray of the flowers for their breakfast table at Christmas, a tradition said to have begun in the reign of Queen Anne.

The trees growing at Glastonbury at the turn of the 21st century are not claimed to be the originals. It is said that the unusual properties of the tree can only be maintained if it is grown by grafting onto another Hawthorn and that trees grown from seed will not flower twice a year. Successive generations of the Holy Thorn have been propagated down the centuries and grafts have also been distributed worldwide to grow in such places as Central Park, New York. At least one of the Glastonbury trees is said to have been cut down by a fanatical Puritan during the Interregnum of Oliver Cromwell; but, according to the 17th-century writer James Howell, the perpetrator suffered for his actions. While wielding his axe, a splinter penetrated his eye and blinded him. Whether or not (judging from the title of Howell's 1644 work, *Dodona's Grove*) the Holy Thorn has been credited with oracular properties is unclear but seems entirely probable:

> He was well served for his blind zeale, who going to cut doune an ancient white Hauthorne tree, which, because she budded before others, might be an occasion of Superstition, had some of the prickles flew into his eye, and made him monocular.

Others who have attempted to damage the Holy Thorn appear to have suffered similar misfortune. In the 19th-century *Folklore of the British Isles* by E.M. Hull, instances are given of vandalism resulting in death of children or cattle, and loss of money. A Worcestershire farmer who felled one of the propagated trees reputedly suffered a broken leg and a disastrous fire soon afterwards.

If any plant can claim the role of 'villain of the piece' in Christian legend, it must surely be the Elder (*Sambucus nigra*). The Elder has earned a special place associated with death, for reasons peculiar to Christianity and entirely different from others such as Othin's gallows tree. Although never stated in the Gospels or the Acts of the Apostles, popular tradition identified the Elder as the tree associated with the suicide of Judas Escariot, the disciple who betrayed Jesus Christ to the Roman authorities.

This particular piece of apocryphal mystique is attributable to the 14th-century English poet William Langland, who named the Elder as Judas' hanging tree in his alliterative tale of spiritual pilgrimage, *The Vision of Piers Plowman*. Not surprisingly Elder, a member of the Honeysuckle (Caprifoliaceae) family, was quickly tagged an unlucky tree in popular folklore. Preferring chalky soils and growing in woods, thickets and waste places, Elder extends through Europe as far as the Caucasus, surviving as a cultivated introduction in more northerly regions.

The myth of the Judas Tree has been aided and abetted by the year-round appearance of a fungus, *Auricularia auricula-judae*, that is particularly associated with *S. nigra*, though it also grows on Beech. The fruit body develops, coincidentally, to look remarkably like a gelatinous human ear and, in medieval times, gained the popular name 'Jew's Ear' in England. Elder has also been described apocryphally as the tree of crucifixion. There is, however, no biblical support for the notion that it was associated with Judas' death, and the brittle nature of the wood makes the choice highly improb-

Above: The myth of the Judas Tree or Elder (*Sambucus nigra*) resulted in the jelly fungus *Auricularia auricula-judae*, which grows on the branches of the Elder, earning its name 'Jew's Ear' fungus.

able as a hanging tree. The unlucky nature of the Elder has, nonetheless, been further enhanced by its placing as the tree of the 13th month in the Beth-Luis-Nion tree alphabet, claimed to derive from ancient Druidic practices (see page 42).

Old local traditions provide constant reminders of how stubbornly ideas of animism have persisted among simple people. Because of the connotations of ill luck, it has been considered that the burning of Elder wood in a hearth will 'bring the Devil into the house', and it has been foolhardy to make a cradle from Elder wood. Folklore also has it that a child in such a cot will be pinched black and blue by the Elder mother who lives in its timber. Stemming from similar folklore, it was believed that burning the wood would reveal the presence of witches and, in apparent contradiction, that planting an Elder near to one's house would keep witches at a distance and would protect the place from lightning strikes! Largely for this reason, Elder is often still to be found growing near to the back door of many old English country cottages. By the 17th century, however, the wood of the Elder was being put to less spiritual purpose. As Nicholas Culpeper commented in his *Herbal*, 'I hold it needless to write any description of this, since every boy that plays with a pop gun will not mistake another tree instead of the Elder'. To this day some countrymen will not cut an Elder growing in a hedge since the act would be a portent of ill luck. In 1966 an article from a local Brighton newspaper in southern England reported that a notice of cursing had been nailed to an ancient Elder growing at the nearby village of Steyning. It stood in the way of a new housing development and the curse was directed towards anyone who dared to take a chainsaw to the tree.

It should be said, in conclusion, that names apparently revealing mystical traditions or links can sometimes be misleading. A plant named the Tree of Heaven or Paradise Tree (*Ailanthus altissima*) would seem a likely candidate for inclusion among a list of Biblical plants, yet it is difficult to find any evidence to suggest spiritual or mystical significance in either Jewish or Christian tradition. The genus *Ailanthus* includes some ten rapidly growing species indigenous to China and northern Australia but now widely introduced in the New World as ornamentals. They are also known as Copal trees since they provide a source of Copal varnish. The name 'Ailanthus' derives from a Moluccan word 'aylanto', which roughly translates as 'tree of heaven' but refers only to the considerable height of the tree. *A. altissima* is not to be confused with various tree species of Central and South America, regarded as sacred by the Mayan Indians because Copal resin has been extracted from them and used in ritual as an ingredient of incense.

麻姑自墦桃會回歸

CHAPTER 7

The Great Herbals

I n the year 804 CE, a Latin scholar named Alcuin, employed to tutor the Emperor Charlemagne, allegedly put the question to his sovereign: 'What is a herb?' To this Charlemagne replied promptly: 'The friend of physicians and the praise of cooks.' Charlemagne's answer probably sums up an attitude to plants that had prevailed for many thousands of years.

We can guess that, in remote antiquity, a utilitarian interest in the plant world preceded one that was based on their mystique, although it is impossible to confirm or deny the argument because the limited amount of art left to us by the prehistoric hunter-gatherers provides insufficiently firm clues. We are by nature, however, omnivorous creatures and plants have been eaten as a prime source of sustenance from the beginning of human experience. It is a reasonable guess that lore and legend arose from the experiences of eating plants or utilising their properties in the treatment of injury and disease. Inevitably, as the effects of certain species on the functioning of the human body were noticed, so these plants became recognised as the natural agents that the earliest physicians used to heal wounds and to treat and prevent disease.

Utilitarian value became inextricably entwined with superstition and lore, however, once it was discovered that eating certain plants could produce a magical effect. A tribesman, ignorant of science, would view the spirituality of a plant that brought about hallucinations, terrifying convulsions or death, quite differently to a species with more beneficial after-effects including powers of healing.

Left: In China, the divinity Ma-Kau is said to have studied magic and been closely linked with medicinal herbs.

There can be few better examples than the genus of plants known as *Agave*, belonging to the Amaryllidaceae family (or Agavaceae according to some authorities). The *Agave* genus includes some 300 species indigenous to the southern United States and tropical America, though they are cultivated in many parts of the world. The plant is unusual in that 60 years may pass before it flowers, and it dies immediately after flowering. Today many are grown for ornamental purposes, but in the past the characteristically tough fleshy leaves that arise from a basal rosette have been a major source of the fibre known as sisal. *Agave* species, however, possess another distinctive property in that the juice or sap can be fermented into alcohol.

Plants from which intoxicants can be extracted or manufactured have earned a special mystique and among primitive people they have frequently been claimed to have mythic origins. The species of *Agave* from the sap of which the alcoholic drink is made is known as the Maguey and the brew is known as pulque. The extracted juice also forms the basis of tequila manufacture. Nowadays the Maguey is grown commercially, mainly in the Oaxaca region of central Mexico.

In the past, however, before Hispanic conquest, the Maguey gained an extraordinary reputation, playing a major role in the religious life of Aztec Mexico as a ritual drink as well as contributing to numerous medicinal remedies, mainly due to its tranquillising properties. A French colonial work, the *Histoyre du Mechique*, provides an extensive source of information on Aztec culture. It relates a mythical tale of how the gods became aware of shortcomings in the lives of people that had been provided with a source of food but little else by way of pleasure. The myth is believed to stem from far back in Aztec history.

The heroic creator god of the Aztecs, Quetzalcoatl, and the goddess Mayahuel descended to earth to improve the humdrum human existence by providing humanity with pulque. In order to do so inconspicuously they became embodied as the branches of a great forest tree. On finding Mayahuel missing from home, however, her grandmother flew into a rage and sent a band of star demons known as *tzitzimitl* to search for her and punish her for absconding. The demons crashed to earth in the form of lightning bolts and one hit the tree, causing it to split in half. Recognising it, in part, to be Mayahuel, they ripped the tree limb from limb and devoured it before returning to the sky. Quetzalcoatl, fortunately left unscathed by the attack, collected what was left of the goddess and buried the shattered remnants in the earth. It was from Mayahuel's grave that the first Maguey plant grew and provided pulque, as he and Mayahuel had intended. Thus she became the goddess of the Maguey plant.

Our understanding of bygone attitudes towards plants becomes much clearer once there is an historical record available, a point well illustrated by the story of the Maguey. It is certainly true in the matter of herbal remedies for our human ills. The oldest existing document describing the use of herbs in medicine is a Babylonian tablet dating from about 1700 BCE, but our medical interest in herbs extends back over some 60 millennia, as the archaeological evidence from Shanidar testifies (see Introduction). During that immense period of time certain plants have been found to secrete chemicals in their tissues that make them important sources of medicines. Much of the modern pharmaceutical industry, although it did not respond to an exact science until the 19th century, has arisen out of this gradually acquired knowledge of naturally occurring plant drugs.

Over the course of many thousands of years, our understanding broadened about the value of such plants as Willow (*Salix*) that produces salicylic acid, which forms the basic ingredient of the painkiller aspirin, and eventually the knowledge became incorporated into the medieval catalogues or herbal lists. The early herbals were generally compiled by philosophers whose interest was transcendental rather than a serious approach to natural history, and they included a hotch-potch of lore, cookery tips and medical advice. Yet the introduction of the written herbals also marked the start of an ongoing path of botanical discovery that was to result in an understanding of plants based on scientific observation rather than folklore and superstition. The herbals formed the basis on which arose the modern *pharmacopoeiae*, the scientifically based reference works on drugs that we know today. The Chinese were probably the first people to write herbals and some of those still in existence date back many centuries before their earliest counterparts in Europe. Such works have become available in the West only in recent times and they have exerted virtually no influence on the progress of European understanding.

Herbalism in Europe is generally accepted to have begun with a Greek philosopher named Theophrastus, born on the island of Lesbos in about 372 BCE. His work in the pioneering field of botany was crude, largely influenced by his philosophical mentors and teachers (he was a pupil of Plato and later of Aristotle, under whom he studied in Athens) and his attempts at classification merely distinguished plants into trees, shrubs and herbs. Nonetheless, Theophrastus' scholarship was accepted without question for many centuries as a foundation of botanical understanding and, in some respects, the slavish devotion to his flawed understanding impeded real progress until the Middle Ages. Theophrastus is thought to have written some 200 works on the

VITA
BREVIS
ARS
LON

subject of plants of which, unfortunately, only two have survived, including studies titled *De causis plantarum* and *De historia plantarum*.

The original works in Theophrastus' hand were probably limited to textual descriptions and carried no visual impressions. From the 1st century BCE, however, botanical drawings of plants were being added to illustrate Theophrastus' texts. An artist named Crataeus of Pergamon was responsible for the creation of these drawings. A herbalist in his own right, he served as the physician to Mithradates VI, king of Pontus. Crataeus set about classifying plants according to their medicinal properties, and his most important work *Rhizotomicon* exerted considerable influence on the development of early herbal medicine. None of the original drawings has survived, but we have copies bearing his name made in about 500 CE.

The next major contributor to our understanding of plants, the person credited with the founding of botany as an exact science, was another Greek-speaking physician Pedanius Dioscorides (*c.* 40–90 CE). Born in a small town in Cilicia (now central Turkey), he worked as a surgeon with the Roman army under Emperor Nero and travelled extensively in Europe recording details of hundreds of plants and their uses. Dioscorides' work *De materia medica* ('On Medical Matters'), compiled in about 70 CE, was the earliest text on botany and pharmacology to be based on first-hand observation. Although reasonably free from the kind of superstition that had distorted Theophrastus' view, Dioscorides' understanding was still conditioned by a considerable amount of nonsense. On the subject of fungi, he had this to say:

> Fungi have a twofold difference, for they are either good for food or poisonous; their poisonous nature depends on various causes, for either such fungi grow among rusty nails or rotten rags, or near serpent's holes, or on trees producing noxious fruits; such have a thick coating of mucus, and when laid by after being gathered, become putrid.

The measure of argument arose from a common misconception that certain plants were capable of absorbing harmful elements from their surroundings. Nor was *De materia medica* based on a classification that would be found acceptable today. Dioscorides grouped his plants according to their *uses* – aromatic, culinary and medicinal. Nonetheless, until the 16th century his work was the 'bible' of every self-respecting physician and herbalist in Europe. No original of Dioscorides' work has ever been found, but the earliest copy in existence, the *Juliana Anicia Codex* of *c.* 512 CE (better known as the 'Vienna Dioscorides') in the Austrian National Library, represents a landmark in the history of western herbal medicine.

Right: The 1st century Greek physician Pedanius Dioscorides is the person credited with founding botany as an exact science. His *De materia medica* was the earliest text based upon first-hand observation of plants.

We do not know for certain if the original Dioscorides manuscript was illustrated but, like Theophrastus' work, subsequent copies of *De materia medica* were illustrated, and in 512 CE one was presented to Juliana Anicia, the daughter of Byzantine Emperor Anicius Olybrius. The artist appears to have based his drawings on those of Crataeus.

In the 1st century CE, the Roman scholar Pliny the Elder compiled a massive 37-volume work on natural history of which 16 volumes are devoted to plants. Pliny was not especially innovative but drew extensively on the works of other Greek and Roman authors. His *Historia naturalis* is riddled with scientific inaccuracy and it serves to shed light on the writings of other early herbalists whose works have not withstood the passage of time and are no longer available. Were it not for Pliny their contributions to our early understanding of plants would have been lost to posterity.

During the European Dark Ages that ended with the European Renaissance of the 14th to 16th centuries, there was a virtual dearth of any further development in botanical understanding and the situation did not change significantly until the mid-1500s. Nonetheless it was the medieval apothecaries with their knowledge of plant action on the human body who prepared and prescribed drugs and paved the way for the 19th-century medical discipline of pharmacology.

The Renaissance movement saw two revolutionary developments that bore considerable influence on progress. The combination of the invention of movable printing type by Johann Gutenberg in the 1430s and Caxton's printing press of 1474 meant that all types of literature, including herbals, became much more readily available, and it resulted in a plethora of published works on botany. This flood on the literary market did not serve to improve our understanding greatly, however, because few if any of the newly circulating books showed much originality. They were still largely based on the classical Greek works of Theophrastus and Dioscorides.

At least one other factor changed our perceptions. The exploration of the New World opened a hitherto locked door on plants. Over thousands of years, the tribes of the Americas had developed their own sophisticated understanding of botany and medicine. When the Spanish conquistador Hernan Cortez reached Mexico in 1519 he discovered that the indigenous people, the Aztecs, were experts in herbalism. Two scholars, Juannes Badianus and Martinus de la Cruz, were appointed to draw up a list of local herbs and their medicinal uses based on a thorough reading of Aztec codices. The original texts of these codices were translated into Latin and became known as the *Badianus Manuscript*. Published in 1552 and now held in the library of the Vatican in Rome, it represents the oldest known Native American herbal.

Right: English herbs and wildflowers depicted in an early 15th-century medical treatise in Latin.

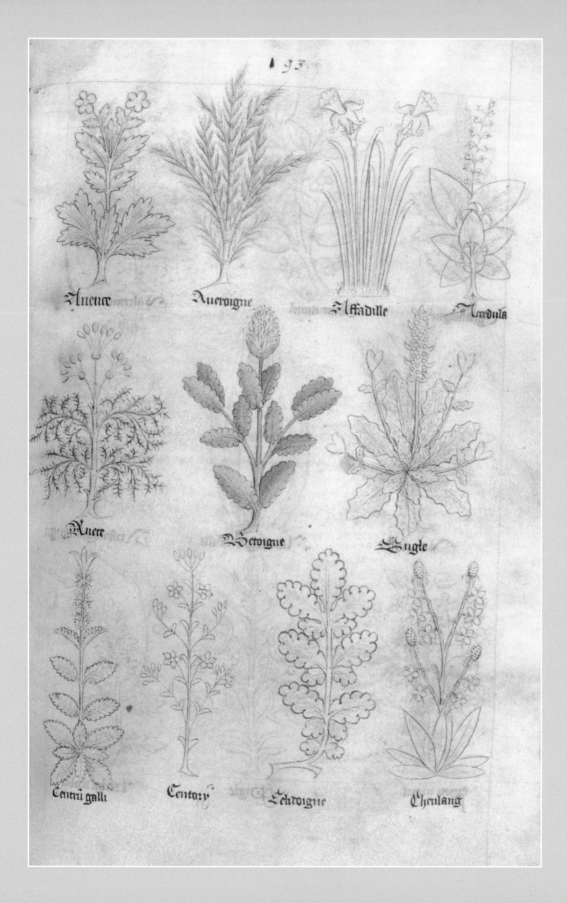

93

Auence   Aueroigne   Affadille   Acedula

Anete   Betoigne   Bugle

Centri galli   Centory   Sechoigne   Chenlang

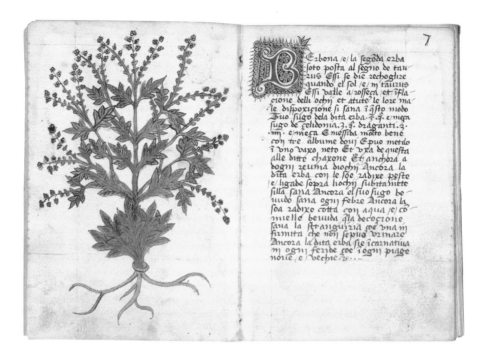

In Europe the early herbals of the medieval period, still largely based on Dioscorides, paid more attention to astrology and religious superstition than to botany. This was not entirely surprising given that even the Christian clergy were placing considerable emphasis on crude magic in the collection and use of herbs. In about 1020 CE, Burchard, Bishop of Worms, exhorted that religious chants should be used 'save only with the Creed and the Paternoster, in honour of God and Our Lord' during the collection of medicinal herbs.

The advent of Caxton's printing press meant that not only text but also illustrations could be conveniently copied, and it stimulated artists to create depictions of plants, mainly in the form of woodcuts that could readily be inked and copied onto paper. A manual by Konrad von Megenberg published in 1475 and entitled loosely *Das Buch der Natur* (A Book of Nature) was probably the first to incorporate illustrations copied from such woodcuts. The illustrations, however, only served to muddy the waters in that they too revealed the same mix of fact and fantasy inherent in the textual descriptions. A work by Jacob Meidenbach, published in 1491, entitled *Hortus sanitas*, shows a flower claimed to be Narcissus but, where the male and female reproductive parts should have been it reveals a human figure emerging from the perianth of petals and sepals.

Above: Illustration from a chapter on the properties of Vervain or Verbena, from a herbal of the 16th century.

Paracelsus, or to give him his full title Phillipus Aureolus Theophrastus Bombastus von Hohenheim, born in Einseideln in 1493, was variously considered the Swiss 'mad hatter'of his age or the darling of the neo-Platonic revival in northern Europe. He was also an informed herbalist. Yet Paracelsus was responsible for some of the misinformation at large. It was he who originated the so-called Doctrine of Signatures, a theory pursuing the logic that the outward appearance of a plant revealed the illness that it was designed to remedy.

The state of misinformation and superstition lessened early in the 16th century, encouraged by the pioneering work of a German botanist and one-time monk, Otto Brunfels. His work (in two volumes) *Herbarum vivae eicones* (Living Pictures of Herbs) is of limited scientific value because the descriptions relate only to aspects of the plants that were of interest to medieval world. The main historical value is that Brunfels' study is one of the first books on botany to include accurate illustrations, prepared by a wood-engraver named Hans Weiditz. In the wake of Brunfels' sterling efforts, his fellow countryman, Leonhard Fuchs, compiled a definitive botanical guide called *Historia Stirpium*. Fuchs' attention was primarily directed towards the medicinal properties of the plants he listed, but he also included illustrations that maintained the excellent standard set by Hans Weiditz. Another influential German botanist was the cleric Hieronymus Bock who presented, again with reasonable accuracy, illustrations of about 700 plant species in his 1539 work *Neue Kreuterbuch*.

In England, study of botany generally lagged behind that of the Continent. The monasteries had been the most valuable repositories of information about herbs until Henry VIII's enthusiasm for monastic dissolution resulted in the irrevocable destruction of most of their manuscripts and learned books. Of works compiled before the Reformation we are left with a scant vestige among which the oldest surviving herbal is the *Leech Book of Bald*, compiled in the first half of the 10th century and containing descriptions of some of the most frequently used herbs in Anglo-Saxon times.

The Elizabethan era saw the opening up of new and uncharted parts of the world by English as well as Spanish and Portuguese explorers. This not only resulted in the acquisition of knowledge about tribal herbalism in the Americas and other far-flung regions of the globe, but also stimulated a peculiarly English passion for collecting exotic plants. With this came a new interest in botany. According to the Elizabethan chronicler William Harrison, it was 'a wonder also to see how many strange herbs, plants and annual fruits are daily brought unto us from the Indies, Americas, Taprobane, Canary Isles and all parts of the world'.

The most significant English herbalist of the 16th century was undoubtedly John Gerard, though his massive *Herball, or Generall Historie of Plantes*, which first appeared in 1597, had been preceded in the early part of the century by several others. The herbal of Richard Banckes (1525), probably the first, was based on an unknown medieval manuscript, and this was followed in 1568 by that of Dr William Turner, Dean of Wells and physician to the Duke of Somerset. In 1548 Turner published a study entitled *The Names of Herbs* which was, in effect, a pioneering attempt to bring nomenclature used in England into line with that of the Continent. Twenty years later he completed his *New Herball* and his work has earned him justly a claim to be the 'father' of English botany.

Gerard's work is, however, by far the best known and, remarkably, is still in print at the beginning of the 21st century. An improved and revised edition was prepared after his death by an apothecary named Thomas Johnson and published in 1633 and 1636. Born at Nantwich in Cheshire, Gerard underwent apprenticeship as a barber-surgeon and established his own London practice as a physician in 1569. He became a dedicated herb gardener in association with his medical profession and eventually was awarded the post of superintendent of gardens to William Cecil, Lord Burghley, one of the outstanding Elizabethan plant collectors, who owned properties in Hertfordshire and in the Strand, London. In 1588 Gerard was responsible for the creation of the famous botanic garden attached to Cambridge University, and he also grew a wide variety of plants in his cottage garden in Fetter Lane, Holborn. One of the most significant of the species that Gerard collected and introduced to English society was the Potato. He had obtained personal stocks from the explorers Drake and Raleigh and had successfully grown crops of Potatoes before the vegetable was more generally available in England. Eventually his personal collection extended to more than a thousand species, many of them rare, and the *Herball* is, in effect, a catalogue of the garden plants he grew.

Criticism of Gerard lies in the fact that he borrowed liberally from the works of others, most notably the Flemish botanist Rembertus Dodoens. Gerard's *Herball* bears considerable similarity in its textual descriptions to Dodoens' work *Stirpium historiae pemptades sex*, published in 1583. Gerard is said to have copied from an English translation of Dodoens, but added 182 new plants and included many personal observations. The great majority of the woodcuts that form the source of illustrations in Gerard's *Herball* were borrowed from the artist Jacob Theodorus Tabernaemontanus and are to be found in his 1590 work *Eicones plantarum seu stirpium*. Gerard himself executed only 16 of the illustrations. The *Herball* provides a good example of an approach to botany

Left: Title page of the *Herball* by John Gerard, which first appeared in 1597. It was not the first English herbal to be printed, but remained the best known of the 16th-century works.

that was typical of the age in which Gerard lived, with a confused mixture of scientific accuracy, old folklore and 'virtues', in other words the popular uses of the plants in medicine and cookery. It is perhaps indicative of Gerard's sentiments that the title page of the *Herball* shows two draped figures in classical pose. On the left is Theophrastus with Dioscorides standing on the right.

In the early 1500s, much of the mystique of plants still arose from the notion that they were planted in the soil by gods and grew under the supervision of the spirit world. Towards the end of the 16th century, however, the invention of the compound microscope allowed the understanding of botany to be moved forward. For the first time, observers were able to unravel the mystery of how plants reproduced, hitherto a matter swathed in superstition since plants do not copulate in an obvious manner as animals do.

The new knowledge gained through examining plant reproductive behaviour under the microscope was available to the famous 17th-century herbalist and physician Nicholas Culpeper in his *British Herbal and Family Physician* of 1652. It did not, however, dispel time-honoured superstitions or the belief that the properties of herbs and plants were governed by astrology. For many centuries such superstitions had demanded that herbs were collected at times dictated by astrologers. Herbal remedies, too, had to be prepared under the correct astrological signs and possess the right virtues. The Elizabethan astrologer John Locke was one among many who believed firmly in the prescribed choice of times for picking herbs, and Nicholas Culpeper solemnly asserted that each and every species was under the influence of some or other heavenly body. All plants governed by Mars were, by nature, hot and fiery, those of Saturn cold and phlegmatic, and anything lucky enough to be overseen by Venus possessed strongly aphrodisiac properties. Hence, under the first entry in Culpeper's book, the government and virtues of *Amara dulcis* (Bittersweet or *Solanum dulcamara*) are listed as follows:

> It is under the planet Mercury, and a notable herb of his also, if it be rightly gathered under his influence. It is excellent good to remove witchcraft both in men and beast, as also all sudden diseases whatsoever. Being tied around the neck, is one of the admirablest remedies for the vertigo or dizziness in the head; and that is the reason (as Tragus saith) the people in Germany commonly hang it about their cattle's necks, when they fear such evil hath betided them.

The power and influence of herbs in the lives of people 400 years ago cannot be underestimated. All too frequently for ordinary folk medicinal herbs represented the difference between life and death. Before the advent of modern medicine there was no ready recourse to a pharmacy when sickness occurred, and even by Tudor times little progress had been made to further the knowledge of medicines and physic available to the Anglo-Saxons. Many of the inconveniences that we take more or less for granted today were major problems and, even as late as the 19th century, frequently proved fatal. Culpeper described practically all herbs as being of value in 'bringing down the woman's courses', an allusion to the constant concern about unwanted pregnancy in an age when childbirth could be an extremely dangerous event for both mother and baby. Many plants were recommended for diuretic complaints while others would assuredly cure an assortment of ulcers, running sores, scabs, itch, French Pox and gangrenous wounds referred to as 'green flesh', all of which could involve complications and ultimately bring death.

All too frequently for ordinary folk medicinal herbs represented the difference between life and death.

In order to understand fully the miraculous powers attributed to plants, one also needs to be aware of the superstitious attitudes towards illness that prevailed until at least the 1800s. Disease was also thought to be spread by noxious vapours and to be allied to sin. Galen (*c.* 129–199 CE) was another Greek physician and scholar whose ideas, despite considerable shortcomings, had influenced European medicine until the Renaissance intellectual study in the 15th and 16th centuries. Galen's theories proved wildly inaccurate. He had proposed the philosophy of humours. The human body was an extension of the universe containing four humours or fluids relating to the four basic elements. Yellow bile was equated with fire, phlegm with water, black bile with earth, blood with air. According to educated opinion, it was necessary to keep these aspects in balance in order to maintain a healthy constitution. Avicenna (980–1037 CE), a celebrated Persian philosopher and physician, had adopted Galen's principles. He relied on Roman and Arabic medicine, coupled with his own medical experience, and by the 12th century his *Canon of Medicine* had been translated into Latin and was the standard textbook in European medical school. Avicenna's views, like those of Galen, were held sacred, such antiquated understanding providing a conservative barrier to progress, slow to be updated.

The mystique attached to plants was strengthened by the limitations in pharmacy and pharmacology that prevailed not only during the medieval period but at least until the end of the 17th century. Antibiotics and other drugs, including sophisticated analgesics, had yet to be invented and the degree of suffering experienced by king and commoner alike, without any easy or effective remedy available, was quite appalling. Hospitals were virtually non-existent and the few that functioned acted as little more than breeding grounds for germs. In London, during Culpeper's lifetime, there were just two hospitals in business, St Thomas' and St Bartholomew's, and they tended to be frequented by the poor and needy since anyone entering such a place almost inevitably increased their chances of dying through infection.

A plant that could offer a cure or even reduce the discomfort of an ailment was, indeed, a gift from heaven. Culpeper made a particularly poignant observation when describing the virtues of the Lesser Celandine (*Ranunculus ficaria*) root that he used to treat his daughter for a massive infection of scrofula, a potentially fatal disease involving tubercular inflammation of the lymph glands in the neck:

> With this I cured my own daughter of the King's evil, broke the sore, drew out a quarter of a pint of corruption, cured without any scar at all in one week's time.

Illustration from *Phytognomonica* by Giovanni Battista della Porta published in Naples in 1588. Printed from a woodcut, as one of many typical depictions of plants and animals.

Yet whether the extract of Lesser Celandine had any therapeutic affect on his daughter's condition is questionable. *R. ficaria* is a common member of the buttercup family Ranunculaceae that occurs in woodlands and hedgerows in the early part of the year and bears pretty star-shaped yellow flowers. Pliny had claimed that swallows fed their young with bits of the plant in order to improve their eyesight, and Culpeper's observations were barely less far-fetched, based largely on the signature of the plant (see page 153). 'If you dig up the root of it,' said Culpeper, 'you shall perceive the perfect image of the disease which they commonly call the piles.' Did he imagine that the signature of Lesser Celandine also bore resemblance to the tubercles in his daughter's neck? The chief effect of the plant juices is actually an irritant one and there are reports that, in bygone times, itinerant beggars used to rub Lesser Celandine into their feet and hands to exact sympathy and donations from passers-by.

As late as the 18th century, physic treatment was often ineffectual, more academic than of any remedial value, and still largely based on Galenic theory. Physicians offered limited relief to the privileged few with enough money to pay and hospitals were almost non-existent. Those hospitals that did exist were still rife with infection to the extent that one was more at risk of death than cure by entering such places. The prospect of surgery, with crude instruments and without proper anaesthetics remained truly terrifying. There is good argument that many people owed their lives to their inability to pay for conventional treatment.

For most people, therefore, medicine began at home. Nicholas Culpeper once observed that 'all the nation are already physicians. If you ail anything, every one you meet, whether a man or a woman, will prescribe you a medicine for it.' The housewife served as the family doctor, having learned a store of private remedies from her mother and grandmother. If she lived in the country, her garden was often her medicine chest, and what she could not grow for herself in the way of medicinal herbs she would obtain from herbalists and wise women. These pedlars of herbs were trusted. Culpeper's contemporary, the English political philosopher Thomas Hobbes (1588–1679), noted that he would 'rather have the advice or take physic from an experienced old woman that had been at many sick people's bedsides, than from the learnedst but inexperienced physician'.

There were, of course, those who decried the arts of the cunning woman dispensing her herbal remedies. In reality, the attribute 'cunning' stemmed from a reputation that she simply knew more than other people and used that knowledge. But the Church argued that her activity came perilously close to that of witchcraft and many

herb women stood accused of witchcraft and wizardry during the height of the 17th century witch-hunts.

In truth the herbal practitioners often relied on a mixture of genuine knowledge of the efficacy of herbs, technique and magical jiggery-pokery. The application, or misuse, of the herb Henbane provides good illustration. Toothache was a perennial complaint from which almost every member of the community suffered and extraction was a gruesome process involving pliers and considerable pain. Remedies for

Above: The flowers of the strongly narcotic Henbane (*Hyoscyamus niger*).

toothache were, therefore, in heavy demand. A member of the Solanaceae family, Henbane (*Hyoscyamus niger*) was probably spread into much of Europe by the Romans. A biennial herb growing up to 80 centimetres (3 feet) tall on erect unbranched stems, it favours sandy soils and ground that has recently been disturbed. The stems and leaves are covered with soft white glandular hairs and become sticky with an unpleasant mouse-like smell. The flowers are trumpet-shaped, yellow or cream with distinctive purple veins, and mature into a fruit capsule with a prominent five-toothed calyx.

As with most members of the Solanaceae family, Henbane produces alkaloids that affect the nervous system and the analgesic properties of the plant have been known for many centuries. The Greek physician Dioscorides was among the first to note its potential and the Romans valued it strongly as a narcotic drug with a wide range of analgesic uses particularly for the easing of labour pains. Nicholas Culpeper also extolled the virtues of the herb, indicating that it was more common in the 17th century than today. 'Whole cart loads of it,' Culpeper observed, 'may be found near places where they empty the common jacks [sewage] and scarce a ditch is to be found without it growing in it.'

It was Gerard, however, in his *Herball*, who provided the fascinating insight into quackery associated with Henbane during the Middle Ages and later. In Gerard's day the seed, in which the greatest concentration of the alkaloids is to be found, was a popular remedy for toothache. Gerard noted that, 'drawers of teeth who run about the country and pretend they cause worms to come forth from the teeth by burning the seed (henbane) in a chafing dish of coals, the party holding his mouth over the fume thereof, do have some crafty companions who convey small lute strings into the water, persuading the patient that these little creepers came out of his mouth.' In reality the fumes from the heated Henbane seeds provided a short-term pain-killing effect. Gerard probably misunderstood what took place subsequently because the underhanded assistance may not have been needed. When the seeds were heated over

Henbane fruits were once resorted to by mediaeval quacks, when the seeds, heated in a chafing dish, produced small white 'worms' – evidencing a 'cure' of toothache.

coals or placed in hot water, the seed coats burst and the embryos protruded looking, for all the world, like small white worms or, as Gerard calls them, 'lute strings'.

Change did, however, take place for the better. In 1673 in the Manor of Chelsea, London, the Apothecaries' Garden was founded to provide a reliable source of medicinal plants. It became known as the Chelsea Physic Garden, and within ten years of its foundation it was recognised as a botanical resource of international importance, running a seed exchange system and pooling resources of knowledge about medicinal herbs. In 1712 the Manor was purchased from one Charles Cheyne and the gardens,

Above: A mediaeval physician selects his herbal requirements
from a herb garden, the most famous of which was created in
London at Chelsea in 1673.

occupying a little more than three acres and including 'greenhouses, stoves and barge-houses', were leased to the Society of Apothecaries for a rent of £5 per year. The first Head Gardener of any note, Philip Miller, was related by marriage to a botanical artist, Ehret, through whom the gardens became the source of inspiration for the flower paintings celebrated in 'Chelsea China'. Today the Chelsea Physic Garden contains about 6,000 species, including medicinal plants in designated areas devoted to the history of medicine, medicine in different ethnic regions of the world (ethnopharmacology) and to pharmaceuticals derived directly or indirectly from plants.

The greatest contributor to our modern understanding of plant systems, and therefore to the elimination of old superstitions, was the Swedish botanist Carl von Linné, or Carolus Linnaeus, who published his outstanding work *Species plantarum* in 1753. It was Linnaeus who formalised the use of the binomial system of nomenclature, the denomination of each species of plant by two words, one identifying the genus, the other the species. The binomial system of naming had been in use for a hundred years or more but was not generally accepted over the more cumbersome formal descriptions of plants.

In spite of advances by scientists such as Linnaeus, fanciful notions about herbs clung with great tenacity; although, once it became possible to observe the processes of pollination and fertilisation, the trend towards botany as a science accelerated and whimsical notions slowly became passé. By the 18th century, botany was firmly established as a laboratory discipline and drugs were being standardised and purified. Herbals ceased to enjoy the same credibility or popularity that they had in earlier times. In 18th-century England, only a single herbal volume of note was produced when, in 1783, Bryant published his *History of Esculent Plants*. The work provides little evidence of advance on Culpeper's ideas after more than a hundred years. In Scotland, six years after Bryant, a two-volume work appeared by Lightfoot, the *Flora Scotica*. Though ostensibly a systematic cataloguing of native Scottish flora, much of it was taken up with a fascinating but inappropriate store of local customs and eating habits.

Early in the 19th century, pharmacy moved on a stage further when chemists in Continental Europe began to extract pure drugs such as atropine, morphine, quinine and strychnine from the plants that had been their crude source for generations past. The only serious attempt to provide a 20th-century herbal was that of Mrs M. Grieve, compiled between the World Wars. This covers both British and North American plants, and although it edits a vast hive of information about useful herbs and other plants, it contains little original material.

KATRIN IDRIS 1998 601

CHAPTER 8

Herb Women
and their Simples

During the European Middle Ages, the role of the physician was strongly supported at local level by herb women, the so-called 'wise women'. These were largely people of peasant and country stock who used their hands-on knowledge of plants to treat disease and injury by imitating their allegedly, though not necessarily, more learned counterparts, the physicians. Often they experimented with herbs following the principle of trial-and-error. In the 15th and 16th centuries the 'establishment medicine' of licensed practitioners was a luxury that the poorer sections of society could rarely afford and so they tended to rely more or less exclusively on herbalists and wise women. Many of these people had genuine knowledge of herbs and roots, their cottage gardens becoming living stores of varieties proven to possess remedial properties. Others prescribed quack treatments that were harmful and even fatal, based largely on lore, fancy and such mistaken beliefs as the efficacy of plants displaying appropriate signatures (see page 135). Beside every quack cure there was probably also an herbal remedy that worked.

Herbal practitioners as a breed tended to be frowned upon by the establishment: a reaction that was hardly surprising, given that such people were taking business away

Left: Mediaeval herb women at work in a German garden of 1512.

from licensed physicians. The antagonism resulted in new laws. In 1512 an Act of the English parliament legislated against the 'great multitude of ignorant persons' practising physic and surgery. In the religious 'minefield' of the troubled medieval centuries the Church not infrequently persecuted such individuals as witches or 'cunning persons', a term roughly synonymous with 'wise women'. A typical indictment in the English assize records is that of a Cambridgeshire woman, Joan Warden. When she was charged in 1592, she declared to the court that she did not rely on any charms but that she did use ointments and herbs to cure many diseases.

Herb lore had been accumulated over centuries and it should be remembered that much of modern pharmacy is based on the age-old knowledge of active principles produced naturally by plants. In a sense each and every 16th-century housewife was required to become her own herb woman. Necessity demanded that a wife and mother gained knowledge of the therapeutic uses of plants, usually handed down from generation to generation. She would either grow plants from seed and cuttings or buy them in the markets where medicinal herbs were readily available. This late 17th-century ballad, and others like it, would have been heard as the herb women hawked their wares:

> Here's pennyroyal and marigolds
> Come buy my nettle tops
> Here's watercress and scurvy grass
> Come buy my sage of virtue, Ho!
> Come buy my wormwood and mugworts,
> Here's all fine herbs of every sort,
> Here's southernwood that's very good,
> Dandelion and houseleek.
> Here's dragon's blood and wood sorrel
> With bear's foot and horehound.

During the European Middle Ages, charms were regularly used to empower ordinary deeds and objects with supernatural properties, and plants were strong recipients. Charms were recited regularly when gathering medicinal herbs, and various rituals were attached to this activity in order to give the herbs particular remedial strengths. The Church authorities, choosing to blend herbal lore with their own brand of quasi-religious ritual, also generally required that the plants were collected to the accompaniment of prayers. This resulted in a belief that they were useless unless picked in an appropriately ritualised manner. The same principle applied when the herbs were dispensed. The patient was required to take them after reciting prayers, and the concoctions gained added efficacy when dissolved in holy water filched from the church.

A typical piece of doggerel is one associated with the collection of Vervain (*Verbena officinalis*), which had to be crossed and blessed when it was picked. Vervain was once heavily relied on for protection against evil and witchcraft. In his *English Physician and Complete Herbal* Nicholas Culpeper extolled the virtues of the herb for curing more or less anything and everything from jaundice, gout and eye defects to snakebite, asthma and piles – yet, in reality, Vervain is a plant with no proven medicinal properties:

> Hallowed be thou Vervain, as thou growest on the ground
> For in the mount of Calvary there thou was first found.
> Thou healedst our Saviour, Jesus Christ, and staunchedst his bleeding wound
> In the name of the Father, the Son and the Holy Ghost,
> I take thee from the ground.

In past centuries when the logic of people was frequently governed by superstition, plants took on mystical properties for reasons that, today, we might find quaint. Sometimes plant species gained associations of mythological proportions without simple explanation. The common herb Centaury (*Erythraea centaurium*), found throughout the temperate regions of the world, takes its name from the famed half-human, half-horse creatures of Greek legend. Said to be descended from Ixion, king of the Lapiths, the centaurs were reputed to live in the mountains of Thessaly in Greece. According to myth, the centaur Chiron (one of the sons of the Titan Kronos), famous for his knowledge of medicinal plants, healed himself with Centaury after being wounded by a poisoned arrow in his epic struggles with the hero Heracles. Dioscorides homed in on the tale and prescribed Centaury for treatment of wounds, but even in Nicholas Culpeper's day physicians were advocating the use of Centaury as being 'singular good both for green [infected] and fresh wounds'.

Usually, however, there was a more tangible logic to the aura that a certain tree or flower gained. Among the strange ways in which associations grew, the signature of the plant – its physical likeness to a human organ or ailment – made it suitable for prescription. 'Signature' plants were relied on to bring homeopathic 'cures', following the logic that they were in sympathy with the problem. Nicholas Culpeper advised confidently: 'The virtue of an herb may be known by its signature.'

Sometimes a characteristic behaviour pattern of a plant was seen to provide evidence of its therapeutic value. The Poplar (*Populus*), of which there are several northern

Centaury (*Erythraea centaurium*) as depicted in the 16th-century *Hours of Ann of Burgundy*. The plant provided a popular treatment for wounds.

hemisphere species and still more worldwide, displays a fluttery appearance. The Latin name of one species, the Aspen, is *P. tremula*, and it is well applied because in a breeze the leaves are in constant shivery movement. This activity lent to a belief that Poplar would provide a magical cure for the ague, the old name for a fever with hot and cold bouts that result in violent shivering. A medieval country rhyme about the Aspen, with quasi-religious overtones typical of many of these plant associations, goes:

> When Christ our Lord was on the Cross
> Then didst thou sadly shiver and toss,
> My aches and pains thou now must take,
> Instead of me I bid thee shake.

More often herbalists and physicians relied on physical appearance of individual parts, including roots, stems and leaves. As children we hold buttercups under the chins of our playmates. The yellow glow determines whether or not we are truthful, but 300 years ago a yellow flower such as a dandelion was believed to be efficacious in the treatment of liver or choleric conditions such as jaundice by enhancing the flow of bile. In medieval times the orchid Lady's Mantle was considered to bear the appearance of the human cervix and, for this reason alone, it was prescribed to ease the pains of childbirth.

Protective powers against diseases for which there was no known cure were often attributed to plants that possessed religious association. Tradition has given a whole plethora of species with spotted leaves the distinction of having grown at the site of the crucifixion on the Mount of Calvary. The leaves caught drops of blood from the wounded body of Christ. Among better-known examples is the Arum Lily (*Arum maculatum*). It produces a basal cluster of dark green, broadly arrow-shaped leaves that are often spotted with purple. Found in woods, thickets and hedgerows throughout much of Europe, though thinning out substantially in more northerly latitudes, it flowers in spring and its clusters of red berries stand out distinctively in late summer as other vegetation is dying back. During the Middle Ages, decoctions of the Arum Lily were considered to safeguard people against contracting the plague because the dark spots are reminiscent of the infected buboes that characterise later stages of infection by the Plague bacterium, *Pasteurella sepsis*.

The Arum Lily possesses another distinctive characteristic, and this has given rise to a quite separate folklore with a strongly sexual flavour. The flower of the plant is striking in appearance and has given it the popular name of 'Lords and Ladies'. From

the basal arrangement of leaves that arise directly from a tuberous rootstock emerges a pale green sheath, up to 25 centimetres (10 inches) tall, known as the *spathe*. When immature, this hides a club-shaped rod, the *spadix* or spike on which the male and female parts develop. As the spathe opens it provides the visual allegory of a purple phallus surrounded by a vaginal sheath. The imagery has given rise to a variety of local names for the plant, including 'Kings and Queens', and even 'Dog's Dick'. For those offended by such risqué connotations, it has been known as 'Parson in the Pulpit'. In some rural areas of southern England it was believed that girls who touched the plant would become pregnant. Young men, on the other hand, could guarantee a maiden's attention by inserting a piece of Arum Lily into a shoe! Physicians of earlier centuries viewed the spadix in a less prurient light, but their reliance on the principle of sympathetic magic was no different. Dioscorides and other physicians of his era had given the plant the Greek name 'Drakontaia mikre', meaning 'little dragon'. They had perceived a resemblance in the spadix to a serpent and, for this reason, had prescribed Arum as an antidote to snakebite. Dioscorides also advocated rubbing the hands with the root of the plant as a preventative measure, to deter snakes from striking.

Above: The Arum Lily or 'Lords and Ladies' (*Arum maculatum*)
provided sensual imagery and gave rise to a wealth of superstitions.

🌿 *Lesser Celandine does indeed seem to be a plant in which the herbalists' correlation of appearance and therapy works in practice because the herb has been introduced in modern times into the British Pharmacopoeia as a treatment for haemorrhoids. Less effective, but based on the same principle of a sympathetic characteristic ... the yellow juice of the plant has been advocated as a treatment for jaundice.*

The flowers of Lesser Celandine (*Ranunculus ficaria*) growing in profusion. It is also known as Pilewort because of the similarity in appearance between the roots and haemorrhoids.

Inexplicable contradictions often accompany folk beliefs. The spots on the Arum Lily leaves may have been looked on as a safeguard against the Plague but other superstitions placed people at risk of contracting tuberculosis when the plant was brought into the house. Doubtless these were based on the notion that the same leaf spotting resembled the discoloured appearance of an infected lung. To add to the confusion, the appearance of another plant with spotted leaves, the Lungwort (*Pulmonaria officinalis*), was sufficient to have it prescribed as treatment for the tubercular disease it was supposed to represent.

One of the more bizarre examples of a signature plant listed among the herbal remedies of bygone times is the Lesser Celandine (*Ranunculus ficaria*). The pretty yellow flowers grace the countryside in early spring, often when there is still snow about. Lesser Celandine is common throughout Europe, and although it prefers life in more damp shady places, including stream banks, wet meadows and woodlands, it can appear more or less anywhere. *R. ficaria* also enjoys the common name Pilewort, because the old herbalists seized on the similarity of the roots to haemorrhoids, which they assumed would be relieved by treatment with the juice of the plant. As Culpeper was drawn to observe:

> I wonder what ailed the ancients to give this the name celandine, which resembleth it neither in nature or form; it acquired the name of Pilewort from its virtues … the true signature of the plant appears; for if you dig up the root of it, you shall perceive the perfect image of the disease which they commonly call the piles.

Lesser Celandine does indeed seem to be a plant in which the herbalists' correlation of appearance and therapy works in practice because the herb has been introduced in modern times into the *British Pharmacopoeia* as a treatment for haemorrhoids. Less effective, but based on the same principle of a sympathetic characteristic seen in the Buttercup, the yellow juice of the plant has been advocated as a treatment for jaundice.

Not all of the herbal knowledge gained was put to benign use. When a plant exhibited properties that caused damage to human health, particularly when it also possessed a distinctive appearance, it gained its own brand of mystique. The Foxglove (*Digitalis purpurea*) is one of the most impressively showy wild flowers of temperate regions. The plant stands more than a metre tall and bears long spikes of bell-shaped, pinkish purple flowers on stoutly tapering leafy stalks. The tissues of *Digitalis* produce a gamut of active pharmacological principles including digitalin, digitoxin, digitonin and others that can give rise to a variety of symptoms, some of which affect the heart

rate and can easily be fatal. The poisons are not neutralised by drying or storage, and deaths are recorded on numerous occasions among horses and cattle that have eaten contaminated hay. In records going back to Anglo-Saxon times, the juice of Foxglove has seen use as an ordeal drug and as a poison applied to the tips of hunting arrows. Since the 18th century, however, when its medicinal value was recognised by a Shropshire physician named William Withering, *Digitalis* has been used extensively in controlled doses to treat cardiac ailments. Though it is now considered an old-fashioned remedy, before the First World War the plant was cultivated commercially in various parts of the world, mainly in the British Isles, Germany and India. All of these attributes have, not surprisingly, stimulated wonderful tales about Foxglove. The origin of the name lies in the belief that wicked fairies provided the flowers to equally naughty foxes so that they could tiptoe silently around chicken roosts without giving themselves away.

Among the most notorious examples of a plant that has attracted an elaborate folklore because of its unusual physical appearance, coupled with narcotic chemical properties, the Mandrake or Mandragore stands close to the top of the list. 'Mandrake' is a common name for one of six related species belonging to the genus *Mandragora*, which is included in the Potato family (Solanaceae). The true Mandrakes are Old World plants and are not to be confused with the North American Mandrake (*Podophyllum peltatum*, family Podophyllaceae) which, although it has been used for medicinal purposes as a purgative, has not gained the same magical reputation. Nor should the true Mandrakes be muddled with the English Mandrake or Devil's Turnip, although this plant has enjoyed scarcely less notoriety. English Mandrake or Tetter-berry (*Bryonia dioica*), with the more familiar name of White Bryony, is a member of the cucumber family (Cucurbitaceae). A common hedgerow climber in the south of England, its rather weak stems, bearing large pale green palmate leaves, rely on more robust supports, which they cling to with masses of coiling tendrils. The small white flowers bloom throughout summer and the clusters of berries, cerise when ripe, can be seen from August onwards.

The true Mandrakes grow in the Mediterranean region and in the Himalayas. The best known species is *M. officinarum*, a plant that bears purple, bell-shaped flowers on a short stem with a tuft of ovate leaves. The fruit is a berry, commonly known as a 'love apple', typically ripening to a bright orange at harvest time which, in the Mediterranean countries, occurs in May. It is, however, the long taproot that gives Mandrake a special place in plant lore. Fleshy and often split along part of its length,

Previous page: Foxglove (*Digitalis purpurea*) gained its popularity amongst physicians as treatment for cardiac ailments during the 18th century. Folklore suggests the flowers were worn on the feet of marauding foxes.

it can be seen, with a little imagination, to be formed like a distorted human body. As if this were not enough for a superstitious mind to cope with, the plant also produces chemicals with strong narcotic and, allegedly, aphrodisiac properties, particularly the roots where the active substances are most highly concentrated. The latter reputation is probably more attributable to the fact that the root, when not divided, looks rather phallic. In a bygone age of ignorance, these qualities made it more or less inevitable that such a plant would become labelled with magical attributes, both good and bad. In Classical Greece and Rome, the narcotic properties of the plant were valued by physicians who used the extract of Mandrake as an anaesthetic during early operations, and its use in this respect was still common among English surgeons in the Elizabethan era.

The anthropomorphic shape of the Mandrake root has led to all kinds of bizarre beliefs, mainly stemming from the worry that the plant is the outward embodiment of a malevolent spirit. This superstition can be found in Roman documents dated as early as the end of the 1st century CE when the Jewish historian Josephus reported on the harvesting of Mandrake. The demonic owner of the plant allegedly shrieked when it was uprooted and the cry was so terrible that those who heard it became insane or dropped dead on the spot. The only safe recourse for the person wishing to dig up the plant was said to be the employment of a dog to do the pulling. When the earth had been partly excavated from around the plant, the dog was tied to the root and then encouraged to drag it from the ground by being offered titbits of food. The exercise was best carried out in moonlight and only when a magical circle had been drawn around the plant with a sword to keep evil influences from escaping. According to various old folk traditions, the dog should be either black or white and should be tied to the Mandrake with a cord knotted around its collar.

Such bizarre beliefs about the Mandrake persisted into the European Middle Ages, when artists frequently displayed the plant in anthropomorphic form. Even in later times, during the Renaissance, illustrators drew the roots looking suspiciously like human limbs. Some botanists were prepared to rise above such fantastic notions and the English herbalist John Gerard openly ridiculed the tales about Mandrake. In his *Herball* of 1597 he assured the reader that he had planted and replanted the roots many times without being driven mad.

Like the true Mandrake and its North American counterpart, *Bryonia dioica* synthesises a toxin, an alkaloid known as bryonine that acts as a violent irritant on the digestive system. This plant also develops a tuberous branching rootstock that can

Fructus mandragore. oplo.fri.mj. sic.i ?. Electo magni odoufer. umani. odovato ? tra sed.i. calam. ? uigilias. emplanto eletmtie ? ifectoib; nigris cutis. nocinni. ebetat sensus. Re nocti. cu fructu edere. Quid gnat no e comestibile puemt ca. ? ? estate ? midianis.

🌿 *According to various old folk traditions, the dog*

should be either black or white and should be tied to the

Mandrake with a cord knotted around its collar.

An Italian woodcut showing a black and white dog being used to uproot the Mandrake plant. The roots were said to resemble the human body and have a mysterious power.

grow to massive dimensions, giving it the popular name of Devil's Turnip. John Gerard described the root in graphic language: 'A root hereof that weied half an hundred-weight, and of the bignes of a child of a yeare old.'

During the witch-hunting craze of the 16th and 17th centuries, it became a punishable offence for a person to be found in possession of Mandrake and, in 1603, three women were sentenced to death in Hamburg for owning the roots. By this time the Mandrake had acquired reputation as an aphrodisiac because its root, when not bifurcated, looks somewhat phallic. This had led the 13th-century Bavarian scholar Albertus Magnus, in his *Book of Secrets*, to promote the inclusion of Mandrake juice in his recipes for several love potions:

> Take of wild teasel and temper it with the juice of mandrake, and give it to a bitch, or other beast, and it shall be great with a young one . . and it shall bring forth the birth.

Medieval witches seized on the claim and were reputed to harvest the plant as a standard ingredient of their aphrodisiacs. English witches are also reputed to have exploited the anthropomorphic shape of the Devil's Turnip root. When young, the base of the plant was carefully unearthed and a clay mould was constructed around it in the outline of trunk and legs. After the soil was replaced, the root then grew to the restricting outline of the mould. When dug up at the end of the season (complete with the necessary paraphernalia) it bore the form of the Mandrake in all its sinister mythical aspects.

The legendary associations of the plant sometimes took bizarre proportions, including a belief that it grew at the foot of the gallows, spawned from the blood of felons. In his *Herball to the Bible*, the eminent 18th-century scholar Thomas Newton commented,

> It [the Mandrake] is supposed to be a creature having life, engendered under the earth, of the seed of some dead person put to death for murder.

In the New World, the reputation of the Mandrake has not only been grafted onto indigenous folk beliefs but, paradoxically, has also invaded the popular lore of Roman Catholicism. During the 1600s, the town of Jacona in Mexico lay on the eastern shores of Lake Chapala, the area of which has since shrunk, leaving Jacona some distance inland. Towards the end of the 17th century, a local fisherman retrieved a piece of distorted wood from the edge of the lake and dried it out. Several people then remarked that the twisted trunk bore strong resemblance to the Virgin Mary cradling the infant

Jesus in her right arm. The object subsequently received extraordinary attention and became celebrated as the Virgin of Michoacan. Firstly, it found its way into the chapel of a local Indian hospital where it gained strong local popularity, to the extent that the Augustinian friars became concerned that interest in the wood was giving it the aura of a pagan totem. Rather than raise antagonism, they moved it to their monastic church where, in the 18th century, an industrious monk improved its anthropomorphic shape, gave it a doll-like face, lacquered it and clothed it in a richly embroidered costume including a floral crown. It became known officially as La Esperanza, not so well known as Our Lady of the Roses at Guadalupe, but gaining the popular idiom Lady of the Mandrake Root. It can still be seen in the church at Jacona.

The association between Mandrake and magic has persisted into comparatively recent times. In the 1930s, two comic-strip authors, Lee Falk and Fred Fredericks, invented a cartoon character named Mandrake the Magician, who became a popular and enduring cult figure.

Another plant secreting a range of dangerous toxins is *Datura stramonium*, the Thorn Apple, belonging to the family Solanaceae that also includes such familiar vegetables as the potato and the tomato. Although the greatest concentration of poison occurs in the seeds, it is present to a lesser extent in the roots. The active principles, including hyoscyamine, hyoscine and atropine, were unfamiliar to medievalists, but they did not take long to discover that ingestion of the seeds of the Thorn Apple could bring on mental confusion and, in the later stages of acute poisoning, long periods of maniacal behaviour. In Europe the plant has attracted some bizarre reports attributable to its effect on the central nervous system:

> We find these plants associated with incomprehensible acts on the part of fanatics, raging with the flames of frenzy and fury, and persecuting not only witches and sorcerers but also mankind as a whole. Garbed in the cowl, the judge's robe and the physician's gown, superstitious folly instituted diabolical proceedings in a trial of the Devil and hurled its victims into the flames or drowned them in blood. (Lewison)

Spices were another indispensable part of the herbal arsenal against disease and other misfortunes. They could not, by and large, be grown by herb women because they were obtained from exotic regions, but they were in strong demand and became a major commercial import to medieval Europe. Spices had played a significant part in the life and death of people as far back as the ancient Egyptians. Hieroglyphics in the Great Pyramid at Giza depict construction-workers eating garlic and onions to give them strength for their task. It is also known from Egyptian funerary documents that, because some spices were known to possess antiseptic qualities in addition to strong masking fragrances, they became indispensable ingredients of the embalming process carried out on the kings, pharaohs and other nobility (see also Chapter 4). This use led to spices becoming associated with the idea of immortality. In later times the so-called 'Golden Road of Samarkand', controlled for centuries by Arab merchants buying and selling spices, was destined to become one of the most famous of all over-land trade routes reaching from China across the deserts and mountains of southern Asia into the Middle East.

By the Classical period of Greece and Rome, spices and certain herbs were still revered far beyond their culinary value and all kinds of spin-offs had resulted. Because of its recognised antiseptic properties, Bay Laurel (*Laurus nobilis*) had become perceived as a symbol of immortality and was sacred to Apollo and to Asclepius, the god of medicine, both of whom wore Laurel crowns. The first victors of the Olympic Games emulated this in their celebrations by wearing wreaths of Bay Laurel and Parsley (*Petroselinum crispum*) and the laurel crown became a widely accepted symbol of victory. The links to Apollo also made Bay Laurel a symbol of poetry and wisdom, and the power of the Laurel's spicy aroma took on such significance that Pythia, the famous oracle of Delphi, was said to gain her powers of clairvoyance by inhaling the smoke of burning Laurel branches. The tree also allegedly provided protection against the light-ning bolts of Zeus, and twigs were often hung up in Greek and Roman homes as household insurance.

Following the same logic, the withering of a Bay Laurel was believed to be a por-tent of disaster. Legend has it that in the winter before the Emperor Nero laid a torch to Rome in 64 CE the leaves of all the Bay Laurels became blighted. Even in the medieval period, Shakespeare maintained the theme of foreboding linked with the tree. The play *Richard III* includes the lines: 'It is thought the king is dead; we will not stay, the bay trees in our country are all withered, and meteors fright the fixed stars of heaven.' In the 17th century, Culpeper turned the belief around and extolled the pro-tective properties of the plant against witchcraft: 'It resisteth witchcraft very potently, as also all the evils old Saturn can do the body of a man, and they are not a few, and I am not mistaken if it were not Mizaldus, that neither witch nor devil, thunder nor lightning, will hurt a man where a Bay tree is.' Today, some of the wilder notions about Bay Laurel have been lost, but the association with poetry is still maintained in the title 'Poet Laureate'

CHAPTER 9

Plants of the Imagination

T hroughout the ages, people have been tantalised by the idea of animals and plants that have only existed in fertile minds. Images of fantastic animals – the unicorn, the yeti and the leviathan – are familiar from myth, legend and folk tale, but we have also invented plants that are wholly imaginary. We cannot know for certain when the first mythical plants were dreamed up, but undoubtedly they existed among the traditions of people in the ancient Near East and the Far East. In Europe, belief in plants of the imagination persisted through the Middle Ages and even extended beyond the period of the Renaissance.

The Tree of Knowledge and the Tree of Life envisaged by the writers of the Biblical Book of Genesis have already been discussed (see Chapter 5), but other fabled growths can be encountered, some of which are truly bizarre. Though most of the plants falling into the wholly mythical category are trees, no doubt because of the spiritual importance already attached to them, some of the plants that never existed are of lesser stature.

The belief that the elixir of life, the key to eternity on earth, lies in the magic of some mysterious and elusive plant began very early in human experience, and it has never been entirely forgotten. As strong symbols of life and fecundity because of their robustness and longevity, trees may have been the most frequently encountered

Left: The distorted growth of this Willow provides a good illustration of the ease with which people once associated aged trees with mystery and magic.

symbols of immortality but, from time to time, lesser plants also shared the distinction. Some of the earliest evidence of a tradition about a herb of life comes in the Mesopotamian *Epic of Gilgamesh*, the vast saga of beginnings first inscribed on clay tablets some 4,500 years ago. The saga contains several elements that were copied by the later writer of the Biblical Genesis story, including a sacred tree, the home of the goddess of life, and a serpent that predated upon it. One of the examples contained in the *Gilgamesh Epic* describes the search of the eponymous hero for a plant reputed to bring immortality.

Gilgamesh who, according to the earliest records, was the king of Sumer (lying in modern Iraq) sometime between 2800 and 2500 BCE, becomes obsessed with searching for the secret means of cheating death. The *Gilgamesh Epic*, compiled from Sumerian word-of-mouth stories, is not merely an account of mythical origins. It contains a recurrent theme of man's quest for immortality that is denied by the gods. In the relevant part of the saga, Gilgamesh had already become deeply affected by the loss of his closest friend and ally, Enkidu, to the land of the dead. He began a desperate quest for some means of avoiding the same dreadful fate that led him to the home of a shadowy personality named Utnapishtim, meaning 'he who has found life'. Utnapishtim alone among men had been granted the boon of immortality by the gods. At first Utnapishtim's wife tried to discourage Gilgamesh from pursuing his dream, pointing out that sleep is a mirror that reminds constantly of the inevitability of death while allowing mortals to bathe in the water of life. Gilgamesh was not to be dissuaded and eventually he was directed by Utnapishtim to travel to the bottom of the primeval ocean, the source of all life, the Abzu. When he reached the floor of the ocean he was told that he would find the Plant of Eternal Life:

> Let me reveal a closely guarded matter, Gilgamesh,
> And let me tell you the secret of the gods.
> There is a plant whose root is like a camel-thorn,
> Whose thorn, like a rose's, will spike [your hands].
> If you yourself can win that plant, you will find [rejuvenation].
>
> (*Myths from Mesopotamia*, translated by S. Dalley)

The hero followed Utnapishtim's instructions and dived into the depths where, as promised, he discovered the mysterious plant. He seized it and returned to the air above, triumphant in his success — but the prize was a cruel and brief illusion. On the long journey back to his capital city, Uruk, Gilgamesh stopped by the side of a lake to bathe and refresh himself. He laid the plant down at the water's edge, but it did not go unnoticed:

> Gilgamesh saw a pool whose water was cool,
> And went down into the water and washed.
> A snake smelt the fragrance of the plant.
> It came up silently and carried off the plant.
> As it took it away, it shed its scaly skin.
> Whereupon Gilgamesh sat down and wept.
>
> (*Myths from Mesopotamia*, translated by S. Dalley)

The snake, eternal and ubiquitous spokesman of evil and knowledge, had cheated Gilgamesh of his dream and, in doing so, became the age-old embodiment of both wisdom and eternal life who repeatedly sloughs his skin and emerges anew in endless rebirth.

Even the illustrious gods occasionally needed to resort to magical plants in order to maintain or restore their immortal status. Stemming from about the same period of Sumerian literature as Gilgamesh is the story of *Inana's Descent to the Underworld*. This is almost certainly the original mythical saga from which the Christian Passion tale ultimately derived. The parallels are impossible to avoid, including Inana being stripped, beaten, judged, executed by hanging from a 'peg' and then restored to life after three days and nights. It is, however, the method by which she was revived from death that makes the story interesting in the context of magical plants. In the earliest Sumerian version of the story, a pair of strange, sexless creatures were sent to the underworld, on the instructions of the gods, with two essential tools that so often go together in matters of fertility or rejuvenation: the Water of Life and an unidentified Plant of Life. They were used to assist Inana's recovery to immortality.

The mythical Mesopotamian hero Gilgamesh seizes the plant of immortality from the floor of the primeval ocean, only to lose it shortly afterwards to a serpent, symbol of eternal life.

Out of the strong symbolic bond that developed between plants and the goddess of life, it is not surprising that certain herbs became associated with the mystical power to induce pregnancy. In the ancient world, barrenness was a very serious matter. Ability to farm the land that a person owned, security in old age and the all-important continuation of lineage, necessary in order to keep property within a family dynasty, were dependent on the regular production of children. The institutions of ancient Israel, for example, under the Law of Levirate, provided for a wife whose husband died prematurely. In such a situation the widow was handed into the care of her brother-in-law in order to bear children. Furthermore, if a man found his wife to be barren he was entitled in law to take concubines.

In purely practical terms, plants secreting chemical compounds that afforded a genuine ability to cure barrenness in women were unknown, but the issue was of sufficient importance that such plants had to be invented in myth. We have only limited detail of these mysterious and fabled growths, but they would seem to have been the property of the fertility goddess. One clear account comes in the Mesopotamian legend of Etana of Kish that was recorded on tablets during the Babylonian era in the 6th and 7th centuries BCE. Its first authorship is, however, much older and the tale was probably composed as early as the middle of the 3rd millennium BCE, because scenes depicting episodes from the tale were inscribed on cylinder seals of the period.

Like Gilgamesh, Etana lived in the mythical heroic age of Sumer, as a king who was desperate for his wife to conceive a child and who rode to heaven on an eagle's back in an attempt to gain the boon of fertility from the goddess Ishtar. In order to achieve his audience with the goddess, Etana prayed every day to the sun god Shamash:

> O Shamash, you have enjoyed the best cuts of my sheep,
> Earth had drunk the blood of my lambs
> I have honoured the gods and respected the spirits of the dead,
> The dream interpreters have made full use of my incense.
> The gods have made full use of my lambs at the slaughter
> O Lord, let the word go forth from your mouth
> And give me the plant of birth,
> Show me the plant of birth!
> Remove my shame and provide me with a son!
>
> (After J. V. Kinnier Wilson)

Probably we shall never know whether Etana's quest was successful or doomed to failure, because at the precise moment when he and the eagle entered the gate of Ishtar's heavenly palace the text ends, and no other more complete copies of the legend have thus far been found.

The ancient civilisation of the Hittites to the north of Mesopotamia in Anatolia (modern Turkey) may also have recognised a fabled plant of birth. Hittites once celebrated a festival known as *Andahasum*. Very little is known about this rite, but apparently it took place to mark the Hittite New Year in springtime and it centred on a mysterious plant. Parts of this plant were apparently eaten as an essential aspect of the celebrations. No information has survived about whether the plant was a symbol of fertility and the bringing of new life to the natural world, but the *Andahasum* is known to have been linked with worship of the Akkadian fertility goddess Ishtar. The document from which the limited information comes includes description of 'bringing forth the Ishtar instruments'.

The Greeks and Romans occasionally dreamed up fantastic plants and these even included fungi. The Greek physician Theophrastus wrote a discourse in the 4th century BCE in which he commented:

> In the sea around the Pillars of Hercules where there is much water, fungi are produced close to the sea, which people say have been turned to stone by the sun.

The objects that Theophrastus was describing were, in fact, not fungi at all but stone corals made by small marine animals. The largely mushroom-like appearance of their communal colonies with radiating plates of calcareous material added to the deception, and people genuinely believed they were witnessing petrified mushrooms. It was in the European Middle Ages, however, that many of the plants were invented. Mythical growths were conjured up to dispel the mystery surrounding unexplained events and superstitions. Impossible species took on anthropomorphic guises to explain to an ignorant population causes of illness and such mysteries as that of fertility. They were also invented to embody diverse abstract concepts ranging from wealth and joy to destitution and sorrow. To no small extent, in later times, the authors of the medieval Herbals kept alive the conviction that such plants actually existed.

Among the best examples is the curious tale of the 'Barnacle Tree'. No one knows where and when the story of a tree that produced fruits maturing into birds originated, but it is recorded from at least the 13th century when the German philosopher, Albertus Magnus (*c.* 1200–1280), described it in sceptical fashion. Since the European Classical period, when Aphrodite stepped glamorously, and in varying stages of undress, from a scallop shell floating on the Aegean Sea, writers have envisaged the foam of the sea to possess generative powers. The idea of creatures being hatched from seashells clearly also captured the imaginations of later medieval writers, who depicted birds emerging variously from shells produced in foam or from a marine tree. In his *Herball* of 1597 John Gerard illustrated a tree allegedly found growing by the seashore on the Isle of Man, which he identified as 'a small Ilande in Lancashire called the Pile of Foulders'. There, according to Gerard's information, the Barnacle Tree produced a fruit in the form of the shellfish known as the Goose Barnacle, so named because it bears a black-and-white pattern like the head of a Barnacle Goose. The 'fruits' allegedly fell into the water's edge and then split open when mature, where they 'gathereth feathers and groweth to a foule, bigger than a Mallard, lesser than a Goose'.

Britanica Concha anatifera.
The breed of Barnacles.

The Barnacle Tree arising from the edge of the sea was not alone in the minds of more enterprising medieval writers. They chose to explain the origins of amber resin in a similar manner. Because its source was unknown, amber was believed by magicians and sorcerers to possess strange powers. Various claimants had it produced from crystallised sea foam, from a fish called the amberfish and from the resin of certain trees. When another of the early physicians and herbalists, Jacob Meidenbach, published his *Hortus sanitatis* in 1491, he combined these various strange ideas and drew a fish swimming beneath a tree emerging from a foaming ocean! Today we know that Meidenbach

Above: Gerard's *Herball* depicts the mythical Barnacle Tree, believed by some to produce Barnacle Geese. Gerard himself was, however, distrustful of the claim.

was not wholly wrong since amber is indeed the fossilised resin of ancient trees that became submerged in lakes and the sea.

Most of the more inventive stories circulated among gullible Europeans during the medieval period were centred on the Middle East and Far East, because the sheer inaccessibility of such distant parts of the world, other than to a few intrepid travellers, made then truly exotic. Distant lands were always to be potential candidates for tall stories.

The mystique attached to spices can be traced back to the ancient Near East, where myths about their origin have probably existed since prehistoric times. Among the first civilisations, those of the Sumerians, Assyrians and Babylonians in Mesopotamia, spices were being traded from at least the 3rd millennium BCE. The earliest report placing spices in a mythical context comes from an Assyrian document of the 1st millennium BCE that not only records the use of sesame seed as a spice but also reveals that the creator god An drank sesame wine on the night before he fashioned the world. In origin, the myth forms part of an oral tradition that may extend over some 7,000 years.

Egypt had acquired a fair share of mystery on account of its Biblical fame, its pharaohs and the knowledge of its fabulous buildings. It was also somewhat less inaccessible than the Far East. In the minds of ordinary people the Nile was imbued with great mystery, not least because its source, deep in the unexplored hinterland of Africa, was beyond comprehension, a place of fabulous bounty. Writers who described the Nile were, not surprisingly, liable to exaggeration and romance. Early in the 14th century, a French aristocratic historian, Seneschal de Champagne, otherwise known as Jean de Joinville (1225–1315), compiled a biography of the canonised King Louis IX with the cumbersome title *Le Livre des saintes paroles et des bonnes actions de St Louis*. Although the first short section contains anecdotal material about St Louis, who died in Tunis in 1270, the second main part is actually an autobiography of Joinville during the Egyptian Crusade of 1250. The original has been lost, but two copies exist in the Bibliothèque Nationale in Paris. Joinville describes some of the reported mysteries of the lands beyond the Egyptian reaches of the Nile:

> Before this river enters Egypt, the people who earn their livelihood from its waters cast their nets into the Nile each evening and let them lie outspread. When dawn comes they discover in their nets such things as are sold by weight and carried into Egypt for commerce. These, it is said, come from the Earthly Paradise. For instance they are ginger, rhubarb, aloes and cinnamon.

The reference to an 'earthly paradise' was probably copied from the writings of the Greek author Pliny, in which case he may have been referring not to Africa but to Sri Lanka. By his era, the legends of an island in the Indian Ocean that he knew as Taprobane, the 'Thrice Blessed Isle' from which spicy breezes were said to blow, were already time-honoured. The stories had been spread by inventive Arab traders keen to maximise on the value of materials obtained from fabled places. Sri Lanka became a land where the rare, the sweet-scented and the ambrosial were commonplace. The gods, it was said, had taken pity on ordinary mortals who could never visit this earthly paradise by arranging that Birds of Paradise collected up aromatic herbs and spices and brought them to the seashore where seafarers sailing the Indian Ocean could collect them conveniently. At this idyllic juncture, commercial interests came to the fore because the local natives quickly realised the value of the plants on their doorstep and developed a keen nose for barter. Spices became expensive! The Arab monopoly was maintained until the 14th century, when the explorer Marco Polo reported seeing spices growing in other parts of Asia. This revelation triggered keen interest among Portuguese mariners of the calibre of Vasco da Gama, Christopher Columbus and Ferdinand Magellan to find effective ocean routes to the spice lands of the Orient. For the Portuguese, Sri Lanka, or Ceylon as it was known by then, became one of the main spice trade stations.

> 🌿 *The gods … had taken pity on ordinary mortals who could never visit this earthly paradise by arranging that Birds of Paradise collected up aromatic herbs and spices and brought them to the seashore where seafarers sailing the Indian Ocean could collect them.*

Spices, because the countries from which they were exported represented faraway, largely inaccessible lands, were strong contenders for legends about their origin and their mystical properties. The very name, the Spice Islands, conjured up a sense of the occult and stimulated eager imaginations. The Spice Islands are, in fact, the Moluccas that lie between Sulawesi and West Irian, now a part of Indonesian territory including Ambon, Halmahera and Ceram. Historically, they were taken over by the Portuguese in 1512, but prior to that time they were governed by Arab Muslims who had made them famous as a source of nutmeg and cloves.

The hot-tasting nature of many spices encouraged folklore linking them with fire, and this led to their association with a no less fabled bird, the Phoenix. Long revered

Right: Sunset over Tetiaroa, one of the Society Islands of French Polynesia that became endowed with legends as the 'Spice Islands', which became famous as a source of nutmeg and cloves.

in Egypt as a symbol of immortality, it was said that only one Phoenix could exist at a time. It lived for 500 years and was then consumed by fire in a nest built with the material of aromatic plants. From the ashes of the old arose a new Phoenix. One medieval source discusses the source of cinnamon, here described as 'canel', in this context:

> Pliny sayeth that men tolde fables of canel and of cassia in old tyme, that is founde in briddes nests and specialle in the fenix his nest, and may nought be founde but what falleth by his owne wight or is smyte down with leded arrows.

Even such common 'hot' commodities as pepper earned their share of similar mystique. Black peppercorn was assumed to be the source of white pepper that had been scorched by flames. According to the 16th-century English writer Bartholomew de Glanville, peppercorns were the fruit of trees growing in forests teeming with venomous serpents that had to be driven away by fire before the pepper could be harvested.

Spices and the mystique associated with them generated a familiar colloquial expression. Sometimes stories of mythical plants were invented simply to 'spice up' the record of a sea voyage to some exotic destination, following in the Classic tradition of the Homeric legends of the *Odyssey* and the *Iliad*. The fabulous lands of the Orient provided one of the most popular settings from which voyagers returned armed with more than tales of sea monsters. The first Western visitors to China (known as Cathay) enlivened audiences with reports of a deadly tree known as the Bohun Upas that allegedly grew on some nearby Malayan islands. Some of the first printed books describing exotic travels included fantastic drawings of the tree, and by the 15th century its repute was well known in the West. Said to produce vapours so toxic that they destroyed all living things for miles around, there are claims that local prisoners were once executed by tying them to the trunk of the Bohun Upas.

Early reports of this imaginary plant were probably based on a real tree growing in the jungles of parts of southeast Asia, the Upas or Bausor Tree (*Antiaris toxicaria*), in the Mulberry family of plants, the Moraceae. The sap or latex has been extracted traditionally by native Malay hunters for use as a poison in blowpipe darts since it contains chemicals that affect the cardiovascular system. The real tree has earned scarcely less notoriety. In the 18th century, the physician Erasmus Darwin, grandfather of Charles Darwin, described the Upas tree in lurid terms after a visit to Java: 'Fierce in dread silence on the blasted fell, Upas sits, the Hydra-Tree of death.'

The Upas also apparently attracted the interest of the Russian poet Aleksander Pushkin (1799–1837) who composed verses to which he gave the title *Anchar (The Poison*

Tree). He may have misinterpreted the habitat of the Upas since his poem implies the surroundings of a dry burning steppe:

> In the pale unyielding desert, on soil that the sunrays curse,
> Anchar like a dreadful sentry stands — sole in the universe.
> The sun-tortured, thirst-racked steppeland gave it birth in a day of wrath
> And fed the dull green of its leafage and its roots with a poisoned broth.
> Through its bark thick poison oozes and, melting when midday comes,
>   congeals again in the evening in smooth transparent gums
> No bird ever alights in its branches, no tiger approaches the tree:
> Alone the black storm-winds brush it and, venom infected, flee
> If a wondering rain-cloud moistens its dense and unstirring leaves,
> The burning sand from its branches a poisonous dew receives.
> But one man to the tree sends another with a glance that, imperious, burns
> And the poor slave sets out on his journey and at dawn with the poison returns.
> He brings with him a poisonous resin and a branch with a few faded leaves,
> And the sweat on his pallid forehead in thick streams trickles and cleaves.
> The poison he brings, and fainting at the feet of his dread Lord lies
> On the bast that the tent floor covers he utters no word and dies.
> But the king, in that poison steeping his arrows with secret art,
> To his enemies sends destruction and death with each poisoned dart.
>
> (English translation by Walter Morison)

Trees have always been strong candidates in the choice of fabulous species. In Hindu mythology, five magnificent trees, not all of which have been identified botanically, grow as the property of the gods in the Hindu paradise on the mythical Mount Meru in the Himalayas. Each of the Paradise Trees is known as a *kalpavrksa* or 'wishing tree', so named because it is believed to grant wishes. The *kalpavrksa* is symbolic of one of the five world periods recognised in Hindu cosmogeny, each of which spans 4,320 million mortal years but a mere day in the life of the creator god Brahma. Of the five, *haricandana-vrksa* is identified as the sandalwood, the paste and oil of which are important in Hindu worship. *Kalpalata-vrksa* may be less of a tree than a fabulous creeper. *Mandara-vrksa* is recognisable as the Coral Tree (*Erythrina indica*). *Parijata-vrksa* is thought to be another type of Coral Tree. The fifth, *santana-vrksa*, is not readily identifiable but is the personification of a minor deity.

The *kalpa-vrksa* is sometimes depicted in Indian art, when it forms part of a decorative carving above the arched doorway of a building. The traditional design of the carving is known as the *prabhatorana* and it is drawn as an aureole or halo of light beams on top of which rests the Paradise Tree.

Still further east, in Chinese Taoist tradition, the tree of eternal life is the Peach, but this is no ordinary fruit tree! Regarded as sacred in China since prehistoric times, peaches carry a fascinating mythology. The Empress of the Western Heaven, Xi Wang Mu, who is also the goddess of longevity, nurtures the Peaches of immortality. Although she probably originates as a plague goddess (in the ancient *Book of Mountains and Seas* she is drawn as a fearsome creature with fangs), Xi Wang Mu became more benign under Taoism and took the responsibility for governing the length of mortal life. As the Ruler of the West, the place of the setting sun, she is naturally associated with autumn and the season of old age but she grants the boon of longevity and, in some instances, immortality.

The legend of the Peaches describes the Empress living in a palace of pure gold somewhere in the K'un Lun mountains in western China. This was once an area of the hinterland virtually unknown to people living in central China and therefore suitable ground for tales of mystery and magic. According to folklore, the fabulous Peach trees grew in the palace garden and each fruit took 3,000 years to form and a further 3,000 to ripen. Xi Wang Mu celebrated her celestial birthday by giving a banquet at which the serving of the Peaches was the crowning moment. One of the most illustrious guests said to have visited the home of Xi Wang Mu was an emperor of the Han dynasty, Wu Di, who lived in the 2nd century BCE. According to tradition, Xi Wang Mu presented Wu Di with the Peaches of immortality on his birthday. We must assume that Wu Di never got to eat his present because, according to the record, he died of normal old age.

As in so many legends about plants that possess the elixir of life, eating the celestial Peaches of Xi Wang Mu was governed by strict taboos. These are illustrated in the legend of the heavenly archer, Hou I. His story is to be found in the *History of the Zhou Dynasty*, compiled in the 2nd century BCE, but almost certainly deriving in part from older oral traditions. Much as the giants of Scandinavian mythology built Valhalla for the gods of Asgard, so Hou I was contracted to build a palace for Xi Wang Mu made of jade (a substance that in its own right is considered an elixir). In return for his services the Empress rewarded Hou I with a potion made from the juice of the Peaches of immortality. There was, however, a condition attached. Hou I was not allowed to take the elixir until he had fasted for a year and, in order to keep it safe, he hid the precious flask in the roof of his home. Tragically, his wife discovered his secret and drank it. As soon as she had swallowed the potion she felt herself float off the ground and out through the window. Despite Hou I attempting to catch her, she floated away so fast and so high that she reached the moon where she turned into a three-legged toad. There is, of course, a moral to this story that reminds us of Gilgamesh and his temporary possession of the Plant of Life. No mortal person can gain immortality. There is always a catch to possession of the elixir. Gilgamesh lost his to a snake, Adam and Eve lost their paradise garden to the same adversary. Hou I lost his to his wife who promptly ceased to be a human being at all. In any case the message is clear that, had Hou I managed to save his prize, he still could not have benefited since he would be dead from starvation long before his year was out!

According to Taoist tradition some mortals did, nonetheless, achieve immortality through their devotion to Taoism. The most famous of these are the Ba Xian (Eight Immortals). One among them, Han Xiang-Zhi, said to have lived during the 9th century CE, was guided by another of the Immortals to the top of the Sacred Peach Tree from the branches of which he plunged into immortality. In traditional Chinese art, Han Xiang-Zhi and at least two of his fellow immortals, Zhong-Li Kuan and Zhang-Kuo Lao, often carry peaches of immortality as attributes.

We have not entirely lost our fascination with the imaginary in the plant world. It lives on in the names we sometimes attach to plants. Though the *Antirrhinum* is a real flower, the animal after which it is popularly titled is not. We call it the Snapdragon because its blooms can be squeezed open and shut like the mouth of a fabled beast.

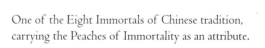

One of the Eight Immortals of Chinese tradition, carrying the Peaches of Immortality as an attribute.

175

Plants of
Special Significance

Of all plants, throughout every region of the globe, that gained a special and mystical aura, a select few stand out above the rest. Given that in the minds of our ancestors, the most profound spiritual power resided in trees, perhaps surprisingly none of them are trees in the true sense. However, one is intimately associated with sacred trees and others can take on certain tree-like characteristics. Two, in particular, hold pride of place in the Western world; and so do three in the East.

Mistletoe

The Mistletoe has earned a truly fascinating repertoire of ritual use, myth, legend and folklore. How many people stop to ask why or from where the bizarre tradition exists of hanging up a branch of this obscure golden-green plant at Christmas time and then manoeuvring someone beneath it in order to give them a kiss? Answers, as with so much of the green mantle, lie among the magical and religious practices of our ancient forebears.

Left: In Europe, Mistletoe has enjoyed a mysterious reputation since prehistoric times. This is largely because of its association with the Oak and Apple and its distinctive golden green color, making it sacred to the Druids.

The Druids regarded the Oak as sacred but they also believed that it had conferred its sanctity, by association, onto the odd parasitic plant that occasionally grows on the boughs. The tradition of this mystical bond was destined to endure down many centuries. As late as the 1600s, Nicholas Culpeper, not only a physician and herbalist but also an astrologer, was writing of the Mistletoe in his *Complete Herbal*:

> It can be taken for granted that that which grows upon oaks participates something of the nature of Jupiter, because the oak is one of his trees . . . but why that should have most virtues that grows upon oaks I know not, unless because it is rarest and hardest to come by.

Three distinct species of Mistletoe are found worldwide, though only one, *Viscum album*, is common in temperate Europe including much of the British Isles, living as a partial parasite that ultimately weakens and kills its host tree. The plant does not occur in Scotland or Ireland. A native North American counterpart, growing most frequently on Red Maple and Elm, is *Phoradendron flavescens*. The third species, a leafless flowering dwarf Mistletoe (*Arceuthobium pusillum*), is very rare in Britain and is a dangerously destructive parasite of coniferous trees.

The Mistletoe of lore and legend is *Viscum album*. Although its traditional host is the Oak, the Roman writer Clusius states that, in his time, it was at least as common on Pear trees. Nowadays *V. album* tends to be associated more with other deciduous tree species, including Apple and Poplar, its familiar branching tufts often growing very high up in the branches. The tufts sprout from the bark of the host by way of a thickened base and the branches, at first succulent and yellowish green, become woody in older plants. The leaves are more or less ovate, thick and leathery-fleshy, and the flowers are very small with tiny petals. Mistletoe is seen in its best-known state in midwinter when it bears distinctive, white, semi-transparent berries that consist of soft, somewhat sticky flesh surrounding a single seed. The name 'Mistletoe' derives from two Anglo-Saxon words — *mistel* meaning 'dung' and *tan* meaning 'twig' — and owes its origin to the way in which the plant is propagated. Birds eat the berries and

How many people stop to ask why or from where the bizarre tradition exists of hanging up a branch of this obscure golden-green plant at Christmas time and then manoeuvring someone beneath it in order to give them a kiss?

the sticky seeds pass through the gut, to be deposited on the branches of trees with their droppings. Seeds are also rubbed from the birds' beaks when they wipe them on bark. By either route, the seeds find their way into cracks and crannies from where they germinate.

The Roman writer Pliny provided a brief but striking contemporary insight into the ritual use of Mistletoe, its mystical link with the moon and the attitude of the Druids towards the plant:

> The mistletoe is very rarely to be met with; but when it is found they gather it with solemn ceremony. This they do above all on the sixth day of the moon, from whence they date the beginnings of their months, of their years and of their thirty years' cycle because by the sixth day the moon has plenty of vigour and has not run half its course. After due preparations have been made for a sacrifice and a feast under the tree, they hail it as a universal healer and bring to the spot two white bulls whose horns have never been bound before. A priest clad in white robes climbs the tree and with a golden sickle cuts the mistletoe, which is caught in a white cloth. They then sacrifice the victims, praying that their god may make his own gift to prosper with whom he has bestowed it. They believe that a potion prepared from mistletoe will make barren animals bring forth, and that the plant is a remedy against all poisons.

To Pliny's brief comments, Clusius added advice that the Mistletoe should not be cut with iron and that the magical effect of the plant was lost if the cuttings were allowed to touch the ground. While Clusius gave no explanation for this, reasons become apparent in the context of medieval witchcraft. A superstition had arisen that anything growing off the ground or kept clear of the ground was impervious to the influence of witches. Mistletoe was believed to be particularly efficacious against witches and this was partly attributable the fact that it does not grow from the ground.

By medieval times, sprigs of the plant were hung above doorways to keep witches at bay, and in the 17th century Nicholas Culpeper advised in his *Complete Herbal* that, when worn around the neck, Mistletoe would provide good protection against witchcraft.

The ritual described by Pliny involved the slaughter of bulls beneath a tree bearing Mistletoe. When growing on Oak, Mistletoe has been considered to possess especially strong magical properties linked with fertility, and bulls were also powerful symbols of fertility throughout the ancient world. Clearly, the magical powers of Mistletoe and bulls were intended to be combined in this ritual. Because of their way of life, the ancient Celts were deeply concerned about fertility, not only among the human population of the tribes but also in their domestic animals. When the Druids had completed the sacrifice it is also probable, if they were following documented Celtic traditions, that divination was involved and that the blood and entrails of the animals were examined in order to detect portents for the future. Two thousand years on, however, we are largely left guessing about the exact meaning and purpose of the Mistletoe ritual. In *White Goddess*, Robert Graves asserts that the slaughter of the bulls symbolised the emasculation and slaying of the old priest of the sacred grove by his more youthful successor in order to propitiate the fertility goddess; but we have no hard evidence that this assassination took place among the Celts.

Mistletoe was revered as a sacred plant not only among the ancient Celts living north of the Alps. Its repute extended to Greece and Rome. There is a clear hint in the writings of another Roman writer, Virgil, that the ceremony of cutting the Mistletoe was performed in winter, perhaps close to the time of the Winter Solstice. At this time the plant would have been fruiting vigorously and clearly visible among the bare branches of the Oaks. Virgil also brings us neatly to a connection between Mistletoe and the realms of death. In Book 6 of his epic saga, the *Aeneid*, the Sybilline seeress instructed the hero Aeneas on how to commune with his dead father, Anchises. The way to the kingdom ruled by the queen of the underworld, Persephone, lay in a gloomy valley but, in order to pass back through the portals of the dead into the world of the living safely, Aeneas needed first to perform a ritual:

> There lurks in a shady tree a bough, golden in leaf and pliant stem, held consecrate to nether Juno (Persephone); this all the grove hides, and shadows veil the dim valleys. But 'tis not given to pass beneath earth's hidden places, save to him who hath plucked from the tree the golden tressed fruitage. This hath beautiful Persephone ordained to be borne to her as her own gift. When the first is torn away, a second fails not, golden too, and the spray bears a leaf of the selfsame ore. Search then with eyes aloft and, when found, duly pluck it with thy hand; for of itself will it follow thee, freely and with ease.
>
> (*Aeneid* vi. 135)

Aeneas reached the place and did as he had been commanded after following two doves sent by the Sybil. Here Virgil indicated that the mistletoe was growing on a Holm Oak (*Quercus ilex*). There seems also, as Sir James Frazer asserted in *The Golden Bough*, to have been a clear intent by Virgil to equate the Mistletoe with the mystical golden bough in the renowned grove at Aricia sacred to the goddess Diana Nemorensis, a scene made famous by the artist Turner (see pages 182–3):

They swiftly rise and, dropping through the buxom air, settle on the site longed for, the two fold tree, whence, with diverse hue, shone out amid the branches the gleam of gold. As in winter's cold, amid the woods, the mistletoe, sown of an alien tree, is wont to bloom with strange leafage, and with yellow fruit embrace the shapely stems. Such was the vision of the leafy gold on the shadowy ilex, so rustled the foil in the gentle breeze.

(Aeneid vi. 200)

Frazer suggested that the rites at the Nemi grove, involving the periodical slaughter of a priest-king became less violent as time went on, and that the killing of the guardian of the grove was replaced by a tradition in which a runaway slave was pitted against the 'King of the Wood' or *Rex Nemorensis*. The challenge was for the slave to break a piece off the sacred tree in the midst of the grove. If he did so and successfully fought the King, he was allowed to take his place for a year. This tradition, Frazer argued, was staged as the symbolic re-enactment of Virgil's legend of Aeneas seizing a piece of Mistletoe as a safeguard before visiting the underworld. By implication the sacred tree of the Nemi grove also bore the plant.

The link between Mistletoe, fertility and death was either transmitted to, or arose independently in, Germanic and Norse traditions. The plant played a key role in the strange slaying of Balder, the ill-fated son of Othin. Balder was the dying and rising god of the north and was, arguably, a fertility deity. Among the Eddaic poetry of the Vikings, the Voluspa, the 'Prophecy of the Seeress', tells how Balder would be killed by a seemingly innocent sprig of Mistletoe that turned into a lethal projectile:

> I saw for Balder, the blessed god,
> Ygg's dearest son, a hidden doom:
> Aloft among the trees there grew
> The green and glossy mistletoe.
> When flung by War, the blind god,
> Became that slender sprig
> A slaying weapon.

(Poetic Edda, translated by Lee Hollander)

The tragic tale was amplified by the 12th-century Icelandic historian, Snorri Sturluson. He described how Balder's mother, Frigg, gained a magical immunity from all kinds of danger for her son after he had experienced dreams of his own doom. Everything in the world had pledged not to harm Balder, with one exception. Frigg was asked by Loki, a Machiavellian adversary of the gods: 'Have all things sworn oaths not to harm

Overleaf: William Turner's famous painting of the Golden Bough in the Sacred Grove of the goddess Diana Nemorensis at Aricia in Italy. The mysticism of the plant was alluded to by the Roman poet Virgil.

Balder?' To this, she replied: 'There grows a shoot of a tree to the west of Valhalla. It is called mistletoe. It seemed young to me to demand an oath from.' So Loki took a sprig of the plant to where the assembly of gods regularly enjoyed the sport of throwing missiles at Balder in proof of his extraordinary immunity. To one side, however, was standing the blind god Hod, and to his unwitting accomplice Loki handed the mistletoe directing where Hod should hurl it. As it flew through the air, the harmless sprig became a lethal dart and Balder fell dead. Paradoxically the plant that killed Balder also brought the promise of new life, for Balder was to rise again and lead a new generation of gods after the apocalypse of Ragnarok. As was so often the case in the beliefs of the ancient world, the themes of death and fertility were inextricably interwoven. These traditions and myths placed Mistletoe firmly in the role of a plant not only acting as a powerful fertility talisman but, ironically after Balder's tragic experience, also providing a safeguard against evil influences. If Virgil's Aeneas had managed to return from the underworld after presenting Mistletoe to Persephone, then it would also protect ordinary people from dark forces.

To the hotchpotch of literary glimpses at the traditions linked with Mistletoe, we can now add some archaeological evidence, though how significant this is remains an open question. Traces of the plant have been analysed from at least one Bronze Age tree coffin found in Yorkshire. Parts of Mistletoe berries were also detected in the stomach of the bog corpse victim of ritual Celtic sacrifice at Lindow Moss in Cheshire (see page 47). It is easy to jump to a hasty conclusion that immediately before his death the man had eaten a ritual meal including Mistletoe, but there may be another reason for its presence in his gut. Pliny noted that the Celts regarded Mistletoe as therapeutic, giving it the name 'All Heal', and Pliny detailed at least 11 conditions that were treatable with the plant extract, including epilepsy and the dispersal of cancerous tumours. It may be, therefore, that the victim of the Lindow bog sacrifice was already a sick man. Epilepsy, otherwise known as the 'falling sickness', was regarded as a sign of possession by evil spirits and this may explain not only why the man was fed with Mistletoe, to guard him against witchcraft, but also why he was condemned to an early death. Alternatively Lindow Man could have been dosing himself with Mistletoe in order to treat a carcinoma.

Of the various mystical associations earned by Mistletoe, that which has survived most tenaciously to the present day is the link with fertility and the turning of the old year in midwinter. It answers the question of why we kiss under the Mistletoe at Christmas. The tradition was begun in the 18th century in England when a ball of

Mistletoe was hung up and decorated with ribbons and ornaments. We are, in fact, performing a small rite, in the part of the year when nature appears dead, guarding ourselves against the powers of the netherworld and strengthening our ability to procreate as winter turns to spring with someone we have taken a fancy to!

🌿 *Lotus*

If any plant may lay claim to an aura comparable to that of the Mistletoe, the Sacred Lotus of India (*Nelumbium nucifera*) must surely rank highly. For Hindus, the Lotus has been regarded as sacred since prehistoric times. It is their Tree of Life and Good Fortune.

N. nucifera belongs to the Leguminosae family. In Sanskrit, the Lotus is called the *padma,* a name that properly refers to a red or pink lotus flower, but, in practice, becomes applied to a lotus of any colour, including the white and blue varieties. The Lotus displays the unusual botanical habit of reproducing from within its own 'matrix' rather than in the soil. It blooms when the fruit is ripe, whereas the flowers of most plants wither and fall before the fruit; this characteristic chiefly brings about a belief that the Lotus is a flower of divine origin capable of spontaneous generation. Thus it became the emblem of the universe and of cosmic creation throughout the sphere of Indian religions, and it is carried as an attribute by many deities. Its symbolic meaning can alter, however, according to the way in which it is incorporated into art, either as a bud or a fully opened flower.

The creator god Vishnu conventionally holds a Lotus bud in one of his hands and in this unopened state it is, in common with Mistletoe, a powerful fertility symbol, its link with Vishnu also emphasising the role of the plant in creation. Conventionally in Hindu iconography the goddess Shridevi, the principal wife of Vishnu, is depicted standing or seated to his right carrying a Lotus with its petals opened to reveal the pericarp (the wall of the developing ovary) and she is also known as Padmavati, the 'Lotus-bearer'. The goddess Bhudevi, Vishnu's second wife, stands to his left holding a blue lotus in her right hand with the petals fully developed but closed. Even the great god Brahma is sometimes depicted sitting upon the pericarp of a Lotus that springs from the naval of Vishnu. If, on the other hand, the Lotus is depicted as a fully opened blossom known as the *vikasitapadma*, it takes on a quite different symbolic role from that of the bud, because in the mature state it becomes the emblem of the Hindu sun god Surya, who conventionally holds two of the blossoms. The ancient poetry of the *Rig Veda*, the earliest religious text of Hinduism, describes Surya's eyes as being like deep blue lotuses and a Hindu prayer at sunrise, for one who wishes to attain greatness, includes the invocation: 'You are the one lotus among the quarters! May I become the one lotus among men.'

Aside from its powers of regenesis, the Lotus has been held in considerable esteem because of its sheer aesthetic beauty. In this it differs markedly from Mistletoe, which is a rather unprepossessing growth. It is not surprising that, in the ancient world, the Lotus soon became a symbol of purity and perfection. The flower has given its name to some of the great teaching scriptures of Hinduism, including the *Padma Sutra* and the *Padma Purana*. According to the Sutras, the Lotus flower possesses four outstanding virtues – its scent, its purity, its softness and its loveliness – perhaps reasons enough why the immortal soul is depicted in various ways including that of a Lotus. Another of the great Hindu scriptures, the *Brhadaranyaka Upanishad*, says that the immortal essence of a person is 'like a golden cloth, or white wool, or a red bug, or a flame, or a white lotus, or a sudden flash of lightning. When a man knows this his splendour unfolds.'

One of the most extraordinary and striking demonstrations of the regard with which the Lotus is held in India can be seen in the Baha'i Temple, inaugurated in New Delhi in 1986. The temple is built from concrete, clad in white marble, in the exact, if modern and contemporary, shape of a Lotus blossom. Three layers of nine petals arise from a plinth which raises the building above the surrounding plain. The first two tiers curve inward around the inner dome and the third layer arches out over the entrances. Such is the fascination with this building that the number of visitors regularly exceeds those at the Eiffel Tower or the Taj Mahal. Less dramatically, symbolic patterns or *mandalas* are also frequently drawn in the shape of the Lotus flower. Some examples include a fine 18th-century Tibetan temple hanging that depicts an assembly of saints in the form of a lotus flower; while in South India, at Tanjore, the layout of the Brhadesvara temple, known as the *padmagarbha mandala*, follows the geometric outline of the Lotus.

The Lotus is a no less powerful symbol in Buddhism, and the fact that it flowers and bears fruit at the same time suggests that it can reveal past, present and future simultaneously. The Lotus represents the throne of the Buddhas, each of whom is believed to have been born from the Lotus, and therefore it also symbolises their purity of descent. The Buddhas are sometimes referred to as the 'Lotus Family'. There has been, however, a more abstract concept, not always easy for someone more famil-

iar with Western culture to understand. The Buddhas are believed to have the power of becoming emanations, the nearest equivalent to which is the idea of spiritual ectoplasm. Among these emanations is one in which the personification of the Buddha is transmitted as enlightened speech. Probably the most celebrated figure of historical times in this context was Padmasambhava, the Tibetan Buddhist founder of Lamaism in the 8th century, someone that had undoubtedly found enlightenment. He is believed to have been an emanation of the Buddha Amitabha. Padmasambhava means 'born of the Lotus', a title which refers to the myth of his birth from a Lotus blossom.

In Vajrayana Buddhism, the most esoteric form of the religion, the Lotus also symbolises the female principle or the female genitals. Thus in Buddhism it replaces the Hindu *yoni*. The symbol of the flower is also a divine pledge of salvation.

In Jain religion, a more extreme ascetic offshoot from Buddhism, the Lotus flower was adopted as the symbol of the *tirthankara* Padmaprabha (Splendour of the Lotus),

Above: 'Throne of the Buddhas',
Lotus blossoms at the lakeside..

the sixth in the line of mythical 'Great Teachers' of Jainism. In Lamaism or Tibetan Budhism, not surprisingly, it became the emblem of the movement's founder.

The 'Lotus seat' or *padmasana* became a favourite attitude of many Hindu, Buddhist and Jain images including that of the Buddha and, to this day, it remains one of the classic positions of yoga. From an upright sitting posture, both legs are crossed and the feet are brought to rest on either the opposite thighs or knee joints.

The mystique of the Lotus became exported far beyond the ancient Near East and India. In the *Odyssey*, the Greek classical writer Homer described how the much-travelled eponymous hero Odysseus encountered a strange people living on the coast of North Africa who ate only the flowers of the Lotus:

> On the tenth day we reached the Land of the Lotus-Eaters whose only fare is that fragrant fruit. We stepped ashore there and drew water, and without delay my men and I took our meal by the ships. When we had had our portions of food and drink, I sent away some of my comrades to find what manner of human beings were those who lived there. They went at once and soon were among the Lotus-Eaters, who had no thoughts of making away with my companions, but gave them Lotus to taste instead. Those of my men who ate the honey-sweet Lotus fruit had no desire to retrace their steps and come back with news; their only wish was to linger there with the Lotus-Eaters, to feed on the fruit and put aside all thought of a voyage home.
>
> (*Odyssey* ix. 39–132, World Classics Edition)

In later times the imagery of the Lotus was also exported to China where it is held in high esteem by Taoists and represents the emblem of summer and fruitfulness. It also became revered in Japan where, in the 13th century, the Buddhism Nichiren Sect was founded, its doctrine based on the teachings of *Padma Sutra*.

Rose

The only other flower that approaches the level of kudos earned by the Mistletoe and the Lotus is the Rose, on account of its outstanding beauty. Some 250 species of Rose occur naturally worldwide, with innumerable hybrids. Members of the family Rosaceae, Roses are prickly shrubs and climbers native to the north temperate regions of the globe, and their five-petalled flowers in white, yellow, pink or red mature into bright red 'hips'. Modern hybrid roses are distinguished into several types, most notably hybrid teas and floribundas.

Since Biblical times, the Rose has been a symbol of love and purity, according to the colour of the bloom. Red roses are associated with love, white with purity. The earliest Rose symbolism is that of the fertility goddess Ishtar (see page 166), but the Rose is one of the most frequent attributes of the Virgin Mary, and Roman Catholic churches are often constructed to include a Rose Window. One of the best known of these is to be found at Arundel in Sussex, England. In the Roman Catholic brevary she is named as 'The Royal Virgin of David's Rose'.

Roses were adopted by two houses rivalling each other for the possession of the English crown in the English Middle Ages. The Red Rose became the symbol of the victorious House of Lancaster in the so-called Wars of the Roses, fought from 1455 to 1485, while the White Rose was the emblem of the House of York. Today, we still speak of the Red Rose of England. During the 19th century, when a romantic interest developed of

the symbolic meanings of flowers, lovers would exchange red Roses as esoteric messages of passion, and it was Robert Burns who penned the immortal lines: 'O my love is like a red, red rose, that's newly sprung in June.' White roses were sometimes contrasted with red, as symbols of sorrow. Thus the poet Tennyson wrote:

> She is coming, my dove, my dear; she is coming, my life, my fate.
> The red rose cries, 'She is near, she is near,'
> and the white rose cries, 'She is late.'

The Rose was also adopted by the Rosicrucian sect of mystics that originated in Germany in the 17th century and spread across much of Europe. Based on a fictitious brotherhood allegedly founded by Christian Rosenkreuz in 1484, the symbol of Rosicrucianism is the Rose Cross.

Above: The Dog Rose (*Rosa canina*) became an inspiration for the White Rose of York.

The Rose should not, incidentally, be confused with the 'Rose of Jericho' or 'Resurrection Plant'. This is an unrelated perennial herb, *Anastatica hierochuntica*, that grows in the Near East. It is so called because during the summer dry season it has the xerophytic ability to shed its leaves and roll itself up so that it looks like a dead wickerwork ball that blows about in the wind. By conserving moisture in this way, it can survive the drought and then regain its vitality. Nor should the Rose be confused with the Rose of Sharon (*Hibiscus syriacus*), another Biblical plant that also goes by the name of St John's Wort.

🌿 *Chrysanthemum and Peony*

In the Far East, two flowers in particular have gained a similar level of kudos to the Lotus and the Rose. They include the Chrysanthemum and the Peony. In China the Chrysanthemum has, by tradition, represented autumn. It is also a plant of fidelity since it is capable of withstanding the frosts of early winter. The name reflects a genus

of about 200 herbaceous plants and shrubs that are found more or less worldwide and which belong to the Compositae family. To the Japanese, the Chrysanthemum flower is a sacred imperial symbol and Japan's royal seat, inherited in what is claimed to be an unbroken imperial line descending back to the sun goddess Amaterasu, is known as the chrysanthemum throne.

The Peony became an important emblem both in imperial China and in Japan with a mystical influence that, in the course of time, extended west as far as Turkey and Iran. The flowers have been cultivated in China for some 1,500 years, not only for their beauty but also for the medicinal qualities of their roots. Two types occur in nature, herbaceous and so-called Tree Peonies,

The Peony became symbolic as an imperial flower in China and thus a celebrated subject in traditional Chines art. An ink painting (detail) by the 19th-century Chinese artist Ichimiosai.

though those grown by devotees in gardens in Europe and North America mainly take the herbaceous form. Tree Peonies are, more correctly, shrubs that grow to a height rarely extending beyond 2.5 metres. The wild form, known as Moutan, is found growing only in China and all the garden hybrids of Tree Peonies are descended from this species.

Like the Rose and the Chrysanthemum, the Chinese have regarded the Peony as a symbol of love and fidelity and, because of the ravishing appearance of its flowers, it has also been associated with femininity. The beauty of flowers and the beauty of women have gone hand-in-hand in the Orient, and Peonies were once frequently embroidered into the costumes of Japanese courtesans. From the 6th century, the flowers were sent regularly as tributes of loyalty to the Chinese emperors by their courtiers and retainers. As recently as 1997, when the territory of Hong Kong was handed back to the Chinese Communists by the British, the Jiangxi Provincial Government presented the Hong Kong regional authority with a porcelain picture of Peonies 'symbolising the joy at Hong Kong's return to China'. The fourth month in the Chinese calendar, Moutan, is also named after the Tree Peony. Peonies flower naturally in shades of reds, pinks, yellows and white. Much as the fabled blue Rose gained legendary properties in the West, so tales arose of a mysterious blue Peony, and in the 1860s excitement was aroused among Peony-fanciers in Europe by reports that blue Peonies of magnificent proportions were growing in the Chinese emperor's gardens.

Other flowers have earned reputations of mystery and magic at various times in history, but none has achieved quite the same level of fame as the Mistletoe, the Lotus, the Rose, the Peony and the Chrysanthemum. One of these has achieved its mystique by reason of association, but the others have done so on account of their sheer beauty to the beholder. Their value to humankind and their spiritual strength may best be summed up in the Biblical quotation from the Gospel of Matthew:

> Consider the lilies of the field, how they grow.
> They toil not, neither do they spin:
> And yet I say unto you,
> That even Solomon in all his glory
> Was not arrayed like one of these.

May Day

Of all the pagan festivals marking seasonal transitions in the year, May Day is probably the most significant since it celebrates the end of winter and the beginning of summer. It stands in a pivotal position midway between long cold winter nights and the long bounteous days of summer. It is also one of the few truly pagan dates in the calendar that exists in its own right and has not fallen to the tendency to place a Christian stamp on such occasions.

In Celtic times, the occasion was known as Beltane, a word deriving from *Bel* meaning 'bright' and *Tan* meaning 'fire'. It almost certainly took the form of a fire festival, when the Celts lit bonfires as a token of sympathetic magic to invoke the safe return of the hot summer sun. Their celebrations, beginning as the moon rises on the eve of 1 May, coincided with the moment at which, by time-honoured practice, the herds of cattle were first turned out into the pastures, having been kept in barns or corrals during the winter. Beltane coincides only with an obscure Christian festival of Walpurgistnacht, but is also given the names Rood Day and Rudemas, derived from the Old English word for a crucifix. The Christian establishment gave acknowledgement to the old pagan festival with a church service followed by a procession around the fields of the parish. The pagan festival placed a strong emphasis on fresh spring growth appearing in the countryside and also on fertility rites to ensure the fecundity of animals and crops during the coming seasons. Recent thinking, however, has tended

Left: Apple in blossom, one of the plants most closely associated with the old English traditions of May Day.

to discount the idea that May Day celebrations focused on a magical ritual to secure fertility of crops and to favour the theme of an expression of hope for the summer season to come, with the emphasis on a spirit of local community strength and unity. In more northerly regions of Europe including Scandinavia where the spring is much later, similar celebrations are held not on 1 May but at midsummer.

The word 'May' is thought to derive from the name of an obscure Greco-Roman earth goddess, Maia. She seems to have originated in pre-Homeric times as a mountain spirit who subsequently became a minor consort of Zeus. The Romans renamed her Flora and made her a barely less inconsequential consort of Jupiter who became the mother of Mercury and enjoyed a fringe cult as the goddess of growth in the fields. It was the Roman festival of Floralia that was adopted by peoples in territories conquered by the Roman empire.

Above: A Syrian mosaic depicting the earth goddess Maia.

In the past, May Day has been a period when the sexual norms of society were relaxed briefly, and on May Day eve courting couples went to the woods to 'make merrie sport' while gathering fresh leaves and flowers. During the 19th century, the character of Jack-in-the-Green became a popular figure in these May Day celebrations. Probably originating in medieval times, it was customary for a man to dress up in a wicker frame covered over with leaves apart from a small aperture for him to see through. He paraded through the streets accompanied by a crowd of revellers, their faces blackened like chimney sweeps, that danced around him banging drums, sticks and shovels, blowing whistles and collecting money.

In Carinthia (now in the southern part of Austria) there was a not dissimilar tradition of Green George, not associated with May Day celebrations but with St George's Day. A young villager was cloaked in birch branches, rather than wicker, and then paraded through the streets to the accompaniment of music. At the end of the celebration, either the individual in the Green George costume or a substitute effigy was thrown into a pond or river to the accompaniment of a chant:

> Green George we bring,
> Green George we accompany,
> May he feed our herds well.
> If not to the water with him.

The symbolism of the action was to provide a sympathetic magic to ensure that the fields were well watered during the summer growing season to provide a good harvest. Characters like Jack-in-the-Green have survived into modern times enshrined through enduring folk traditions, but there is no evidence that he was a dying-and-rising personality directly associated with the harvesting and sowing of the corn. He was probably a spirit of greenery, more associated with springtime in general and May Day celebrations in particular.

By tradition in many parts of Europe, including England, country people have elected a May King and Queen who preside over the proceedings of the day. They have often been portrayed as popular characters from national folklore, such as Robin Hood and Maid Marian, but once they probably represented the maidenly aspect of the earth goddess and her youthful consort. In Catholic countries such as France, the pagan colours of the May Queen have been thoroughly purged by the Church, and the young girl who plays the part has now become a representative of the Virgin Mary, leading a May Day procession in her honour.

During the Reformation, the Puritans in England and some of their contemporaries in Europe condemned the May Day celebrations. The Puritan settlers who sailed out across the Atlantic to what was to become the United States carried the disapproval with them, and May Day never achieved the same popularity in North America as in Europe. Nonetheless in many American towns and cities celebrations of a kind take place, with children electing May Queens and taking small paper baskets of spring flowers to hang on the doors of friends and neighbours.

The English parliament passed a statutory prohibition against May Day in 1644 and this restriction was upheld until the relaxation of austerity authorised by Charles II as part of the restoration of 1660. The old sexual connotations on the occasion remained, however, the subject of disapproval and did not make any noticeable return. In Victorian times, May Day became thoroughly imbued with moral fibre and was turned into an occasion of innocent spring jollity, with girls wearing the white of purity and carrying posies of flowers.

One might imagine that sacred tree traditions died out under the advance of Christianity, yet forms of tree worship have proved remarkably tenacious. The erection of a Maypole continues to be a major focus of May Day celebrations throughout Europe. It has been claimed that this object offers phallic imagery, but it may well be possible to trace the origins of the Maypole back either to the sacred trees of the ancient Near East or to the *Yggdrasil* of Norse tradition. Traditionally on May Day a living tree was hewn from the woods, stripped of its branches and carried into the village. Old English engravings show the pole to have been a massive object encircled by garlands of flowers and decorated with ribbons. From about 1888, in England, a shorter form of the pole was introduced and this became the norm, though occasionally a tall Maypole is still to be seen. The poles were erected traditionally on the village green close to the church, and this proximity of an object with clear pagan origins also incurred disapproval of the Christian establishment. Many of the village Maypoles, which eventually ceased to be freshly cut trees and were stored away year on year, were destroyed under the orders of the Church.

It may well be possible to trace the origins of the Maypole back either to the sacred trees of the ancient Near East or to the Yggdrasil of Norse tradition

Occasionally one can discover vestiges of Maypole sites in old names. In Nottinghamshire a Maypole was last erected in 1780, but a pub, long since demolished, bore

the name of The Old Corner Pin. In England, the Maypoles that become the focus of village activities are small compared with the size that used to be familiar, but a striking example of a tall traditional Maypole is still erected each year on May Day in the village of Barwick in Elmet in West Yorkshire. In the City of London there is a church with the curious title of St Andrew Undershaft. Sited in Leadenhall Street, it takes its name from an enormous Maypole that Chaucer once referred to as the 'Great Shaft of Cornhill'. This object stood until Cromwell's Puritans destroyed it during the Interregnum.

Elsewhere in Europe, the association between the Maypole and fertility was retained more strongly. In most parts of Europe the May Day traditions used living trees, particularly young firs and birches, that were cut freshly and carried into the villages with great celebration, having been decked with ribbons and flowers. In Germany and in the Czech Republic, there were old customs wherein on May Day eve young

Above: May Day celebrations around a decorated pole date from ancient times and are surviving remnants of pagan tree worship.

lads placed small Maypoles before the bedroom windows of their girlfriends. In terms of size, some of the tallest Maypoles, up to 40 metres 130 feet) in height and known as *maibaumen*, are still set up in Bavaria were they are traditionally decorated with 'branches' depicting local crafts and silhouettes of the principal village buildings such as the church. These traditions go back to the 16th century.

The ritual dance of the Maypole is performed in a complicated pattern around the periphery of a circle with the dancers holding the ends of coloured ribbons streamed from its top. As the dancers weave in and out of each another, they bind the ribbons around the pole until it is covered, and the practice is almost certainly a faint echo of those very ancient traditions wherein sacred trees were decorated with bands of metal and coloured cloth. These ribbon dances around trees or symbolic poles are extremely widespread around the world. In Spain, they are known as the *baile del cordon* and are derived from pre-Hispanic conquest dances known throughout Latin America. Similar dances can also be found in the folk traditions of India.

> *The practice is almost certainly a faint echo of those very ancient traditions wherein sacred trees were decorated with bands of metal and coloured cloth.*

Although May Day is the most popular of the festivals honouring the green mantle, it is by no means alone, though most of the others have taken on Christian colours. At Easter and Whitsun, the old sacred plants such as Yew and Mistetoe used to be cut and hung inside churches, as were garlands of Roses and other spring flowers. In almost all cases, the traditions have little to do with Christianity and a great deal in common with the sacredness of the living world.

Rogation Sunday ostensibly has been an occasion to give blessing to the rising crops but it once included a ceremony known as 'beating the bounds'. This too owes little to Christian dogma. According to old records, at the small village of Burpham in the south of England a procession took place that included a stop at an old Ash tree that was stripped on the east side. From this tree those involved went directly south to a place known as Lady's Coppice and to a Maple in the hedge, beside which they erected a cairn of stones. From here they processed to a well and finally ended up beside a Walnut tree, where they drank a gallon of ale and ate cheese and cakes. This ritual was nothing more or less than the blessing of sacred, and probably guardian, trees around the four cardinal points of the village.

As so often is the case, traditions associated with the green mantle are not always quite as they may seem. People dressing themselves in flowers or leaves sometimes do so for reasons that have little to do with agrarian festivals, and their ceremonies can appear misleading unless the background is understood. In Malaysia, for example, the festival of Thaipusam takes place each year in late January or early February. It involves ritual participants carrying an object known as the *kavadi*. This takes the form of a frame looking not unlike a tree with decorated branches, and its hangings include coloured paper, tinsel, fresh flowers and fruits. It would be easy to interpret the activity as a celebration akin to that of May Day with its Jack-in-the-Green. The intention is to make a form of appeasement — not, however, to a nature deity.

The Thaipusam ceremony is dedicated to the Hindu war god Skanda in his variety of Subrahmanya or Murukan. Hindu worshippers in Kuala Lumpur make an annual pilgrimage to the Batu Caves in Selangor with the *kavadi*. Of some considerable weight, it is carried as a form of penance and placed in a huge cavern containing an image of the deity. Malaysia does have a form of May Day celebration known as the Flora Fest, which takes place in July. At the end of a week of festivities, a floral parade takes place with a succession of spectacularly decorated flower floats.

Flora Fest is not specifically a religious event but an occasion for people to recognise and enjoy the beauty of the country's year-round subtropical profusion of flowering plants.

In pre-Christian times, Birch trees were often carried into village as part of the May Day celebrations. The delicate tracery of their leaves and branches give the tree its feminine attributes.

CHAPTER 12

Blessings and Curses

In some instances, the chemical principles produced by plants have resulted in
their developing a special kind of mystique far broader than that acquired
because of medicinal properties alone. Certain plants have become part of the
fabric of society, and their use has often attracted rituals of an almost religious
nature. Most possess chemical properties that affect the central nervous system, altering our state of mind. These are known as psychoactive drugs, and they fall into two
main categories: stimulants and narcotics. Species of *Camellia* (Tea), *Coffea* (Coffee)
and *Theobroma* (Cocoa) provide the main source of caffeine, the most universally popular social stimulant generated naturally in plants.

Tea

Camellia sinensis, better known as the Tea Tree, can probably claim the strongest impact
on commerce and social habits during a long period of history. A member of the
Theaceae family, it is native to China and grows as a medium-sized, rounded shrub
up to 2 metres (6 feet) in height. It has considerable tolerance to heat and drought and
bears white flowers in the leaf axils in autumn.

Tea drinking originated in China and undoubtedly the use of leaves from the
Tea plant goes back some 5,000 years. According to tradition a Chinese emperor, Zhen

Left: Harvesting the tea in Sri Lanka, a plant that constitutes
a major industry there.

Nong, discovered the delights of infusing the leaves of tea with hot water to make a beverage in about 2737 BCE while on a royal tour of his kingdom. He and his entourage had paused for some roadside refreshment when leaves from *C. sinensis* by chance fell into a cauldron of hot water. Curious about the change in colour of the water and the aroma, the Emperor investigated the taste, and the rest is history.

Tea drinking was taken up by the Chinese chiefly as an adjunct to meditation. It became useful as an aid to keeping practitioners awake, and such has been the influence of tea on Chinese culture that the first definitive book on the subject, the *Ch'a Ching*, was compiled there in about 800 CE. It was written by a Zen Buddhist monk, Yu Lu, who had gained considerable experienced of the husbandry of Tea plants and laid down the various methods of Tea cultivation.

The tea drinking habit may have been invented in China but it was the Japanese who turned it into an art form. Tradition has it that in about the 8th century CE the seed of Tea plants was taken from China to Japan by an itinerant Buddhist monk called Yeisei. Whatever the truth of this, the Japanese have been drinking tea enthusiastically for about as long, and from the outset the tea culture gained royal approval in Japan. Records show that the 8th-century Japanese emperor Shomu invited 100 Buddhist monks into his palace on one occasion to drink tea.

In Japan, tea drinking was to become a ritual with almost a religious character, but in the early stages sipping tea was a fairly informal business. The idea of attaching a ceremony to taking one's beverage was not introduced into Japan until 1267 by the Zen Buddhist monk, Dai-O, and it was only in the 15th century, during the Muromachi period, that it attracted widespread interest. Known as the Tea Ceremony or *cha no yu*, its ritual aspect was largely promoted by the Zen master Ikkyu (1394–1481) and one of his pupils, Shuko (1422–1502). It was further refined by another Zen monk, Sen-no Rikyu (1521–1591), and it was through his influence that ceremonial tea drinking evolved into an activity of almost cultic proportions. Sen-no Rikyu was actually keen to maintain the basic simplicity of the Tea Ceremony, but wanted to establish strict rules about how and where. These included specifications on the type of utensils to be used (often very beautiful), the layout of the tea room and even the design of the gardens that surrounded the tea pavilion. The idea inherent in the design and spirit of the pavilion was to recreate the atmosphere of a simple country cottage. Such was the fervour stimulated by Sen-no Rikyu for the art of tea drinking in Japan that, towards the end of the 15th century, the shogun Yoshimasa (1435–1490) had an ostentatious silver Tea Pavilion, the Dojinsai, built on his royal estate near Kyoto. This became the

model for all future tea houses known as *cha shitsu*. The service of the Tea Ceremony also became a special preserve, that of the Geisha, the professional Japanese hostess.

Unfortunately, as years went by, the early simplicity associated with the ceremony was lost and it became ever more ostentatious and elaborate. Among the wealthy Japanese elite, competitions were held, known as tea tournaments, in which participants challenged one another to games including the naming of blends of tea for which the victor won extravagant rewards. All was thoroughly alien to the beliefs and practice of Zen Buddhism.

The first Westerner to describe the joys of tea drinking seems to have been a Portuguese Jesuit priest, Jasper de Cruz. It was through his description compiled in

Above: Japanese geisha captured on film around 1900 and standing beside a traditional tea house.

1560 that European imaginations about the brew were titillated and the effect was to stimulate a rapidly burgeoning tea trade, first through Lisbon and then, principally, with the Dutch capital, The Hague. Yet it was not until the 17th century that the fashion truly caught the public imagination both in Europe and the newly emergent American colonies.

In the mid-16th century, tea was still strictly a luxury commodity affordable only by wealthy European patrons. The fad did not reach England for almost another hundred years when the first shipments to London were made in 1654, strangely enough several years after the imports had begun in North America. The Stuart king Charles II was already familiar with the delights of a cup of tea, having spent much of his youth in The Hague, and he was also married to a confirmed tea drinker in the shape of the Portuguese *infanta*, Catherine de Braganza. By the early 1800s, however, the English had romped past other nations in the tea popularity stakes and were leading the way as the major tea drinkers of Europe. England was importing, on average, over 100 tonnes of tea each year, having seen ale relegated to second place as the national beverage.

It was on the back of the burgeoning tea trade with the Orient that the East India Company first achieved prominence and then grew steadily more affluent. Negotiation between European buyers and Chinese traders even resulted in its own language, 'Pidgin English', where 'pidgin' is an adulterated form of the Mandarin expression for business activities. Tea planting was still limited to China, a country fiercely possessive of what was rightly regarded to be a prized commodity and the amount of money potentially involved in buying tea led to a system of barter, exclusive to England, using opium as the currency. Paying for tea with narcotics avoided the undesirable necessity to export sizeable reserves from the English treasury, but it created a scourge that carried much greater social penalties, and the opium trade to China became one of the great stains on the English commercial record.

American traders eventually broke the English monopoly on tea because they settled their payments to China in gold rather than the currency of drugs. For a long time the Americans had been obliged to deal through the East India Company and it was, in part, the objection to tea tax imposed on the colonists by Britain that led to the American War of Independence. The colonists had been drinking tea for about 50 years before the craze caught on firmly on the other side of the Atlantic and the first Tea Gardens became established in Boston and New York in about 1700. Following the colonial war that the British fought in support of their emigrees to the New

World against the French, it was considered right and proper that the colonists should shoulder a reasonable amount of the massive financial burden that had been incurred in maintaining hostilities across the Atlantic. The British government's redress took the form of various punitive taxes and among them, in 1767, the imposition of a levy on tea. The colonists were less than happy and reacted promptly by importing tea from Holland, boycotting sources from England. The British attitude to this serious loss of revenue was equally swift. The government attempted to sideline American importers by authorising sales direct to American tea drinkers. Outraged colonial housewives thwarted the scheme, however, and matters came to an acrimonious head when Bostonians elected to dump a large quantity of British tea into the harbour in an act of sabotage. The incident became known as the Boston Tea Party. The English authorities responded by closing the Boston port to all traffic and imposing martial law in the city. This draconian action amounted to a final insult and urged the colonists into rebellion. This in turn led to the outbreak of wholesale hostilities known as the American War of Independence.

After hostilities ceased, the Americans chose to sail to the Far East and obtain their tea supplies directly, and by the mid-1800s the fast tea clippers sailing between China, Europe and America had become renowned for their record-breaking voyages. Competition between skippers led to the Anglo-American tall ships' races being established as regular events. During these events China still maintained a strict monopoly on the supply of tea. The illegal export of seed and seedlings was resisted until after the opium wars of the late 19th century, when a Scottish botanist named Robert Fortune succeeded in smuggling viable tea seed out of China. His exploit led to experimental growing of tea in India and other parts of the Far East. At first these exercises in commercial farming were somewhat 'hit and miss', but eventually techniques were improved to the extent that extensive tea plantations became established in India and across more or less the whole of South East Asia.

In certain respects, English society of past centuries emulated the Tea Ceremonies of the Japanese, though perhaps inadvertently. The practice of drinking tea accompanied by small sandwiches and cakes was first made fashionable by Anna, Duchess of Bedford, at around the turn of the 19th century, and the novel idea of creating outdoor meeting places in the form of Tea Gardens followed not long afterwards.

Each country joining the 'tea cult' has tended to develop its own customs and tea-making equipment. The brown pot eventually became familiar in England as the basic brewing vessel but in some countries, such as Russia, apparatus in the form of the

Samovar was distinctly more elaborate. The Samovar was developed from a crude water-heating device used in Tibet and was a familiar feature in Russian homes, prominently placed and gently boiling throughout the day. The combination in which tea is drunk also varies from one culture to another. In England it became fashionable to drink tea with milk, while in Russia it was taken in a glass contained in a silver holder and with the addition of strong sweetener and even jam.

Today the art of tea drinking has largely been forgotten in China, though not in Japan. The caring but simple reverence attached to dealing with everyday matters, an ideal fundamental to Zen, still finds its highest expression in 'The Way of Tea', the ritual that was first practised by monks in Zen temples. In modern times, the tea ceremony has become largely a polite accomplishment for well-bred Japanese women.

Modern tea is produced from the dried leaves of numerous *cultivars* of the species and is classified into different tea types according to the degree of fermentation that has been permitted after harvesting. Among the varieties, most of the teas drunk in Europe are so-called black teas, where the oxidisation process on the leaves has been completed, resulting in a strongly flavoured, amber-coloured brew. English Breakfast tea is perhaps the most popular mix of black teas, although in China a blend known as Keemun is preferred. Green tea, one in which the leaves have not been subjected to oxidation, is the standard blend used in the Japanese tea ceremony. The resultant beverage is much paler in colour than that of black tea and possesses a delicate taste. Green tea is mainly consumed in the East and accounts for less than 10 per cent of total consumption, although its popularity is growing in England and America. In Japan the main area of tea planting lies in the district of Uji, not far from Kyoto. A third type of tea, Oolong, a cross between black and green tea possessing a distinct fruity taste and aroma, is especially popular in China. Originally the production of Oolong tea was centred in the Fukien province, before the main area of cultivation moved to the island of Taiwan.

Coffee

The second most widely marketed source of caffeine is Coffee, an evergreen shrub belonging to the genus *Coffea*. The genus, part of the Rubiaceae family, includes several related species found today in tropical regions throughout the world. The coffee beverage, obtained from the seeds ('beans') of the plant, contains the highest concentrations of caffeine, compared with tea and cocoa. The average cup of coffee

delivers between 65 and 115 milligrams of caffeine, while a similar volume of tea is unlikely to contain more than 60 milligrams.

Historical records from as early as 900 BCE show that the Arab nations were the first to drink a beverage made from the crushed beans of *Coffea* soaked in boiling water, and coffee is mentioned in the Moslem holy book, the Koran. Predictably, various legends arose to account for the discovery that coffee acts as a stimulant, and among the best known is a simple tale about an Ethiopian goatherd named Kaldi. He began to notice how lively and energetic his animals became after browsing on reddish-coloured berries from a certain bush. Tempted to eat some of the berries himself, he discovered that it was not only the goats which remained alert and active, so he passed his newly found secret to the inmates of a local monastery. The monks were naturally interested in any useful aid to staying awake during long periods of meditation and prayer, so they began to experiment for themselves. Chewing the beans, they quickly learned, was not the most enjoyable way of taking coffee. A marginally more palatable alternative was to prepare a drink made from the seeds, crushed and dissolved in hot water. It took several centuries for the advantage of roasting the beans to gain approval, probably at some time between 1000 and 1200 CE. With the more attractive flavour, the

Above: The fruits or 'beans' of the Coffee plant (*Coffea arabica*) have been cultivated since around 900 BCE as a source of the beverage.

interest in coffee drinking then spread rapidly throughout the Middle East, though the beans were still being harvested from the wild. By the close of the 15th century, coffee houses had become a common site throughout the Ottoman empire, with Turkey providing the hub for the fashion. So great had the social impact of coffee become that various administrators attempted to ban its use, believing that the stimulant effect had the potential to induce public unrest. The most notable of these included the Grand Vizir of the Ottomans who, in 1656, attempted widespread prohibition, including the mandatory closure of all Turkish coffee houses; but the ruling proved impossible to enforce and the exercise failed in common with all subsequent edicts against coffee drinking.

Coffea arabica cultivation probably began during the 1600s in the Yemen, but from the outset, throughout the Middle East, the industry was carefully controlled, much as tea planting was the jealous preserve of China. The coffee-growing countries placed a strict prohibition on the export of coffee plants or viable seeds that could be germinated, only allowing the sale of infertile sun-dried or roasted beans. The Arab monopoly on coffee growing might have remained static were it not for the smuggling (or inadvertent transportation) of a young viable sapling from the Arab port of Mocha (the origin of the name *mocha* coffee) to Amsterdam during the early part of the 17th century. The plant was then shipped, with careful attention, to the Dutch East Indies. The first coffee production outside the Arab world began in earnest on the island of Java, and Amsterdam became the internationally recognised trading centre for coffee.

The taste for drinking coffee in Europe apparently began in Venice, the first port to receive coffee imports in any kind of quantity early in the 17th century. The fashion is said to have been received with a royal seal of approval in western Europe by the French King Louis XIV, the 'Sun King'. According to conflicting reports, he became a firm devotee of the coffee-drinking fashion after a visiting Turkish ambassador in 1669 considered it would be a novel experience for 'the man who had everything' to be presented with a gift of coffee beans. Another tale suggests that royal interest was aroused in 1714, when the Mayor of Amsterdam, presumably following similar logic, dispatched some young coffee plants to Louis XIV as a gift. The seedlings were then grown on in the Paris Jardin des Plantes. French society soon gained a serious interest in coffee drinking and the first Parisian coffee shop *Le Procope* (it remains in business to this day) was opened in 1686. From the mid-17th century, coffee houses also became highly fashionable in England as places in which men of the world might discuss business and politics, though coffee drinking among the English has never reached quite the level of popularity seen in some parts of Continental Europe, most notably France. It was the French who were responsible for promoting coffee to the North American colonists early in the 18th century. The Americans took to coffee with gusto, while the English remained staunchly loyal to tea as their national beverage.

> *The Americans took to coffee with gusto, while the English remained staunchly loyal to tea as their national beverage.*

By the mid-18th century, such was the Continental fervour for coffee drinking that Johann Sebastian Bach even composed a slightly tongue-in-cheek cantata in praise of the drink, the Kafee-Kantate. He described it as 'lovelier than a thousand kisses, sweeter far than muscatel wine'. In all this time, however, coffee prices remained under the control of a limited number of growers and were kept artificially high. Coffee drinking was still largely a luxury to be enjoyed by society's wealthy elite.

Romantic tradition surrounds the introduction of coffee to what is now the largest growing region in the world, South America. The story goes that in the 1720s a Brazilian emissary to the Dutch colony in Guyana had an affair with the wife of the governor. The Dutch were no less determined to maintain their monopoly on coffee production as had been the Arabs in earlier centuries and prohibited the export of seedlings from their territories. The mistress, however, secreted fertile coffee seeds in a gift of flowers handed to the philandering Brazilian diplomat on his departure. It was her passing gesture of love that created Brazil's vast coffee-growing industry and was forever to bring coffee drinking within the financial reach of ordinary people.

In modern times the main coffee-producing areas include South and Central America, East Africa and Jamaica. A limited amount of coffee growing also takes place in Mysore in India. Among the species of commercial value, *C. arabica*, indigenous to North Africa, is generally considered to produce the best coffee. *C. liberica*, grown mainly in Malaysia and Guyana, gives an inferior quality. The *Coffea* species all develop attractive foliage and bear small white flowers in clusters at the bases of the leaves. These mature into berries that are at first green, becoming yellow and then cherry-red when ripe. When grown commercially, the trees are generally pruned to a height of 3–5 metres (10–16 feet) to facilitate harvesting. The process of producing coffee suitable for making beverages involves fermenting the harvested seeds and then sun-drying before roasting and grinding.

☙ Cocoa

Cocoa (the word is a corruption of cacao) is the third major source of naturally occurring caffeine. Cocoa powder is produced from the seeds of *Theobroma cacao*, the so-called 'chocolate plant', a member of the Sterculeaceae family whose members generally grow as small trees in the understorey of equatorial and subequatorial rainforests.

The Aztecs were the first recorded users of cocoa as a stimulant. In the Classical Period of Mexican history, the last emperor, Moctezuma II (*c.* 1466–1520) is alleged to have drunk as many as 50 cups of chocolate a day before he was assassinated. An Aztec document that survived the ravages of the conquistadors, the *Codex Mendoza*, records a tribute delivered to Moctezuma as a tax payment that amounted to 100 'cargas', or loads of cocoa bean. One load amounted to 24,000 seeds.

Above: The Aztecs were the first recorded users of Cocoa (*Theobroma cacao*) as a stimulant. The emperor Montezuma II is reputed to have drunk 50 cups of the chocolate beverage every day.

It was the leader of the Spanish expedition to Mexico, Hernan Cortes, who introduced cocoa to Europe in 1527. European society soon gained a passion for chocolate and this resulted in a rapid growth in demand for imported cocoa beans. Cocoa has been used in an assortment of folk remedies. It is claimed to possess antiseptic and diuretic properties, and to kill parasites. Cocoa butter has also been prescribed for alopecia, burns, dry skin, fever, listlessness, malaria, kidney complaints and rheumatism, as well as getting rid of wrinkles. There is also a considerable argument that cocoa in the form of chocolate increases sexual desire!

Theobroma is most commonly found in lowland and lower montane areas of Central and South America, especially the warm and humid valleys of the Amazon and Orinoco rivers in Brazil. The fruit arises from small white flowers, and is a large pod, up to 25 centimetres (10 inches) long and 10 centimetres (4 inches) wide, that contains seeds surrounded by a sweet, juicy pulp. It is the seeds, rich in fat and otherwise known as 'cocoa beans', from which cocoa butter is extracted and the cocoa powder is manufactured. The fruit, cut from the tree by machete, is harvested throughout the year and the wet beans are fermented for about a week before being dried in the sun and roasted. The next stage in the process is to crush the seed to remove its hard outer coating and from the resulting 'gravel' to produce butter and powder. Chocolate is derived from cocoa by addition of sugar and other flavourings such as vanilla.

Today the annual harvest of cocoa beans runs to over one million tonnes in the principal production areas of Central and South America, West Africa and Borneo. The quantities of chocolate consumed in Europe alone are fairly staggering. Switzerland tops the league table with an annual consumption, per person, of about 9 kilograms (20 lb). British chocolate 'addicts' are not far behind, digesting about 8 kilograms (18 lb) each year.

The Florentine Codex reveals the Aztecs cultivating and harvesting Cocoa beans.

🌿 *The Great Plant Poisons*

It is paradoxical that although two plants may look alike superficially, one may be harmless to human beings while the other may result in considerable discomfort and, *in extremis*, an agonising death. There is no logical explanation as to why nature should create such pitfalls, but they have undoubtedly served to whet our appetites still further in respect of the mystique already attached to plants. Plant poisoning is currently described by official poisons information bodies as 'creating a serious departure from the normal state of health, when a small portion of vegetation, root or seed, is consumed by an individual susceptible to its effect'. In other words, plant poisoning cannot be viewed exclusively in terms of straightforward toxicity because, in some instances, it amounts to an allergic reaction. It is not hard to imagine the response of a superstitious person, ignorant of medical science, to what seems a selective punishment, delivered by the gods and affecting one person while his or her neighbour walks free.

The poisons synthesised by plants can be of great value if judiciously used, and they have provided the basis of much of modern drug preparation in the pharmaceutical industry. Knowledge about these toxins, however, has only recently been introduced to the public domain and for many thousands of years it was shrouded in mystery and ritual. Over centuries, people learned that certain plants possessed magical properties of death or cure. A certain plant in the forest had the power, magically, to heal wounds; another would strike dead the person who consumed it; and yet another would transport its user to a celestial height where he or she was able to grasp the power and insight of gods.

It is difficult for us, living in the 21st century, to comprehend some of the superstitions that accompanied certain plants and their effects until fairly recent times. Yet lurid and graphic reports of symptoms generated by toxic plants give some idea of how easily fear was generated in a public lacking any of the modern understanding of disease, and frequently convinced that sickness was the work of the devil. The following description is drawn from a case history of a Victorian child who died after eating the root of Cowbane (*Cicuta virosa*), a member of the Umbelliferae family, that had been mistaken for an artichoke:

> His first symptom was a pain in the bowel, urging him to an ineffectual stool after
> which he vomited about a teacup of what appeared to be recently masticated root, and
> immediately fell back into convulsions which lasted on and off continuously till his

death. The doctors found him in a profuse sweat and convulsive agitations, consisting of tremors, violent contractions and distortions with alternate and imperfect relaxations of the whole muscular system, astonishing mobility of the eyeballs with widely dilated pupils, stridor dentum, trismus, frothing at the mouth and nose mixed with blood, and occasional violent and genuine epilepsy.

The 20th-century German author L. Lewin rendered another stark insight into past attitudes wherein reality and superstition about plants were hopelessly entwined. In *Phantastica, Narcotic and Stimulating Drugs* (1931) he discusses the hallucinogenic herb *Datura stramonium*, known in Europe as Thorn Apple and in North America as Jimson Weed:

> We find these plants associated with incomprehensible acts on the part of fanatics, raging with the flames of frenzy and fury, and persecuting not only witches and sorcerers but mankind as a whole. Garbed in the cowl, the judge's robe and the physician's gown, susperstitious folly instituted diabolical proceedings in the trial of the devil and hurled its victims into the flames or drowned them in blood.

A member of the Solanaceae family, the plant grows extensively throughout the warmer latitudes of the northern hemisphere as an annual. In Britain and other more northerly parts of Europe it is an occasional escape from cultivation. Growing to a height of 1 metre (3 feet), its branches bears long, delicate pale blue flowers followed by large fruits reminiscent of a spiny horse chestnut. All parts are toxic with the greatest concentration of poison occurring in the seeds. The course of poisoning is fairly slow and may run for several days, commencing with mental confusion not unlike inebriation, but eventually resulting in the victim becoming delirious and even maniacal. In severe cases, death results from asphyxia.

A certain plant in the forest had the power, magically, to heal wounds; another would strike dead the person who consumed it; and yet another would transport its user to a celestial height.

In medieval medicine *D. stramonium* seeds were used as the main constituent of an ointment that was popular as an external analgesic, and so effective are they when taken as a 'knockout' drug that in parts of Africa the plant has earned a secret name 'lukuma'. It has also been fed to unsuspecting schoolchildren by their classmates in South Africa in an initiation ritual where the seeds are known as 'laughboontjie'.

For the people of classical Greece and Rome, Hemlock (*Conium maculatum*) was among the most notorious plants with a danger label attached to its name. A biennial herb, it grows in tall clumps in damp meadows, hedgerows and open woodlands throughout the temperate regions of the northern hemisphere. Hemlock was used in ancient Greece as an official method of dispatching political prisoners condemned to death, of whom the philosopher Socrates is probably the best known. Socrates, seen as a disruptive radical in a strongly conservative society, was accused of impiety and corruption of youth in 339 BCE and condemned to swallow a lethal draught of Hemlock. The effect of the toxin is not unlike that of the South American arrow poison, curare,

causing progressive paralysis of the nervous system by affecting the bodily extremities first and progressing inwards until death results from heart and respiratory failure. According to contemporary reports of his death, Socrates remained fully conscious until the end.

In small quantities, the toxic principles provide a non-fatal numbing effect, and it was apparently with this in mind that Hemlock was employed in the sexually charged Mysteries of the Greek Rites of Eleusis. These included a symbolic act of intercourse between the High Priest and Priestess of the fertility goddess Demeter, and the drug apparently kept the libido of the priest under reasonable control. In later times, the herbalist Nicholas Culpeper noted that a cold poultice of the leaves 'applied to the privities, stops its lustful thoughts'.

The magical and mystical nature of Hemlock was not lost on William Shakespeare, who introduced it into the witches' brew in *Macbeth*, and Banquo complained of eating 'the insane root that takes the

Hemlock (*Conium maculatum*) was used as a narcotic in the ancient Greek Rites of Eleusis. It kept in check the libido of the officiating priests during the sexually charged ceremony.

reason prisoner'. It was also, allegedly, an ingredient of the so-called 'flying ointment' of medieval witches.

Aconite or Monkshood (*Aconitum* spp.), which occurs throughout the temperate regions of the world, is among the most poisonous of all flowering plants. A member of the Ranunculaceae family, it is frequently grown as the garden hybrid *A. napellus*, on account of its spikes of attractive blue flowers and deeply cut, pale green leaves. The compound responsible for its fatal properties is the alkaloid aconitine, and death, from paralysis of the respiratory system, occurs up to 24 hours after ingestion of a fatal quantity (as little as 2 milligrams). The intervening symptoms include dizziness, hallucination and convulsions.

So concerned was the Roman Emperor Trajan, who reigned from 98 to 117 CE, about the lethal nature of Aconite that he prohibited its cultivation on pain of death. In Europe, from the time of the Anglo-Saxons, the juice of the plant was favoured as an arrow poison, hence one of its common names, Wolfsbane, and occasionally during the 16th century it was used experimentally on condemned prisoners. As in the case of so many toxic plants, however, tincture of Aconite has also been used in pharmacy as an external treatment for rheumatism and gout. To add still further to the confusing mystique, the antidotes for aconitine poisoning include atropine (extracted from *Atropa belladonna*) and digitalin (from *Digitalis purpurea*, the Foxglove). Yet *D. purpurea* extract was, in itself, used during the medieval centuries as an arrow poison and an ordeal drug.

The Romans put another dangerously poisonous member of the Solanaceae family, the Deadly Nightshade (*Atropa belladonna*) to less menacing but thoroughly bizarre purpose. The plant is a shrub-like woody perennial that is found more commonly in the warmer temperate latitudes of the northern hemisphere but has become naturalised in places which saw Roman occupation. The erect stems, up to 1.5 metres (5 feet) tall, arch out from the base, bearing long ovate leaves and dull purple, tubular flowers that mature into shiny black berries. All parts of the plant are toxic but the attractive appearance of the berries (reminiscent of fruit lozenges) has made them responsible for most cases of poisoning in children. Not unlike *Datura stramonium* poisoning, the symptoms commence with the victim becoming extremely excited, often verging on violence with rapid and jerky movements, flushed appearance and widely dilated, more or less immobile pupils that give the eyes a glassy, staring appearance. This phase is followed by lethargy, intense thirst and, *in extremis*, coma followed by death from asphyxia. Such is the course of poisoning from ingestion of Deadly

🌿 *It was considered a mark of attractiveness for*
a woman to possess 'large dark eyes', and the tincture
of Belladonna served to dilate the pupils in
tantalising fashion.

Fruits of the Deadly Nightshade (*Atropia belladonna*). The plant was
so called from a combination of the name of the alkaloid chemical
atropine, and the Latin for 'beautiful lady', after Roman society ladies
used the tincture on their eyes, as described above.

Nightshade, but ladies of the Roman court habitually used an extract of the plant for cosmetic purposes, hence the epithet 'belladonna' or 'beautiful lady'. It was considered a mark of attractiveness for a woman to possess 'large dark eyes', and the tincture of Belladonna served to dilate the pupils in tantalising fashion.

Sometimes the poisonous nature of a plant has led to strange associations. For many centuries from Roman times, the leaves of Ivy (*Hedera helix*) were regarded, fallaciously, as an antidote to drunkenness. Hence Bacchus, the god of wine who was the Roman successor to Dionysos, wears an ivy crown. This theme was pursued during the Middle Ages when wine goblets were frequently carved from Ivy wood. In reality, although eating the berries results in an assortment of unpleasant symptoms including nausea, vomiting and diarrhoea, the leaves have more of a sedative (or sobering) effect and have also been used for soothing toothache. This narcotic property has, in turn, given rise to other legends. Leonardo da Vinci once observed that wild boars always went away and rolled in beds of Ivy when wounded.

Flowering plants have not been the only providers of danger in the botanical and related kingdoms. It was during the Classical Era that certain fungi gained their darker reputations. In Rome, the Death Cap toadstool (*Amanita phalloides*) was employed with deadly effect in 54 CE by Agrippina, the scheming wife of the Emperor Claudius, who arranged with the imperial cooks that her husband's supper was laced with several of the fruit bodies. *A. phalloides* is a deceptively innocuous-looking agaric fungus with an olive-greenish, somewhat silky cap, white gills and the characteristics of a ringed stem associated with a volval bag at the stem base, both remnants of the protective veils that covered the immature fruit body. The species is typically associated with Oak, which from the viewpoint of the Greeks and Romans would have made it a plant sacred to Zeus and Jupiter. Tradition has it that one of Claudius' favourite delicacies was the related but edible *Amanita caesarea*, the culinary virtues of which had been highlighted by the celebrated Roman gourmet Apicus who lived during the reign of the Emperor Tiberius (14–37 CE). *A. phalloides* was introduced into this dish so clearing the political path for the accession of Nero.

CHAPTER 13

Mind Benders

The chemicals synthesised by species of *Camellia*, *Coffea* and *Theobroma* are accepted as indispensable elements of cultural traditions throughout the world. Tea, coffee and cocoa are viewed generally as harmless stimulants though there are some arguments that their consumption becomes addictive and medical evidence suggests that they can cause adverse effects when taken to excess. Other drug-producing plants have gained less acceptance, and some have been the cause of great social misery and deprivation because of their narcotic and addictive nature. Cannabis finds widespread use as a recreational drug on a par with alcohol, but enjoys a mixed political reception. Some other chemicals produced by plants cause severe social, physiological and psychological damage and have become the *raison d'être* for large-scale organised crime. They include the so-called 'hard drugs'. Some act on the central nervous system as stimulants, others as narcotics.

Cannabis

Among various plants that have been used and abused by humankind as a source of intoxicants, some members of the Hemp family have acquired the greatest notoriety in modern times. They are the source of the hallucinatory drug, cannabis. *Cannabis sativa* and *C. indica* grow throughout the world, although commercial production takes place

Left: The leaves of *Cannabis sativa* produce a hallucinatory drug that has been widely abused. Yet, Cannabis has also been employed in medicine since ancient times as a painkiller.

mainly in the Indian subcontinent, North Africa, the Carribbean and Lebanon. The drug occurs in the greatest concentrations in the buds, young leaves and flowers of the plants, and the quality of the material varies from country to country. The dried buds and flowerheads constitute the herbal form of cannabis popularly known as 'grass', but it is also sold as a resin, typically extracted in the country of origin and known as 'hash' or 'hashish'. A third form of cannabis is a thick, sticky oil, refined from the resin and referred to as 'hash oil'.

Since ancient times, the plant has been employed extensively in medicine, largely as an analgesic. The earliest recorded use of cannabis comes from China at around the beginning of the 3rd millennium BCE, when it was included in a medical codex prepared for the emperor T'sien Nung. Egyptian records from Thebes during the time of the Pharaohs also mention Hemp being made into a drink with an opium-like effect.

Curiously, in view of its mind-altering properties, cannabis seems not to have found much interest among Native American tribes, though a notable exception is to be found among the Tepeccano Indians in northwest Mexico and pueblo Indians living in the state of Veracruz. Both use cannabis socially. The first-choice hallucinatory drug among these indigenous tribes is mescal obtained from the Peyote cactus, but if this is not available they will recourse to *C. sativa*. Under Christian influence the plant has become known as Santa Rosa and is used, it is said, to gain communication with the Virgin Mary.

The species *C. indica* finds more extensive use in Asia, particularly in Hindu tradition. It has been tentatively identified with the mysterious Soma plant, the apotheosis of which is the god Soma, and it forms the basis of a drink known as *bhang* sacred to various important deities including Indra and Shiva. Cannabis extract is mixed with water and milk and this liquid is also used to bathe the phallic symbol of Shiva, the stone linga in the Lingaraj Temple at Bhubaneswar. *C. indica* is also regarded as a holy plant in Tibet, where it is harvested on the lower slopes of the Himalayas. Tantric Buddhists use cannabis as an aid to meditation and, according to one tradition, the Buddha survived each day on a single cannabis seed while he was achieving enlightenment at the Bodhi tree. Closer to home, Queen Victoria is reported to have imbibed a tincture of cannabis to ease period pains.

The drug acts as an intoxicant and, for this reason, it has been subject to various restrictions in different countries. From the 1950s in the UK it was being used as a

Queen Victoria is reported to have imbibed a tincture of cannabis to ease period pains.

social drug, at first among West Indian immigrants, then more widely among teenagers at parties and clubs. Cannabis is either smoked neat or mixed with tobacco and known as a 'joint' or 'reefer', or eaten as an ingredient of a cake or biscuit. It can also be dissolved in hot water and drunk. Although prior to 1928 cannabis could be used freely in the UK, its use is currently illegal. There are, however, strong moves among members of the medical profession and other concerned groups to legalise cannabis because of its known efficacy in alleviating pain associated with such chronic conditions as multiple sclerosis and terminal cancer.

Tobacco

Of all the plants with properties affecting the human nervous system, the best known and most widely used throughout the world is tobacco (*Nicotiana* spp.). A member of the Solanaceae or Nightshade family, the genus includes several members, among which the wild form occurring in the New World is *N. attenuata*. Tobacco gained its popularity when it was discovered that droplets of the alkaloid nicotine, produced in the leaves, had a distinct physiological effect when absorbed through the lungs.

One can imagine that the effect of tobacco-smoke inhalation was first discovered by accident, perhaps when someone was burning the material on a cooking fire. What is thought to be the first recorded deliberate use has been found in the form of a picture on a piece of Mayan pottery from Uaxactun, Guatemala, sculpted in about 500 CE. It shows an Indian smoking a roll of leaves tied with string. The effects of tobacco must, however, have been known to man for a much longer period of time. Palaeobotanists now believe that the tobacco plant recognised today first evolved in the Americas in about 6000 BCE, and that by about the 1st century BCE native inhabitants had discovered the therapeutic use of the leaves by chewing or smoking.

Many of the North American Indian tribes have used the dried leaves of tobacco not only for social and medical purposes, for which it has been employed widely as a painkiller, but also in religious ceremonies.

Tobacco is still one of the most important features of ritual when it is smoked rather than chewed, and the Indian's pipe is among his most treasured possessions. It is laid beside him in the grave when he dies in order to give him comfort on his way to the Happy Hunting Grounds. Stems of the plant have been used as well as leaves, but these make an inferior tobacco and have generally been set aside as 'gifts' to the spirits or to be offered to guests!

Among the many myths that have grown up about the origin of the tobacco plant, one describes how the Great Spirit was asleep by the side of his fire, deep in the forest. All was peaceful until another more mischievous spirit came by and decided to push his rival into the flames, rolling him over until his hair was set ablaze. So upset was the great spirit that he leapt up and ran headlong through the forest with a trail of sparks and pieces of singed hair in his wake. Where these fragments came to rest on the soil they took root and became tobacco plants.

The origin of the Pipe of Peace is told in another myth involving the Great Spirit and set at the Red Pipestone Rock, which has long been held as a sacred place by North American Indians. It is from here that the material for all ceremonial pipes,

Above: A Native American shaman carrying a ceremonial pipe
of peace in this 19th-century engraving by Paul Legrand.

made of stone not wood, must be dug. At least 40 tribes are known to have made pilgrimages to the site. It is formed by a sheer wall of polished quartz, some 10 metres (30 feet) in height and running for nearly 3 kilometres (2 miles), at the source of one of the tributaries of the river Missouri, known as Big Sioux. At the base of the cliff the red stone is exposed. According to the myth, the Great Spirit gathered together all the tribes and in their presence fashioned a huge pipe from the red stone, telling them that its colour symbolised their flesh and blood. From it they could make their pipes of peace but, in this place, the war club and the scalping knife must never be raised in anger. The Pipe of Peace, owned by each male Indian, is distinct incidentally from the Medicine Pipe, a special instrument elaborately decorated and used only on ceremonial occasions.

The earliest known written reference to tobacco, as a plant used in medicine, is to be found in the *Codex Barberini*. This was a Latin work produced by two 16th-century pupils of the college at Tlatiluco in Mexico, one of whom was Martin de la Cruz, who recorded much Aztec herbal knowledge. The Latin original, prepared in 1552 and currently housed in the Vatican library, was translated into Spanish and published by Nicholas Monardes under the title *Dos Libros* in 1569. Three separate passages mention *Nicotiana* species. *N. rustica*, described as 'piciyetl', is considered effective against 'rumbling in the abdomen' and 'recurrent disease'. Another species, identified only as 'quappo-quietl', is prescribed for gout.

The first European explorer to report tobacco use was Robert Pane, who sailed with the Portuguese mariner Christopher Columbus on his second voyage of discovery in 1493. In October of the previous year, when Columbus stepped ashore on the island of San Salvador, thereby discovering the New World, the native Arawaks offered him a variety of gifts including 'certain dried leaves, which gave off a distinct fragrance'. Columbus' diary records that the leaves were considered worthless and were thrown away but it was not long after this that Europeans became aware of the effects of tobacco smoking. In Cuba, in November of 1493, Rodrigo de Jerez watched natives rolling the leaves into a tube, igniting one end and 'drinking' the smoke. In copying them, Jerez appears to have been the first European to actually smoke tobacco. The newly acquired habit turned out a mixed blessing for de Jerez. When he returned home keen to demonstrate the technique, the smoke billowing from his nostrils led the Spanish Inquisition promptly to mark him down for Devil worship and he was incarcerated for seven years. By the time he was released from prison, tobacco smoking in Spain and Portugal had become highly fashionable, though the Pope saw fit in the 1600s to place a ban on smoking in holy places. Tobacco was introduced independently into France in 1556 by an explorer named Thevet who brought back plants of *N. tabacum* from Brazil.

The tobacco-smoking craze was carried to England from the New World, not in 1586 by the Elizabethan explorer, Sir Walter Raleigh, as has been widely credited, but some years earlier. Walter Raleigh had been introduced to the use of tobacco by another English mariner, Sir Francis Drake, who had seen it employed by Indian medicine men. Drake had reported it as a 'wonder drug' that would cure more or less anything! In 1564, however, the writer William Camden (1551–1623) had observed some of the Virginian colonists disembarking from a ship under the command of Sir John Hawkins at Plymouth and causing a local stir when they were seen smoking their newly acquired pipes. Camden noted that 'these men who were thus brought back were the first that I know of that brought into England that Indian plant which they call Tabacca and Nicotia, or Tobacco'.

For centuries, tobacco was considered a route to good health. Records of Eton College show that in 1665 the pupils were required to smoke a pipe of tobacco, which became known in the popular Elizabethan idiom as 'softweed', every day in order to maintain fitness and acquire what was believed to be yet another effective protection against the Plague.

In spite of rapidly gaining popularity, tobacco soon had its detractors. In 1612 an imperial edict forbade the planting and use of tobacco in China. A year later a similar prohibition was made in Russia under the early Romanoffs. The ban lasted until 1676, though as late as 1674 Russians caught smoking could risk the death penalty.

Even among the American colonists there was dissent about the virtues of tobacco, and in 1639 a ban was placed on smoking in New Amsterdam (later to become New York City). The habit also had its detractors in England, who considered that it rendered men impotent. In 1617, Dr William Vaughn penned a less than complimentary verse about the 'weed':

> Tobacco that outlandish weede
> It spends the braine and spoiles the seede
> It dulls the spirite, it dims the sight
> It robs a woman of her right.

The European fashion of making cigarettes, as distinct from smoking tobacco in a pipe, probably began with the French and Turkish armies during the Crimean War.

Troops smoked tobacco rolled in paper, known as 'papirossi', and were copied by their British counterparts. The automatic rolling machine first appeared in 1881, and it was this invention that triggered large-scale, worldwide commercial cigarette production.

Tobacco is part of deep-rooted tradition in various parts of the world other than the Americas, including Turkey, the Near East and India. In more of a social than ceremonial custom, tobacco is smoked in the *nargile*, more commonly known in the West as a 'hookah'. This instrument is an elaborately constructed system of tubes and vessels in which the smoke from the tobacco is filtered and cooled by drawing it through a receptacle filled with water. Smoked mainly by men but also, in the past, by fashionable women, the *nargile* was invented in India and the fashion spread first to Iran and then to the rest of the

For centuries, tobacco was considered a route to good health.

Arab world. It achieved its greatest popularity, however, in Turkey where it became an indispensable part of coffee-shop culture from the 17th century onwards, after the first tobacco arrived from the New World in 1601. As was so often the case with the spread of tobacco culture, not everyone approved of the new fad and in 1633, faced with what he saw as an unacceptable vice, the Sultan of Turkey, Murad IV, authorised the death penalty for anyone caught smoking. The edict lasted for 14 years, but ultimately proved impossible to enforce because of the sheer numbers of people prepared to flout the law.

Nargile smokers elaborated the procedure for lighting and smoking the pipe into a form of ritual to which strict rules of etiquette were applied. Only strong dark tobacco from Iran was to be used, washed several times to reduce its excessive potency and ignited with oak charcoal. The original Indian *nargiles* were made from coconut shell but they were fairly crude, and as the fashion developed and spread craftsmen began to make the main body of the pipe out of crystal or silver while the mouthpiece was generally formed from amber, considered less likely to transmit germs.

Although first and foremost *nargile* smoking has been a social custom, it does bear some similarity to the pipe-smoking rituals of North American Indians in that it became an important symbol of trust. If a host did not offer the *nargile* to his guests it was considered an insult, and this actually generated a diplomatic row between the Ottoman Empire and France in 1841 when the Sultan declined to smoke with the French ambassador.

Cultivated varieties of *Nicotiana* raised for commercial tobacco production mainly include *N. tabacum* and *N. rustica*. Growing to a height of 1–3 metres (3–10 feet) the plants bear pink, white or greenish flowers and, after collection, the leaves are dried for up to two months, then fermented for as long a period again. Today, outside North America the main growing regions are China, India and parts of the former Soviet Union in central Asia.

🌿 *Betel and Areca*

In India and other eastern countries, chewing betel tends to take over from smoking tobacco, and has similar physiological effects to a mild stimulant, although medical evidence suggests that it is no less injurious to health than tobacco. 'Betel' is a mixture of the seeds of a tree, *Areca catechu*, locally known as the Areca or Betel Palm, combined with the leaves of *Piper betle*, the Betel Pepper. The Areca seeds or 'betel nuts' are dried and boiled. They contain an alkaloid that has limited effect in removing intestinal

Betel nuts on sale in an Asian market. The effect of
chewing betel is mildly stimulating and the habit replaces
that of smoking tobacco.

worms, but the seeds also contain high levels of copper, which increases the risk of contracting oral cancers. The risk is particularly high when the betel is mixed with tobacco and lime in a concoction known as *mawa*. As with tobacco, the chewing of betel constitutes an important part of religious ceremonies in some cultures.

The Areca has attracted an assortment of stories to account for its origins. In Vietnam, a tale is told of two sons, Tan and Lang, whose appearance was almost identical and who were very close to each other. Tan, the elder brother, married the daughter of his teacher and the two brothers drifted apart, to the considerable sorrow of Lang. He left home and became an itinerant. One day his travels brought him to a riverbank where he sat down to await a ferryboat, but none came. Day after day he waited in vain until he died. He was transformed into an Areca nut tree. Meanwhile Tang had also left home in search of his lost brother, and fate took him to the same riverbank. In his anguish at being unable to find Lang, he hit his head against the Areca nut tree so hard that he died and became transformed into a limestone rock. Tan's wife became distraught at the loss of both her husband and brother-in-law and she too went off in search, arriving at the fatal spot on the bank of the river. Clinging unwittingly to the limestone rock she also died and became a Betel Pepper plant creeping around the rock.

Years later, the king of the country was on his travels and came to the riverbank. He chewed some Betel Pepper leaves with some Areca seed and found the taste agreeable, as well as producing a great deal of saliva. When he spat the juice onto the white limestone rock he saw that it turned red (from the pigment in the seeds). Understanding that this was the spot where Tan, Lang and Tan's wife had died out of love for one another, he proclaimed that the colour of the juice symbolised that bond and had a shrine dedicated to the trio built at the place. It was on the basis of this legend that the Betel Pepper leaves and Areca nuts became traditional bridal gifts at Vietnamese weddings.

Nutmeg and Yohimbe

Less familiar in its use but with a comparable effect, Nutmeg is obtained from the fruits of *Myristica fragrans*. The plant is an evergreen tree growing to a height of about 15 metres (50 feet) with big ovate leaves, in the axils of which the flowers form. When mature these develop into small pear-shaped fruits with an outer fleshy husk and an inner seed or kernel, the nutmeg, separated by a leathery crimson layer marketed

separately as mace. The nutmeg kernels and mace contain a combination of oils that affect the adrenal glands regulating the body's energy supply.

Nutmeg has been traded by the Arab world since the 5th century CE, and the sailors carrying nutmeg cargoes discovered that chewing the kernels created a sense of euphoria and alleviated pain. In the 15th and 16th centuries, nutmeg oil was regarded as an important aid in medicine and it has been prescribed for a variety of physical ailments including rheumatism and indigestion. It is also claimed to produce an aphrodisiac effect and to combat nervous fatigue. In later times, nutmeg was sold in Europe as an abortifacient, and its street purveyors were known as 'nutmeg ladies'.

Above: In this 18th-century engraving, a merchant weighs
small quantities of nutmeg. Obtained from the fruits of
Myristica fragrans, it acts as a mild stimulant.

Myristica is by no means the only plant alleged to possess properties that heighten sexual excitement and ability. The bark of *Corynanthe yohimbe* has been described as the 'most potent aphrodisiac known' and, predictably, it has acquired a mythology. The tree is found growing to a height of some 15–18 metres (50–60 feet) in tropical forests of West Africa, Congo and Cameroon, where its bark has been traditionally served at wedding dances. Bantu tribesmen have reportedly used Yohimbe for prolonged orgies 'lasting for more than a week', during which the drumming, dancing and communal love-making went on continuously. The bark is ground to a powder and mixed with boiled water as if making a pot of tea. It can also be smoked. Recently, the pure chemical has been extracted in the form of a powder, yohimbine hydrochloride, and extract of Yohimbe is marketed around the world through health-food shops.

🌿 Cactus juice

Among the most potent of the naturally occurring drugs affecting the nervous system and altering the normal state of mind, the alkaloid mescaline is obtained from several species of cactus. The most familiar of these, and the most extensively investigated, is *Lophophora williamsii*, which grows in arid locations. Known commonly as Peyote, the cactus is indigenous to Central America, and its range extends as far north as Texas. It is found mainly in the Chihuahuan Desert, often growing in profusion in the semi-shade beneath other shrubs or larger succulents where it develops as a spineless cushion with a blue-green coloration.

As a psychedelic drug, Peyote was recorded in Mexico in pre-Hispanic times, but its use by man probably dates back to the first millennium BCE or earlier. In more recent centuries, the popularity of Peyote has spread north to various American plains Indian tribes, including Navajo, Comanche, Sioux and Kiowa, who have used it extensively in religious ceremonies. In their belief, the Peyote permits contact with the spirit world and allows the flow of understanding into the hidden depths of the mind.

The original extraction of mescaline as a pure substance was carried out in 1896 by an American chemist, Arthur Heffter, and it is believed to have been the first plant-based hallucinogen to be isolated in the laboratory. The use of mescaline is now illegal in North America, with the exception of the Native American Church where it has been an integral part of their religious tradition since the 1800s. Members are permitted to use it in their rituals.

🌿 *Its use by man probably dates back to the first millennium* BCE.

Other cactus species that have undergone limited research into their psychedelic properties include *Coryphantha macromeris*, commonly known as Donana, from northern Mexico, and *Trichocereus pachanoi* or San Pedro, native to the Andes range in Ecuador and Peru. Both are grown these days as ornamentals. Mescaline is not to be confused, incidentally, with a drink local to Mexico and known as 'mescal'. The latter does not contain mescaline and is made from the Maguey plant or Agave, a large succulent member of the *Amaryllis* genus from which sisal fibre is produced (see Chapter 7).

🌿 Opium

Of all naturally occurring and socially abused drugs obtained from plants, the narcotic alkaloids synthesised by the Opium Poppy (*Papaver somniferum*) are the most notorious. The true Opium Poppy originates in central and eastern Europe and Asia, but is hardly ever seen in western Europe or the British Isles. It is grown as a commercial crop mainly in Turkey and India. The plant is a member of a small family, the Papaveraceae, that includes Poppies and Fumitories. Poppy species (of which there are about 50 worldwide) are annuals and opportunists that favour growing in open, well-drained areas, and this is the main explanation of why they appear so frequently in cultivated fields. Most are valued not as a source of narcotics but as ornamentals because of their showy blooms. The Opium Poppy flowers throughout the summer months as a handsome erect herb growing to a height of 1.5 metres (5 feet). The leaves that clasp the unbranched stems are coarsely toothed and hairless with a rather waxy appearance, and the large flowers are white. The fruit capsules are large and rounded, and when ripe contain black seeds that are valued in baking. They are also the source of a commercially important drying oil.

The so-called Opium Poppy of western Europe, *Papaver somniferum* subsp. *hortense*, is a native of the Mediterranean region that has been extensively cultivated and occurs as an escape in Europe and the British Isles, generally growing in waste places, particularly in fens and adjacent to the sea. A distinct species, its flowers have lilac petals each with a purplish spot at the base. The capsule splits and the seeds emerge from pores beneath the 'crown'. It differs from the true Opium Poppy in that it does not synthesise the narcotic principles to the same extent.

The history of humankind's relationship with the Poppy can be traced back over many millennia and fossil evidence from sites in Switzerland indicates that Poppy seeds were used in baking by Neolithic man. The first records of use of the Opium

Poppy as a source of a mind-altering drug go back at least 4,000 years to the earliest texts from Sumer in the ancient Near East. Written on clay tablets, these writings refer to a 'plant of joy', *hul-gil*. The potential of the plant was certainly known to the Arab world from that time onwards, and there are some indications that it was also recognised by the ancient Egyptians.

In Classical Greek myth, the gods caused the Opium Poppy to spring up around the mother goddess Demeter as she searched vainly for her daughter Persephone, who had been abducted to the underworld by Hades. As she knelt to examine the flowers, she inhaled their heady aroma and was tempted to taste their seeds. Thus the gods calmed her anguish for her lost child and gave her rest. The Greeks were familiar with the narcotic potential of the plant, and the word 'morphine' derives from the Greek word for 'form', a reference to the ability of morphine to induce dreaming or 'form-

Above: Opium Poppy harvesting in central Asia.
The commercial crop originates chiefly from Turkey
and India.

shaping' in the mind. It is from the same etymological root that the name Morpheus is derived. Morpheus, the son of Hypnos, god of sleep, himself the son of the night, became the Greek god of dreams.

In the 3rd century BCE, the Greek scholar Theophrastus provided what is probably the earliest medicinal reference to the plant, describing it as *meconium*. The physician Hippocrates (460–357 BCE) prescribed the juice of the white poppy as an analgesic, but indicated that it should be mixed with Nettle seeds for best effect. This curious combination may be explained by a comment of the 17th-century herbalist Nicholas Culpeper. He wrote that the seed of Nettle, under the dominion of Mars, 'being drank, is a remedy against the stinging of venomous creatures, the biting of mad dogs, the poisonous qualities of hemlock, henbane, nightshade, mandrake, or such like herbs that stupify or dull the senses.' The European word 'Poppy' probably comes from the Saxon *popig*, which stems from the same root as *pap* and suggests that child-bearing woman may have mixed Poppy seeds with breast milk in order to lull their infants to sleep.

The use of opium spread through the Middle East to Turkey and it is thought that Arab traders exported opium, first to India and then to China in the 7th or 8th century CE, where it was employed principally as a medical drug. The first records of opium use in China, however, come from several hundred years earlier. The Chinese physician, Hua To (220–264 CE), administered opiates to his patients before surgery.

Sometime during the 17th century, the Chinese discovered that opium could be smoked. Dutch traders had introduced the practice of tobacco smoking in pipes to China from Java, and Chinese users began to mix opium and tobacco. From this moment, opium became recognised as a recreational drug and serious problems began to arise with addiction. Opium demand increased dramatically with Britain playing a key role in the international trade in opiates that led, ultimately, to two short opium wars with China.

The first European country to supply China in any quantity was Portugal, but the role was shortly to be taken over in the late 1700s when the British East India Company became the world's largest dealer in opium. The company exercised a virtual monopoly in the marketplace and was able therefore to fix prices and control supply, much as Britain had done when supplying the New World with tea. This resulted in massive revenue coming to Britain. France also became involved in the opium trade. The Chinese government placed a ban on the import of the drug, but the transactions on the British side, though morally indefensible, were carried out legally. The Opium

Poppy was grown and the opium sold legitimately in India, at that time the world's main growing region, before being smuggled into China. The response of the Chinese authorities was first to approach Queen Victoria for assistance but their request was ignored. In consequence, the Chinese emperor ordered the interception and destruction of some 20,000 barrels of opium before they reached China's borders. The British government, faced with losing large amounts of money, went on the offensive, attacking the city of Canton. The objective was to force the opening of ports such as Shanghai in order to sustain the trade in opiates which were being used to pay for costly British imports from China, including tea and silks. Hostilities continued until

Above: Chinese opium dens were supplied via the British East
India Company, which fixed prices and controlled supply.
Ultimately, the trade led to the Opium Wars of the 19th century.

1856 when treaties with China earned the expanding British Empire the territory of Hong Kong, the legalisation of opium imports, extensive trading rights in commodities other than opium and a compensation settlement of £60 million.

Among the more modern legends of the Opium Poppy there are hints in the books of Sir Arthur Conan Doyle that Sherlock Holmes was addicted to opium. It is certainly true that many members of Victorian society were dependent on the drug, and they generally took opium in the form of laudanum (opium dissolved in alcohol). Opium pills also became popular.

The alkaloids synthesised include the narcotics morphine and codeine, both of which are effective painkillers but also produce feelings of pleasure and euphoria. Continued intake of the opiates, however, can lead to dependency, after which users are faced with an extremely unpleasant withdrawal process. Morphine was isolated in the laboratory in 1805 by a German pharmacist who named it morphium. Subsequently, other alkaloids were extracted from the Opium Poppy. Codeine was isolated in 1832 and papaverine in 1848. Heroin or diamorphine, a water-soluble derivative of morphine with stronger action and fewer side-effects, was first manufactured in 1874 as 'a safe, non-addictive alternative to morphine'. It became apparent, however, that heroin induced massive dependency in certain individuals with appalling side-effects, and both heroin and the opiates were made illegal in Britain under the Dangerous Drugs Act of 1920. Similar legislation followed in North America.

Opium derivatives are still used legally by the medical profession, chiefly to alleviate suffering during terminal illness as part of what used to be known popularly as a 'Brompton Cocktail', first concocted by the Brompton Hospital in London. In terms of illegal use, however, it is reckoned that, currently, there are more than half a million heroin-dependent people in the United States alone, with growing numbers in Britain and Europe.

Today, the raw opium from which heroin is manufactured comes chiefly from southwest and southeast Asia, Mexico and South America. Southeast Asia accounts for about half the world's annual production of heroin, calculated at over 200 tonnes. The highlands of Laos, Burma and Thailand as well as parts of south China and northwest Vietnam are notorious sources of illegal production and have become known as the 'Golden Triangle'. Typically, the Poppy fields are owned by small farmers who grow 0.4–1.2 hectares (1–3 acres) of the plants each season, sowing before the end of October in order to take advantage of the long summer days in the southern hemisphere during November and December.

Opiates are derived from the dried 'milk' or latex of the Opium Poppy, secreted as a sap in the walls of the unripe or immature capsules. The harvesters make their collections by scoring the capsules about two weeks after the petals have fallen and then scraping off the latex. In its commercial form, opium is a brown soft and sticky mass that hardens and darkens with age.

Cocaine

The shrub *Erythroxylon coca*, indigenous to the South American highlands but also found in parts of Australia, India and Africa, is the source of another mind-altering chemical that has exerted a major social impact – cocaine. The alkaloid, found in its greatest concentration in the leaves, acts as a powerful stimulant on the central nervous system and also induces a sense of long-lasting euphoria. If taken in greater concentration, it also induces dependency in the user. *E. coca* leaf is exported mainly from Peru and Bolivia, but the plant is also grown commercially in Sri Lanka, Java and Taiwan.

The effects of cocaine have undoubtedly been known to South American Indians for many thousands of years, but the people of the Inca civilisation in Peru that reached its peak during the 15th century CE were the earliest recorded users of the drug. Traditionally the leaf has been chewed mixed with lime to release cocaine in the saliva. The active ingredients are absorbed through the mucous lining of the mouth. At one time it seems that coca leaf was gathered strictly for benefit of the Inca royalty but its popularity spread to all classes. They discovered that the juice of the coca leaf reduced feelings of hunger and increased physical stamina.

When the Conquistadors invaded South America they attempted to ban the use of coca among the *coqueros* or coca-chewers, arguing that the practice was hedonistic and immoral. Once deprived, however, the ability of the native Indians to work in the fields and the silver mines deteriorated so markedly that the Roman Catholic Church reversed the policy and began growing *E. coca* in plantations in order to keep the native workforce supplied. During the 16th century, Spanish colonists brought coca back to Europe and it rapidly achieved popularity as a recreational drug. Discussing the effects of chewing the leaf to reduce hunger, in 1814 an issue of the English periodical *Gentleman's Magazine* appeared with the suggestion, accompanied by 'a measure of levity', that further investigation might permit coca to replace other sources of food, 'for a month or more'.

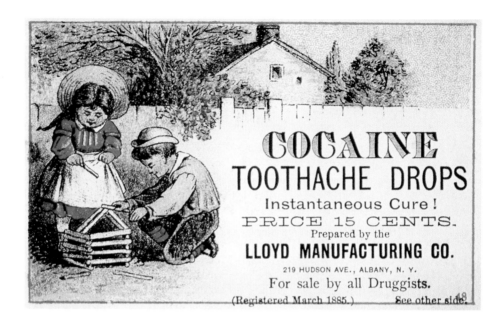

An individual coca leaf contains comparatively small amounts of cocaine, between 0.1 and 0.9 per cent, but if the leaves are processed the resulting coca paste contains 60–80 per cent cocaine. The pure active ingredient was isolated in the laboratory in 1860 by a German chemist, Albert Niemann, and became available as cocaine hydrochloride. Initially it was used in patent medicines that were claimed to cure a wide variety of conditions, and cocaine also served as a local anaesthetic. In Europe, the newly found experience of taking cocaine as a recreational drug earned the marketing tag 'elixir of life'. It was discovered that the potency was increased if the alkaloid was dissolved in alcohol, and during the 19th century the drug was added to several popular wines, particularly a brand labelled Vin Mariani. Sigmund Freud became one of its most fervent supporters, compiling papers extolling the worth of cocaine. At different times in its history the powder has been sniffed ('snorted'), injected and smoked, often resulting in dependency with serious long-term effects on health. In consequence, the sale of cocaine in many countries has been restricted since the early years of the 20th century. In Britain, before sales were restricted in 1916, cocaine even became widely available in such reputable London stores as

❧ Until about 1903, the drink [Coca Cola] still contained a quantity of cocaine and was promoted as a 'valuable brain tonic'.

Above: Cocaine was once a fashionable painkiller and tonic until sales were restricted in the early years of the 20th century. The drug gave its name to the beverage Coca-Cola, which originally included small quantities of the drug.

Harrods. Before prohibition was introduced in North America, undoubtedly the most successful form in which *E. coca* leaf was marketed was in the soft drink Coca Cola, first produced in 1886 by an Atlanta pharmacist, John Stith Pemberton. Until about 1903, the drink still contained a quantity of cocaine and was promoted as a 'valuable brain tonic'. Today, the Coca Cola company is said to import some 8 tonnes of the leaf from South America annually, although the drug is removed during processing and the leaf is incorporated only for flavouring.

Morning Glory

Among plants that have gained powerful spiritual significance for the indigenous tribes of Central America, Morning Glory and Salvia stand out. Both produce chemicals that have a mind-altering effect when eaten and have therefore been used by tribal shamans to enter a state of trance for communing with the spirit world, discovering the source of illness in a sick person and for recovering lost objects.

The genus *Ipomoea* in the family Convolvulaceae includes some 500 species growing as trees, shrubs, climbers and other herbaceous plants. On account of their large showy flowers they are commonly known as 'Morning Glory'. Two distinct species develop large root tubers. *I. batatas,* known commonly as Sweet Potato, is now grown widely as a food source in tropical and subtropical regions of the world, but was probably once indigenous only to South America. *I. purga*, or Jalap, is restricted to tropical Mexico, bears reddish flowers, and its turnip-like roots are a source of purgative.

The Common Morning Glory (*I. purpurea*) is a vine-like climber found extensively in southeastern areas of North America. It bears heart-shaped leaves and large, showy flowers with a variety of colours including white, pink and purple. Perennial Morning Glory (*I. indica*), indigenous to South America, has also become naturalised throughout much of the United States where it is popular as a garden plant, grown for its blooms. These species and others thrive as weeds, much as white-flowered *Convolvulus* grows wild in many parts of Europe and the British Isles.

I. violacea, known as Heavenly Blue Morning Glory, produces the drug lysergic acid (a naturally occurring form of LSD) in its seeds and the hallucinogenic properties made it sacred to the Zapotec Indians of Mexico, who continue to use it today in religious ritual and for medical purposes. The seeds are ground, wrapped in cloth and soaked in water before being eaten. Today the seeds sold commercially in the United States are treated with noxious chemicals to deter their use for illegal purposes.

Salvia

Salvia divinorum belongs to the Labiatae family of mints, and is a small perennial bush up to 1.5 metres (5 feet) in height with ovoid serrated leaves that possess a silvery appearance. It is the only member of the genus known to produce mind-altering chemicals in its tissues. Known variously as the Sacred Healer and Leaves of the Virgin or Yerba de Maria, *S. divinorum* may have originated in Asia, and some experts believe that it was brought to Central America before the Hispanic conquest. Today it is restricted to the Mexican province of Oaxaca. Favouring the banks of mountain streams, it grows at fairly high altitude (up to 1,800 metres/6,000 feet) in cloud forests in the Mazatec region of the eastern Sierra Madre range. *S. divinorum* survives only in highly inaccessible ravines and, because of its rarity and spiritual value, individual Indian tribes tend to keep locations for the plant a closely guarded secret. So rare is the plant that it was unknown to Western botanists before being described by J.B. Johnson in 1939, and there is some argument that it is actually a cultivar that cannot reproduce properly in the wild since its seed is not generally viable. It has proved almost impossible to grow in cultivation, though numerous attempts have been made in North America. One cultivar, the Wasson strain, has been grown successfully, having been collected in Oaxaca and brought to Hawaii in 1962 by a horticulturist, Gordon Wasson.

Alkaloids classed as terpenes and known as salvanorin are produced in the leaves of Salvia. These chemicals, similar in effect to those of Morning Glory, alter the normal state of mind and the plant is highly prized as a means of obtaining trances and gaining powers of divination. Mazatec shamans, who know the plant as Pipilzintzintli, chew the leaves.

Fungi

Green plants are not of course the only growths to produce mind-bending drugs in their tissues. Many fungi, of which the Fly Agaric (*Amanita muscaria*; see Chapter 1) is the most notorious, secrete hallucinogens. Others include *Psilocybe semilanceolata*, more popularly known as the Liberty Cap. This and several related species produce the chemicals psilocin and psilocybin. In terms of effect, the properties of these 'magic mushrooms' were probably familiar to most witches in pre-industrial times throughout much of Europe. Their descent into comparative obscurity doubtless began with the persecution of witches in the Middle Ages. Today they are avidly though illegally sought by users wishing to 'get high', and in Wales a clandestine *Psilocybe* festival is held each year at a discreet location.

A similar mushroom, *Psilocybe mexicana*, occurs in many parts of Central and South America, where it holds enormous social value and is frequently employed by elderly women dispensing their magic and cures in the villages.

The combination of lethal substances in some fungi and hallucinogenic properties in others, coupled with esoteric appearance and mysterious nature, has resulted in some bizarre rituals associated with eating the more palatable species. In some countries, Britain included, the consumption of wild mushrooms has long been regarded as dangerous and has only recently gained limited popularity. Elsewhere in Europe, history reveals much greater interest over the long term. Among the rituals that, at one time or another, have been associated with mushroom cookery, the Roman gourmet Apicus, who lived during the reign of the emperor Tiberius, produced a recipe book that included sections on the preparation of fungi. In Roman times any toadstool-like fungi growing on soil, as distinct from wood, were termed *boleti*. This sounds a little confusing because it conflicts with today's terminology wherein *boleti* are more specifically those mushroom-like fungi bearing tubes rather than gills under their caps.

Apicus described how special vessels called *boletaria* were reserved for cooking fungi, and woe betide any servant of a Roman household who used the *boletarium* for inferior purposes. When the craze for exotic and unusual foods began to wane in Roman high society, a contemporary writer and satirist, Martial, quipped, 'although boleti have given me so noble a name, I am now used, I am ashamed to say, for Brussel's Sprouts' (translated by Houghton, 1885).

Fly Agaric (*Amanita muscaria*) produces hallucinogenics that have made it popular amongst north European and Siberian shamans as a means of them entering into contact with the spirit world.

CHAPTER 14

The Holiest Trees
in the World

The Mesopotamian civilisations and the ancient Celts were by no means the only people to appreciate the sacredness of trees. Separate traditions have developed among cultures throughout history and all over the world. For some, a great tree marks the centre of the earth and forms a ladder or connecting stairway between the heavens, the earth and the underworld. It represents the focal point of their belief and, not surprisingly, each of these cultures, at some time or other, has made the claim that they are the possessors of such a unique growth.

The mythology associated with the Ceiba (pronounced *say-ba*) tree (*Ceiba pentandra*) is not untypical. In Central America, tribes descended from the ancient, pre-Hispanic Mayan civilisation considered that this was the tree at the centre of their world. Related to the Baobab trees of Africa, the Ceibas occur throughout the tropical regions of South and Central America and are representatives of a large genus belonging to the family Bombacaceae. Most grow to great size, and when fully mature *C. pentandra* towers above virtually all other vegetation in the rainforests at a height of more than 40 metres (130 feet).

Left: In the mythology of Central America, the towering
Ceiba tree (*Ceiba pentandra*) was regarded by the descendants
of the Maya as central to their very existence.

241

The overall shape of the Ceiba tree is striking, quite apart from its majestic dimensions, and the appearance explains some of the mythology that has come to surround it. The trunk rises perpendicularly and is very straight, covered with a light grey bark. At the top, it erupts into a distinctive flat-topped crown whose branches radiate out almost horizontally, bearing palmate leaves and large, bell-shaped flowers. At the base of the trunk, the massive rooting system forms aerial buttresses. It is not surprising that the Ceiba became the Sacred Tree of the Maya, the centre of their universe. Its topmost branches seem to reach to the skies and spread like a platform in the heavens, while its exposed roots plunge deep into the nether world. Other mystical factors come into play co-incidentally. The largest of the South American eagles, the Harpie Eagle, one of the symbols of the Mayan creator god, favours the crown of the tree as a roosting site, while bats, symbols of the Mayan underworld, occupy the spaces between the roots and the trunk. The tree provides for an enormous diversity of animals and plants. Aerial plants including Bromeliads thrive in the crown, as do many species of animals from insects to mammals. Vines hang from the canopy to the ground and form what appeared to the Mayan Indians to be a ladder between heaven and the terrestrial earth below. Today in Central America, loggers will often avoid felling a Ceiba and examples of these magnificent growths can often be seen standing alone casting their shade over fields where there was once forest.

In addition to its spiritual role, the Ceiba has a commercial value. Known in this capacity as the Kapok tree or the Silk Cotton tree, its fruit is a capsule that includes large amounts of fibre, a cotton-like substance that is extremely light and elastic. Although now largely superseded by synthetic materials, kapok has been used in many applications from life-jackets and stuffing of thermal clothing to car upholstery. Before the advent of modern alternatives, the main commercial supplies of kapok came from Java in Indonesia.

In Indian Hinduism, several of the more familiar earth-bound tree species have become sacred, of which probably the most important is the Holy Fig (*Ficus religiosa*). The genus *Ficus* includes about 800 species of tall trees, shrubs and vines of the family Moraceae. The common commercial Fig (*F. carica*), a low deciduous tree, is native to Asia Minor (Turkey), but cultivated worldwide for its edible fruit. *F. religiosa* and *F. sycamorus*, the Fig Tree of the Old Testament (see Chapter 5) are favourite shade trees in the regions of the world where they are cultivated, and the Holy Fig is known throughout much of India as the *asvattha*, translating literally as 'horse-stand' or 'the tree under which horses stand'. Another less frequent local term is *pippala* or *pipal*.

The *asvattha* is dedicated to all three of the great trio of Hindu creator gods – Brahma, Vishnu and Shiva – preserver, creator and destroyer. It is also sacred to Thakur Deo, the generic name of any village god or *gramadevata* in northern India. An ancient Hindu invocation declares that 'Brahma shaped at the root, Vishnu shaped in the middle and Shiva shaped at the top, we salute you king of the trees!' In the *Bhagavadgita*, the great central discourse of the Hindu epic the *Mahabharata*, the god Krishna also reveals to the mortal prince Arjuna that 'Among trees I am the *asvattha*, the sacred fig'.

Fertility connotations are attached to the Holy Fig not least because of its prolific fruiting. It also possesses remarkable regenerative ability, and in this it shares a reputation with other plants associated with fertility rites such as the Yew (see page ooo). New shoots grow up through the parent tree so that it continually renews itself. The name *asvattha* is significant in this respect because the horse is a powerful symbol of virility in Hindu belief. In popular Hindu tradition the Holy Fig is also an emblem of love, and there is a legend that any virgin who kicks the tree will cause it to blossom with red flowers.

Fertility connotations are attached to the Holy Fig not least because of its prolific fruiting.

Ficus bengalensis, the Banyan Tree, known in Indian tradition as the *vata* or *nyagrodha*, is also sacred to the Hindu gods Vishnu and Shiva. In Hindu mythology, these contrasting protagonists of creation and destruction are inseparable. The Banyan symbolises a cosmos in which nothing can be created unless something else is first destroyed.

Another tree, the Wood Apple (*Aegle marmelos*), known in Indian mythology as the *bilva* or *bel*, is, however, more closely associated with Shiva, the ascetic god of cosmic destruction. The fruit of this forest tree, the 'apple' or *sriphala*, is revered as evidence of Shiva's great potency. Its leaves traditionally form an integral part of the services in the main annual festival in honour of Shiva – the Shivaratri – that takes place in February and March. *Bilva* leaves and fruits are taken to the temple by Shiva devotees or are bought from vendors selling their wares outside. As a vivid illustration of cultural connections, the word *bel* is almost certainly derived from the same Indo-Aryan language root as the Celtic term for a sacred tree, *bile*.

The holy trees of Hinduism have, predictably, found their way into Buddhism, founded in northern India in the 6th century BCE. The *kalpavrksa* or 'wishing tree' is often to be found in art as a symbol of the Buddha, and a *kalpavrksa* in a jar may be held in the hand of a Buddha-designate or *bodhisattva* such as Gaganaganja or Ksitigarbha.

In Buddhism, the Fig (*F. religiosa*), is held sacred, since it was at the foot of one of these, the *bodhivrksa* or 'Tree of Enlightenment', that Gautama Buddha, the 'living Buddha', attained his perfect understanding of existence after gazing at the tree for seven days. The tree is also known as the *ashoka*, which means 'absence of sorrow', a name honouring the Indian king Ashoka's conversion from Hinduism to Buddhism in the 3rd century BCE.

The Tree of Enlightenment grew at Bodh-Gaya on the west bank of the Nairanjana, a tributary of the holy river Ganges, and the earliest records about it are to be found in a manuscript known as the *Kalingabodhi Jataka*. Although the original Fig has long since died, its association with the Buddha has given rise to an assortment of legends. Among the more bizarre is a suggestion that the Bodh-Gaya tree was cut down by monks from the Hindu Brahmanic tradition, apparently as retribution for his desertion from the Hindu faith, who burned the trunk as a fire sacrifice; but Asoka piled earth around the stump and poured milk on the roots. Miraculously a new *bodhi*-tree, or *bo*-tree, rose from the remains of the old and Ashoka was so awed by this miracle of nature that he converted to Buddhism and became a staunch champion of

Above: In a carving in the Gangarama Temple in Colombo,
Sri Lanka, The Buddha sits in contemplative repose beneath
the Bodh-Gaya tree, or Tree of Enlightenment.

the faith. He also arranged for the Bodhi replacement to be nurtured regularly with cows' milk. Such was Ashoka's dedication to the well-being of the tree that he visited it regularly until his wife, in a fit of jealousy, had the replacement demolished too. Fortunately the miracle repeated itself and the next tree grew to a height of 37 metres (120 feet), at which Ashoka had it surrounded by a protective stone wall some 3 metres (10 feet) high.

In the 6th or 7th century CE, the Bodhi Tree suffered again from vandalism when King Sesanka, a militant Bengali ruler of the Saivite sect, attacked and damaged it. On this occasion, 1,000 diligent cows came to the rescue with their milk on the orders of the Buddhist leader Purnavarma of Magadha. He authorised the planting of a new Bodhi tree sapling in about 620 CE.

Visitors to Bodh-Gaya are sometimes told that the present tree is the original but, according to the more realistic record, its most recent predecessor succumbed to old age and infirmity in 1876. An English archaeologist, Cunningham, who first visited the site in 1862, noted that the tree was in a highly decayed condition with only three viable branches. When he returned three years later it had clearly died, and its only remaining portion of trunk collapsed during a storm in 1875. Some of the legends about the indestructible nature of the Bodhi Tree are, however, probably true because of the regenerative ability of *F. religiosa*. When the old trunk decayed, young trees were already well established within the bole.

Bodhi trees exist elsewhere. Tradition has it that a cutting of the first *bodhivrksa* was carried to Sri Lanka, at sometime during the 3rd century BCE, by the daughter of Ashoka, a nun named Sanghamitta. She planted the sapling in the grounds of the Mahamegha monastery at Anuradhapura where a tradition is maintained that the second-generation tree still survives, not withstanding the fact that the plant would now be more than 2,000 years old. Fired by the idea that this is the oldest continually documented tree in the world, devotees worship it with offerings of milk, sandalwood and camphor essences.

More reliably documented history records that in 1931 Anagarika Dharmapala, the founder of the Mahabodhi Society, took a cutting from the Fig growing at Anuradhapura. He carried it to Sarnath, a few miles from the ancient city of Varanasi (Benares), and planted it at the place where Gautama Buddha is supposed to have delivered his first teachings. The Sarnath Fig is now held to be the third generation of *bodhivrksa* from the original. Yet another and separate tradition, however, contradicts this sentiment by alleging that the tree beneath which the Buddha delivered his sermon was not *Ficus religiosa* but its relative, *F. bengalensis*, the Banyan tree. More cuttings from the Bodh-Gaya tree have been rooted at various places of Buddhist pilgrimage around India. One of the best known of these, known as the Jetavana Bodhi Tree, stands in the grounds of the Jetavana monastery near the ancient ruins of Sravasti in Uttar Pradesh.

The Buddhist sacred tree has found its way extensively into Indian religious art and it can be used as a symbolic representation of the Buddha. In some sculptures the tree sprouts as a sapling from the row of curls or *usnisa* on his head, but in the earliest forms of Buddhist art it is depicted with an empty throne at its foot indicating the precise moment at which the Buddha received his enlightenment. The tree is also dedicated to a Buddhist 'goddess' named Mahapratisara, the 'Great Protectress', one of five spiritual beings that are the personification of amulets or *mantras* designed to guard people against evil influences. In addition, the *bodhivrksa* is a wider Buddhist symbol, particularly of the goddess Parna-Savari, whose name means 'woman dressed in leaves'.

Nature worship in India has not been particularly strong by comparison with Europe, but the Tamils, who live in the south and whose culture and language are accountably different from those in the north of the subcontinent, have actively worshipped trees for thousands of years. Tamils probably combined Hindu belief with that of their ancient tribal culture and their traditions include a bevy of local guardian spirits living in the forests and known as *vrkshakas*. In Indian art, these minor tree deities are depicted, according to sex, as dwarfish and pot-bellied dryads or as voluptuous, sexually charged nymphs.

At about the same time as the rise of Buddhism, another less familiar religion, called Jainism, developed in northern India. Its founder, Mahavira, found an appeal in the well-nigh global idea of a World Tree and so he invented his own. The World Tree of Jain belief is the 'Rose Apple Tree' (*Eugenia jambolana*), known in mythology as the *jambu*. In common with its *Yggdrasil* counterpart in Europe, the Rose Apple Tree was destined to become a symbol of Jain nationalism. Tradition maintains that a huge specimen of the tree grows on the summit of Mount Meru, the mythical Himalayan mountain of the gods lying in the centre of the continent of Jambudvipa (India) around which the seven other continents are arranged.

Mahavira considered that all life is sacred irrespective of its level of evolution, and although plants in general were placed in a lowly position he recognised a possibility that plants could become spiritually perfect through rebirth. He predicted that an unnamed tree and two separate branches, devastated by drought, heat and fire, would be reborn as sacred trees, and from there would advance to birth and subsequent enlightenment as human beings. Mahavira claimed that plants not only are born, grow and die, much as do higher forms of life, but also demonstrate a level of intelligence because they are capable of emotions, including fear and moral reactions. They also show a demand for food and sexual reproduction. Jain belief accepts that plants in general possess consciousness, with the same sentient powers as animals, and that they are aware of their surroundings.

On the question of morality, one Jain myth relates how a man of particularly greedy disposition, named Samaraditya, died and was reborn as a coconut tree that happened to grow above a horde of treasure. The tree exhibited the same characteristics of avarice as its human ancestor, by stretching its roots down to encircle the treasure. The Coconut tree and its fruits, on the other hand, have also been thought of as sacred in India, and parts of the plant are regularly offered to Hindu deities.

In Chinese and Japanese Buddhism, the Maidenhair Tree (*Ginkgo biloba*) is afforded similar sacred credentials to those of the Holy Fig. *G. biloba* is the only living representative of a large ancient Order of conifer-like trees that flourished mainly during the Jurassic period when the dinosaurs roamed between 200 and 135 million years ago. *Ginkgo* has been cultivated for many centuries, especially in the grounds of temples, but it only became known to Westerners in the 18th century when the first specimens were brought to Europe. A *Ginkgo* tree, planted in 1762, can still be seen at the Royal Botanic Gardens, Kew, England.

The Tree of Eternal Life

A tree that symbolises life immortal has gained universality in myth, and it also reveals a concurrence of ideas. Norse mythology places the Apple as a source of eternal life. Popular Christian tradition identifies the Apple with the Tree of Life named in Genesis, yet there is no hard evidence that the Scandinavian myth-makers borrowed from Christianity. According to the Eddaic poems, the goddess Idunn, consort of the poet god Bragi, guarded the golden apples of eternal youth for the Aesir gods of Asgard (the Scandinavian heavenly realm). When she was abducted by a renegade god, Loki, and handed over to the giants, the adversaries of the gods, in payment for the construction of the castle of Valhalla, the gods began to age. Their lamentable deterioration continued until Idunn, still fortunately in possession of both her fruit and her virtue, was rescued.

Less certainty is attached to whether the golden apples belonging to the Hesperides, who lived at the extreme western edge of the world and who are described variously as the daughters of Hesperus or the goddess of the night, fall into the same category. In Greek myth, the four Hesperides sisters were personified as the clouds made golden by the setting sun. In classical Greek, however, the word for 'apple' and 'flock of sheep' is the same and the Hesperides may actually have been celestial shepherdesses looking after a flock of golden sheep rather than guardians of apples.

Probably any fruit tree is a potential candidate for the role of Tree of Life. Far from Europe and western Asia, it is arguable that the theme also surfaces in Hindu religion. The *kinsuka* or *palasa*, the fruit-bearing species *Batea frondosa*, is sacred to the god Soma, who is the personification of the Hindu sacrificial drink. As a Tree of Life, *B. frondosa* is also sacred to the Khmer of Cambodia, who know it as the *talok*.

In China, the Mulberry (*Morus alba*) also emerges as a sacred tree associated with life-giving powers. A story set in the Hsia dynasty some 2,000 years BCE tells of a woman who disobeyed celestial command and drowned in a great flood. When the waters subsided, it was discovered that she had turned into a Mulberry tree from whose trunk were coming the cries of a baby. A local woman reached into the bole of the tree and discovered a newborn infant. The child grew to be a great statesman of China, named I Yin, who was instrumental in throwing out the corrupt Hsia rulers and founding the Shang dynasty (which eventually turned out to be no less corrupt). Here is a mishmash of themes, including a fruit tree as the progenitor of life and an inundation in which the original corrupt inhabitants of the earth are replaced by a new 'cleansed' society, closely matching those in the Biblical Genesis account of the Paradise garden and the Flood.

Able to grow in very poor soils *M. alba* is indigenous to China, Japan and other parts of southeast Asia, though a related species, *M. nigra*, is to be found in western Asia and parts of the Middle East, and a third, *M. rubra*, grows in North America. On a more utilitarian level the Mulberry species are grown for their soft edible fruit, but during the 18th and 19th centuries the Mulberry became popular in Europe where it was widely cultivated as a source of food for silkworms.

Almost the same elements of death and renewal described in the Chinese myth are to be found in the Scandinavian account of the *Yggdrasil* World Tree. It stands in one respect as the herald of Ragnarok, the day of doom when first fire, then water, are destined to cleanse the earth, burning and washing away the sins of the old order of gods. With the *Yggdrasil* another common theme associated with the Tree of Life emerges —

the link with snakes, which appear to have earned a complex reputation for wisdom, immortality and evil wherever in the world they slither. In common with the Biblical tree described in the Book of Genesis, the *Yggdrasil* has a resident serpent in the form of Nidhogg. As Snorri Sturluson reveals, Nidhogg is an adversary that gnaws away destructively at the roots of *Yggdrasil*:

> Three of the tree's roots support it and extend very, very far. One is among the Aesir (gods), the second among the frost giants (adversaries of the gods), where the Ginnungagap once was. The third extends over Niflheim (the underworld) and under that root is Hvergelmir (a spring or well), and Nidhogg gnaws the bottom of the root.
>
> (*Prose Edda*, translated by Anthony Faulkes)

The Eddaic poem, the *Lay of Grimnir*, takes up the same theme of the predatory serpent homing in on the weakness of life already withering and beyond repair:

> The Ash Yggdrasil doth ill abide,
> More than to men is known:
> The hart browsing above, its bole rotting
> And Nidhogg gnawing beneath.
>
> (*Poetic Edda*, translated by Lee Hollander)

Many years before the rise of the Scandinavian cultures, and hundreds of miles to the south in the Mediterranean region, the Classical artists of Greece and Rome may have fallen short of adopting a Tree of Life *per se*, but they translated the imagery into the Bacchic vine and the wand or *caduceus* of Mercury. The *caduceus* also stood both for personal inviolability and for the resolving of conflict or dispute. Not surprisingly, since ill-health was perceived as an inner conflict of the body, the *caduceus* became the symbol of the Greek physician god Aesculapius. The Greeks and Romans were no less reluctant to separate the symbol of life from its snakes, and Aesculapius' 'wand of life' was sometimes depicted in the form of a tree trunk encircled by a single serpent.

If one traces the origins of much of Greek tradition, one arrives at the Minoan civilisation that bridged the time gap between the Mesopotamians, their contemporaries in western Asia and the Bronze Age Mycenean culture in Europe. The Minoans appear to have been dedicated to the worship of deities closely associated with sacred trees, as were the Myceneans.

At Knossos, on the Mediterranean island of Crete, one of the great 19th-century British archaeologists, Sir Arthur Evans, uncovered evidence of a Tree and Pillar Cult that had thrived during the heyday of the Minoan capital during the 2nd millennium BCE. He described how he found painted scenes of processions carrying images of a fertility goddess. This seems to relate closely to a Hittite rite involving a deity that was taken down to a sacred wood and washed (see page 000). Some Hittite traditions were almost certainly exported to Europe in antiquity. The scenes found by Evans showed worshippers making their way to an enclosure where the image was placed on a throne beneath a sacred tree. Quantities of large gold rings were also unearthed during the excavations at Knossos, and many of these depict a large imposing tree, generally a Fig or Olive, frequently surrounded by a wall indicating that it grew in a sacred enclosure. The tree is often depicted in close proximity to an altar or a building thought to be a temple or sanctuary. A ring discovered at Naxos shows a Palm Tree, beside which is a table carrying vessels for libation rites and a man carrying a spear. Sometimes the scenes depicts human figures dancing before a tree, and the inference is that the tree symbolised the embodiment of a deity, usually a goddess, much as it did in Mesopotamia.

The Greeks and Romans could claim to have reached the first real botanical understanding of plants through the studies of such writers as Dioscorides and Pliny, but their new-found scientific awareness did little to stem the more sentient interest in the green world. Trees were sacred in classical Greece, and the concept of the sacred grove or *temenos* probably arose there independently from that of Mesopotamia. The *temenos* was either an enclosure around a single tree or was also associated with a tract of woodland where festivals took place.

When the early European sanctuaries evolved into the Classical Greek *temenos*, they included both a tree and a stone pillar, but the tree was the more important feature and different tree species became sacred to individual deities. In the Acropolis of Athens, the city of the goddess Athene, an Olive has traditionally represented the vitality of the city. A legend exists that when in 480 BCE the Persians burned down the temple to the minor goddess Pandrosos, in whose vicinity the tree stood, it broke into fresh leaf immediately. It is also clear that the Greek *temenos* witnessed human and animal sacrifice, and these rituals probably stemmed from myths telling of the goddess or her priestesses being hung from sacred trees. Animal skins hung in trees were features of age-old hunting customs.

Almost invariably in the Classical period, trees or groves marked the presence of goddesses, and coins have occasionally been discovered showing goddesses sitting in the branches of personal trees. The Olive was sacred to Athena, and in Athens the great statue of the goddess was carved from olive wood. At Olympia, twigs were broken from a sacred Olive, with which to wreathe the heads of the victors of the Olympic Games. The Olive was also sacred to an emanation of Zeus known as Zeus Morios.

The Oak was revered by the classical civilisations of Greece and Rome almost to the same degree as by the Celts. One of the most famous sacred Oaks dedicated to Zeus grew in his sanctuary at the ancient site of Dodona near Epirus in the mountains of northern Greece. The Bay Laurel was sacred to Apollo, and one of the most famous of these special trees stood at the Apollo sanctuary in Didyma. The White Poplar was dedicated to Heracles. On the island of Delos, a Palm was dedicated to the goddess Leto, and tradition has it that she leant against either a Palm or an Olive, or that she grasped the trunks of two Bay Laurels, while giving birth to Artemis and Apollo. This points strongly to a belief in Greece that certain trees, associated with fertility goddesses, would aid delivery. Such was the dedication to some sacred trees that a Willow dedicated to the goddess Hera, the wife of Zeus, growing in her sanctuary on the island of Samos, was actually incorporated into the great altar.

Trees were also seen to be oracles – sources of divine utterance – particularly when their leaves rustled. Socrates wrote of a tradition that an Oak first gave prophetic utterance in the Temple of Zeus at Dodona, and Homer mentioned this tree in more than one of his epic works. In the *Odyssey*, the eponymous hero Odysseus visited Dodona 'to hear from the tall and leafy Oak what Zeus himself counselled' and in the *Iliad* the hero Achilles prayed to its oracle for victory over the Trojan army:

> Zeus of Dodona, god of Pelasgians,
> O god whose home lies far! Ruler of wintry harsh Dodona!
> Your interpreters, the Selli, live with feet like roots, unwashed,
> And sleep on the hard ground.
> My lord, you heard me praying before this, and honoured me
> By punishing the Achaean army.
> Now again accomplish what I most desire.
>
> (*Iliad* xvi. 215–88)

The Selli or Selloi of the passage were originally priestesses believed to have been brought from Egypt to Minoan or Mycenean Crete several hundred years before the Trojan Wars. In later times, they were joined by priests and their cult was exported to Greece where the priestesses were eventually phased out in favour of their male counterparts. The job of the Selli was to interpret the oracular utterances. There was some difference of opinion among Classical writers about the nature of the Dodona tree because Herodotus identified it as a Beech, but the majority opinion favoured Oak.

Tree worship was still keenly followed in imperial Rome. The Greek writer Plutarch, who was born in about 46 CE, wrote a series of biographies on famous Greek and Latin personalities, and these included a profile of Romulus, the mythical founder of the city of Rome. Plutarch describes how the royal twins Romulus and Remus were cast into the river Tiber on the orders of a jealous king of Alba. In a small vessel, they floated downstream and came to rest at the site of Rome where they would be reared by a she-wolf. At this spot on the riverbank there germinated a Fig tree sapling (*Ficus*) and, based on this story, the Fig became sacred to Romans. One especially venerated tree grew in the Forum and this plant, or its descendants, apparently survived almost to the sacking of Rome in 410 CE by the Visigoths.

Aside from trees in Greece and Rome, some notable flowers were identified with deities. The Narcissus was dedicated to Persephone, the ill-fated daughter of Demeter, who was destined to become the Queen of Hades. The Lily belonged to Aphrodite and the Rose to Dionysos.

The linking of trees with immortality and longevity has also been a reason to make them barometers for the well-being of people, and this theme has also persisted into modern times. The connection between the life of a person and the life of a tree can be discovered as early as the Classical Greek era. In Homeric mythology, the Dryads are described as female spirits of the woods who live in trees, particularly Oak trees from whence their name derives, since the Greek word for the Oak is *drys*. In Classical art, they are depicted dancing around the Oaks wearing oak-leaf crowns, and sometimes carrying a weapon such as an axe with which to guard their homes against attack. Some, the Hamadryads, are so closely united with trees that the one is an integral part of the other. The fate of the tree nymph was, therefore, dependent on the survival and health of the tree in which she lived.

In European countries, including England, France, Italy, Germany and Russia, the link between human life and trees has encouraged the planting of a tree to mark the birth of a child. The tree then becomes something of an *alter ego* and, as it grows with the child, it receives special care. If the birth-tree is felled during a person's lifetime it has been considered that the death of its human 'partner' will soon follow. This link has persisted into modern times and, today, the planting of birth-trees is being

revitalised as part of the trend away from more orthodox rites associated with birth, such as baptism, and towards alternative ceremonies. The bonding of a person from birth to death with a personal tree is not entirely surprising because trees are not only the most enduring of all living things but many of them share a similar life span to our own.

Similar tribal traditions can be found around the world. In various parts of Polynesia, including the Maori homeland in New Zealand, birth rituals have involved the burying of part of the umbilical cord of a newborn infant beneath a birth-tree sapling. If the tree withers or dies, so the life of the person will be affected more or less severely. Birth-trees have also assumed subjective and anthropomorphic character-istics. Tree species associated with boys have tended to be the resistant, rugged ones like Oak and, particularly, Apple, while the more feminine trees have included Willow and Birch. Hazel is a tree that has long been associated with wisdom. On the other hand, certain trees that are taboo to celebrate an infant's birth include Elder, associated with the betrayal of Jesus Christ, and Yew, which is a tree of death. Rowan, Blackthorn

Above: The Weeping Willow (*Salix babylonica*) has been linked
with sorrow for thousands of years and has biblical connotations
associated with the Israelites languishing in Babylon.

and Ash have all been strongly linked with aspects of less desirable witchcraft and are to be avoided.

Occasionally the well-being of a tree is not merely linked with that of an individual but also of a family dynasty. A celebrated Oak tree, known as the Edgewell Tree, that grows near Edinburgh in Scotland, has been regarded as a 'barometer' of the good health of the Earls of Dalhousie in a tradition which, although surviving into modern times, is thought to be of very ancient clan origin. A morbid legend recalls that in July 1874, when a massive bough fell from the Oak on a calm day, it signalled the fate of the 11th Earl, Fox Maule, who died at the precise moment the bough crashed to the ground.

Our ancient bonds with trees live on in various ways, though not always in the most likely surroundings. In large parts of communist China, people from all walks of life are turning towards ancient tree ceremonies in order to benefit from their innate strength. The sight of early morning callisthenics of the Mao era is being replaced by a spiritual 'wake up' whereby people are following the popular fashion of holding, rubbing and embracing trees in order to gain from their mystical aura.

Some trees have gained mystical reputations for reasons that, at first glance, appear to fall under the heading of magic, yet the claims of their powers may possess elements of truth in ways that we do not fully comprehend. The divining or dowsing rod provides an example. Native Indians in more arid regions of North America have called for centuries on this technique, employing a flexible forked branch of the Witch Hazel (*Hamamelis virginiana*) that reacts when water or precious minerals are nearby. The two prongs of the Y-shaped wand are gripped lightly in the hands and twist as the dowser nears water. In Europe, wands or twigs of the common Hazel (*Corylus avellana*) have been used in the same manner.

Corylus grows throughout temperate Europe and Asia in woods, hedgerows and thickets as a small tree or tall deciduous shrub bearing ovate toothed leaves that are heralded in early spring by the distinctive yellowish male catkins. The fruit is a nut or 'cob' clothed in a green, jagged-edged husk or *cupule*. In distant times, Hazel was revered by the Celts as a highly magical plant, though more in association with fertility rites and with the fire festivals at midsummer. Cattle were once driven through the bonfires and their backs singed by smouldering hazel rods, then employed for herding until the following season. In Ireland, the tree was known as the Coll, and is one of the holy or Bile trees for which the unauthorised felling was once a capital offence. In the Irish *Dinnshenchas* one can discover a description of the Nine Hazels of Poetry. These

Hazel (catkins shown above) gained strong magical connotations
for the Celts. It is one of the holy trees of Ireland, and is also used
as the source of dowsing or divining rods.

overhang a sacred pool known as Connla's Well near Tipperary, and in folklore they produce flowers and fruit simultaneously. A quaint tale relates that the salmon frequenting the pool eat the Hazel nuts and that the spots on their backs are regulated by the number of nuts they swallow. In Irish legend, the salmon has been regarded as a wise fish and Hazel nuts have been among the sources of its great knowledge. Hazel has also been one of the trees said to provide protection from lightning strikes if twigs are hung up in the house. The term 'cobnuts' to describe Hazel fruits is a recent one. During the 19th century, children used to play a game, the forerunner of marbles, called 'cobs'.

Where the reputation of Hazel for identifying underground sources of precious commodities came from is unclear, and the mechanism by which dowsing works is equally uncertain. Dowsing rods are known to have been in use from at least the 16th century, but the lore attached to them probably stems from the Biblical traditions of the Hebrews. According to the Book of Exodus, before leaving Egypt for the Promised Land God invested the wooden staff belonging to Moses with miraculous powers. While the tribes were journeying through the Wilderness of Sin and were unable to find drinking water, Moses was instructed by God to use his rod and strike a particular rock:

> Behold I will stand before thee there upon the rock in Horeb: and thou shalt smite the rock, and there shall come water out of it, that the people may drink.
>
> (*Exodus* 17. 6)

There is, incidentally, a separate Biblical tradition concerning a magical rod that belonged to Moses' brother Aaron. The Book of Numbers relates the occasion on which Moses handed out 12 rods, one to each leader of the 12 tribes. These were disciplinary sceptres, issued at a time of rebellion against Mosaic law:

> And Moses laid up the rods before the Lord in the tabernacle of witness. And it came to pass that on the morrow Moses went into the tabernacle of witness; and behold the rod of Aaron for the house of Levi was budded and brought forth buds, and bloomed blossoms and yielded almonds.
>
> (*Numbers* 17. 7, 8)

The apparent miracle actually results from a horticultural technique known as truncheoning (see also Chapter 6). If the stem of a fresh sapling is cut and planted in the ground it can, under the right conditions, regenerate fairly rapidly, first putting down roots and then shooting buds.

In the 16th and 17th centuries, divination was introduced to England from Germany, where it was employed largely by miners and treasure hunters, though it was also called on to find hidden wells and springs. The Moses Rod was also employed in a curative capacity. In 1523, a wise person named John Thornton from Sapcote in Leicestershire claimed to have been curing animals with his staff for 30 years, and a number of medieval formulae for Moses Rods still exist. This period of history was marked by the height of religious fervour against witchcraft, and the skills of the dowser could be a hazardous asset to advertise. Divining came perilously close to sorcery but, in reality, was always part of a different tradition from that of witches and sorcerers. It was allied more with the preventative magic and astrology of the 'Cunning Person' who gained a popular following from use of unorthodox methods in an otherwise rather traditional society. In the hands of one of the great astrologers of 17th-century England, William Lilly, the divining rod was said to be an impressive tool, and the services of the country dowser were much sought after in an era before the installation of services to provide piped water. Today, metal detectors have largely overtaken the use of the rods in treasure hunting, but rods are still favoured by many water diviners to estimate the depth and flow of underground streams, often with considerable success. Divination has also become a recognised part of modern witchcraft. Hazel rods have been replaced by metal because of the difficulty in finding forked stems with a proper balance.

Lore has arisen about when and how the Hazel wands should be cut. The traditional time throughout much of Europe is on the Eve of St John's Day, 23 June, although variations can be found. In the Austrian Tyrol, for example, the wands may only be cut on Good Friday if they are to be effective. Modern witchcraft requires that they should be cut with a proper ritual at the correct time of the waxing moon and the right conjunction of plants, particularly Mercury, under whose dominion Hazel grows.

A 17th-century French or Dutch dowser uses a forked stick
to search for anything from a watercourse to lost valuables.

CHAPTER 15

Gardens and the
Green Mantle Today

L ooking back over the last 300 years, attitudes towards the plant kingdom began to change appreciably during the 18th century, and they were aided by scientific advances in botany. In summary, most attempts at cataloguing plants had been based on their value to mankind rather than scientific characteristics. As we have discovered, the 'position' of any given herb in the order of nature was to a large extent predetermined by two totally irrelevant factors. The first was an astrological connotation that each and every plant was governed by the influence of some heavenly body. The second was the indication of a plant's useful properties relationship through examining its shape, colour and appearance. The Lesser Celandine was seen to possess roots like haemorrhoids, so it was identified as 'Pilewort', but the fact that it might be related to another plant such as the Buttercup (both are members of the Ranunculaceae family) either never entered people's heads or was deemed an irrelevance.

Outmoded approaches to the plant kingdom, having persisted more or less since Saxon times, changed under the influence of Linnaeus (1707–1778) when he established scientific principles for naming plants and animals. His studies of botany led

Left: The great gardens, such as Sheffield Park in Sussex, with native and introduced species, represent our sentient interest in plants and the green mantle.

him to draw up a system of classifying plants, based not on the quaint morphological characteristics that had attracted medieval herbalists but on evaluation of flower parts. He observed that plants could be grouped according to the type, number and arrangement of petals, sepals and stamens and, especially, the construction of the ovary in which the seeds developed. After the *Genera plantarum* appeared in 1737, followed by *Species plantarum* in 1753, Linnaeus' classification had given each type of plant a clear and internationally recognised identity. It was in recognition of Linnaeus' great contribution to the science of natural history with his Binomial System, still relied on today, that the Linnaean Society of London was founded in 1788.

The work of Linnaeus and others triggered a passionate interest in finding and collecting plants around the world. A whole rash of dedicated plant hunters sprang up, pioneered most notably by the 18th-century English eccentric Sir Joseph Banks (1743–1820), who has become regarded as the father of modern plant collectors. All of these individuals were of sufficient private means to indulge in their fascination with botany. Banks began by securing the position of naturalist on an expedition to

Above: The famous Victorian plant hunter Sir Joseph Hooker receiving plant specimens. Such entrepreneurs were largely responsible for the enormous increase in the number of exotic species brought into cultivation in Europe.

Newfoundland and Labrador in 1766, and his collection of dried herbarium material from that seven-month trip is still held by the Museum of Natural History in London. In 1768, he joined Cook's famous expedition to the South Seas aboard the *Endeavour*, and during the three years of the voyage he assembled a vast collection of plant material. So prolific were some of his findings that he named the area of the New South Wales coast where the party first stepped ashore on the continent of Australia 'Botany Bay'. When the *Endeavour* sailed back into English waters in July 1771, Banks had amassed 1,300 new species of plant and identified 100 new genera, although sadly none of the material with which he returned was viable.

Banks' exploits may not have resulted immediately in the planting of new and exotic flora in English gardens. They had, however, attracted royal interest, and he was invited to visit one of George III's residences at a village a few miles to the west of London, named Kew. Eventually he persuaded the king that the newly laid out gardens at Kew, designed by Capability Brown, were an ideal site in which to grow and study all the flora of the British colonies. The Kew estate was already no stranger to rare and exotic plants since an earlier owner, Sir Henry Capel, had started a botanical collection in the previous century. Thus the Royal Botanic Garden of Kew was commissioned under royal seal of approval.

Although the botanists of the 18th century awakened a scientific interest in plants, they also re-invigorated the more sentient and romantic view of nature that had been regulated largely by the European classical landscape painters of the 17th century, such as Nicholas Poussin and Meindert Hobbema. These artists had conveyed an idyllic, often Arcadian view of trees, fields and water. Suddenly the European public was confronted by an array of plant exotica 'in the flesh' that a hundred years earlier would have been either beyond experience or the subject of weird and wonderful folk tales and drawings brought back by mariners and explorers. The general fascination that resulted encouraged the art of accurate botanical engraving and drawing. Yet by the 19th century this was also taking a distinctly romantic turn. Exotic flora was rendered in perfect, if somewhat glamorised, detail by wood engravers and printers such as Benjamin Fawcett, whose volumes *Beautiful Leaved Plants* (1861) and *New and Beautiful Leaved Plants* (1870) were the much sought-after triumphs of freshly developed technology in colour reproduction. Authors of children's books such as *The Story without an End* (1868) by Sarah Austin were able to romanticise the magical and mysterious nature of plants through the skills of engravers and printers like C.G. Leighton. *In Fairyland* (1870) by Richard Doyle paid similar tribute to our more imaginative ideas about

🌿 *The biblical Book of Genesis has it that God first created*

a paradise on earth, and dwelling place for Adam and Eve,

in the shape of a garden and, down the centuries, the myth of

Eden has captivated poets and artists alike.

'Spring' by the French painter Nicholas Poussin (1593–1665)
captures the Arcadian romanticism of the age.

plants when he had the engraver Edmund Evans create delicate illustrations from woodcuts that depicted elves and fairies playing among flowers.

We became captivated by the notion of the garden as a secret place full of wonders, and many well-to-do estates incorporated hidden gardens, surrounded by walls or high hedges, into their layout. Nowhere was this romanticism captured more succinctly than in the Victorian classic novel *The Secret Garden* by Frances Hodgson Burnett (1849–1924) that appeared in 1909 and has been virtually in print since first publication.

Gardens and gardening represent one of the truly modern illustrations of our sentient interest in the green mantle. The passion for gardening varies from country to country, but in England it takes on almost religious dimensions. The garden-centre and nursery industry is a substantial one, and we spend sizeable sums of money on maintaining our properties as personal paradise gardens, whether these include rolling acres of country estate or city window boxes. Frequently one reads of planning laws being flouted as this or that person converts farmland into a landscaped garden and runs into trouble for doing so.

The mystique of gardening may seem like a present-day phenomenon but it can be traced back into ancient history. To look back on the evolution of recreational gardens is difficult because they are, by nature, fragile and ephemeral, but the history of the garden created strictly to please the eye and nurture the soul goes back thousands of years. The biblical Book of Genesis has it that God first created a paradise on earth, and dwelling place for Adam and Eve, in the shape of a garden and, down the centuries, the myth of Eden has captivated poets and artists alike. The Hebrew word *eden* means 'delight', although it is arguably derived from an older Akkadian noun *edinu* or 'wilderness'. As to where the Garden of Eden lay, all attempts at identifying its location remain largely hypothetical. The Genesis writer identifies only that it is to be found 'somewhere in the East' which, in the Palestinian view, would make it somewhere in Mesopotamia (modern Iraq). The text also describes four rivers flowing from the garden, yet only the Tigris and Euphrates can be positively identified. Trees, including the Tree of Life (the forbidden source of immortality), the Tree of Knowledge, Olives and other fruit trees feature strongly in Eden, and we are told that God created the garden for the benefit of mankind. Adam was instructed to 'dress it and to keep it' (Genesis 2. 15), and it is from these terse commands that much of our sentient view of gardening stems.

Gardening was practised extensively, however, in parts of the ancient world that cannot have come under the immediate influence of Judaic culture and tradition.

Gardens formed important features of the royal palaces of Babylonia and Egypt and the properties of wealthy Egyptian families where flowers, vegetables, spices and fruit trees were cultivated. There is also contemporary evidence from the Old Testament that private gardens were used as burial plots:

> And Manasseh slept with his fathers, and was buried in the garden of his own house, in the garden of Uzza. (*II Kings* 21. 18)

In the euphemistic Biblical language, the garden became a symbol of pleasure and prosperity:

> For the Lord shall comfort Zion; he will comfort all her waste places; and he will make her wilderness like Eden, and her desert like the garden of the Lord; joy and gladness shall be found therein, thanksgiving and the voice of melody. (*Isaiah* 51. 3)

A later chapter of Isaiah goes further with analogy and likens the redeemed soul to a fertile garden. The association of the garden with water provides for two elements of spiritual purification and echoes the sentiments found in Genesis:

> And the Lord shall guide thee continually, and satisfy thy soul in drought, and make fat thy bones: and thou shalt be like a watered garden, and like a spring of water whose waters fail not. (*Isaiah* 58. 11)

The legendary Hanging Gardens of Babylon may have achieved comparable fame to that of Eden, yet there is some argument that they never existed except in the imaginations of Greek-speaking poets and historians. According to Diodorus Siculus (90–21 BCE), in his *Bibliotheca Historica*, King Nebuchadnezzar II (604–562 BCE), who reigned in the height of Neo-Babylonian prosperity, is credited with the building of the Hanging Gardens. Diodorus Siculus alleges that the main objective was to satisfy the yearning of Nebuchadnezzar's wife for the mountainous surroundings of Media in which she spent her childhood. Strabo and Philo of Byzantium, who first proposed the Seven Wonders of the Ancient World, also wrote about the Gardens in glowing detail, yet never actually visited Babylon:

> The Hanging Garden has plants cultivated above ground level, and the roots of the trees are embedded in an upper terrace rather than in the earth. The whole mass is supported on stone columns. (Philo of Byzantium)

Curiously, although Babylonian writers who were contemporaries of Nebuchadnezzar II compiled detailed descriptions of the palace and city, there is no contemporary

record on the subject of royal gardens. Old Testament mention is also practically non-existent, other than a passing oblique comment in the Book of Esther, whose eponymous heroine lived among the Jews, remaining in exile during the reign of the Persian king Ahasuerus, better known as Xerxes I (485–465 BCE):

> The king (Ahasuerus) made a feast unto all the people that were present in Shusan the palace, both unto great and small, seven days, in the court of the garden of the king's palace.
>
> (*Esther* 1. 5)

We do, however, have some modern archaeological evidence. Excavations on the east bank of the Euphrates about 50 kilometres (30 miles) south of Baghdad and near the southern palace of ancient Babylon have revealed a vaulted building with thick walls and an irrigation system dated to about 600 BCE. It has been argued that this is too far from the River Euphrates, which, according to Diodorus Siculus, flowed by the gardens and supplied it with water. On the other hand, it is known that the courses of the Tigris and Euphrates have altered substantially over the centuries. Other excavations have uncovered massive walls along the riverbank that may have been terraced, a feature also suggested in the description given by Diodorus Siculus:

Above: A romanticized idea of the Hanging Gardens of
Babylon, by the 18th century German artist Friedrich Bertuch.
Whether the gardens ever really existed remains unproven.

> The approach to the garden sloped like a hillside and the several parts of the structure rose one from another, tier upon tier . . . on all this the earth had been piled. The garden was clothed densely with trees of all kinds giving pleasure to the beholder in their great size and charm. Water was lifted from the river in great quantity by machines that were hidden from the observer.
> (Diodorus Siculus)

Gardens have also been a time-honoured source of fascination in the Orient. Nowhere have gardening and cultural aesthetics been blended with greater effect than in Japan, where landscape designers have been heavily influenced by geomancy, Shinto and Buddhist symbolism. The Zen garden undoubtedly represents the extreme development of rustic, but sometimes almost abstract, simplicity in a man-made setting of flowers, trees, water, rocks and gravel. The art was perfected by the Tea Masters of the 16th century who pursued the ideal of *wabi* or subdued taste. In a Zen garden symmetry, blended with the skilful use of contrasts, lines and space, creates perfect tranquillity and harmony. The maxim of 'less is more' can be seen revealed in designs where a single stone, strategically placed, may encompass the idea of an entire mountain.

For most of recent European history, gardens were the indulgences of the rich, and we can gain some idea of their make-up from original plans, drawing and paintings in the possession of wealthy landowners. Landscape gardening in England reached its heyday in the 18th century under the influence of such grand designers as Capability Brown (1716–1783). Surprisingly, hitherto, we were still designing and planting gardens and parks based on formulae that had not changed a great deal since the classical empires of Greece and Rome. The Classical styles frequently bowed to geometric formality. Brown, however, developed the ideas of William Kent (1685–1748), the real founder of the landscape gardening style. He promoted a distinctly English fashion that departed from the formal designs still favoured in continental Europe and typified by the Tuileries Gardens in Paris. Brown's objective was to create gardens with a more casual appearance, offering a stylised imitation of nature. Among his greatest triumphs were the gardens of Blenheim Palace, created in 1765.

In Europe, in the 19th century, gardens became imbued with a special kind of mystique that arose from Capability Brown's innovations, and these new botanical paradises had a sentient purpose that has little in common with herb gardens cultivated for practical reasons by yesterday's country wife. A sentimental Victorian rhyme, sometimes seen inscribed on garden plaques, sums up the attitudes that had developed:

> The kiss of the sun for pardon, the song of the birds for mirth;
> One is nearer God's heart in a garden than anywhere else on earth.

Gardens were beginning to provide a refuge from reality, giving us the illusion that all was well in the wider natural world.

Interest in gardening ranged from the creation of grand landscapes, among the affluent members of society, to public parks and gardens. Yet during the 20th century the interest in gardening spread to more modest estates in the form of our own small private preserves of lawns, paths and flowerbeds. We created a rural idyll in tens of thousands of suburban plots, but this changing style has been recorded less effectively than the 'grand designs' of such visionaries as Capability Brown. Nonetheless, in North America the Smithsonian Institute owns a priceless collection of about 30,000 colour transparencies of gardens from colonial times to the present, and nearly 3,000 hand-coloured glass lanternslides dating from the 1920s. The Garden Club of America donated these to the Smithsonian in 1992, and the archive has been enhanced by gifts of architectural drawings, plans and personal papers. The archive currently documents gardens in 43 states across North America, with images dating from the early 1890s to the present.

Above: The gardens created in 1765 by 'Capability' Brown at Blenheim Palace near Oxford, in a contemporary depiction. They remain as an enduring legacy of his inspirational work at the height of his achievement.

One of the most recent developments in Britain, realising the need for greenery on our doorsteps, is the concept of the Garden City. A response to chronic urban over-crowding produced by the industrial revolution, it is a town surrounded closely by countryside and designed in such a way that the community owns land and recreational space. The British town planner, Sir Ebenezer Howard (1850–1928) first conceived the idea of the garden city, and among the earliest examples of his inspiration is Letchworth in Hertfordshire, created in 1903. Hampstead followed in 1908 and Welwyn Garden City in 1920. Howard's inspiration was to be emulated across Europe.

In the modern world, we retain a bevy of mystical traditions associated with old plant lore. Sometimes the colour of a flower is still taken as a 'signature' association. Many white flowers are considered unlucky if brought into a house, particularly those that flower in spring. The blossoms of May and Blackthorn are particularly shunned. The reasons are confusing. A white flower may be regarded as a symbol of virginity and purity but, confusingly, it is also linked with death. In ancient times it was believed that death was contagious and it was necessary to take precautions in order that the dead should not get at the living. White, as a symbol of purity, was though to provide the best insurance and this is the underlying reason for the white colour of the traditional funeral shroud.

Other historical traditions have played their part in the linking of white with death. Julius Caesar was assassinated while wearing a white toga and, after his death, white was proclaimed the national colour of mourning throughout the Roman Empire. In Classical Greek mythology the thespian Narcissus was punished by the gods for spurning the love of the water sprite Echo, and died from the boredom of being condemned endlessly to gaze at his own reflection in the waters of Echo's spring. It is from Narcissus that the term narcosis is derived, and the ancient Greeks believed that the flower gave off a perfume that led to headaches and, *in extremis*, death. The underworld goddess, Persephone, is said to have been gathering white flowers in a field when the ground opened and she was abducted forever to the kingdom of Hades. White flowers that hang their heads are particularly identified with death, so white Lilies and Lily-of-the-Valley are favourite flowers not only at weddings but also at funerals. Among the common names for Lily-of-the-Valley is Tears of Our Lady, a Christian association that has it growing where the Virgin Mary wept for Christ.

Predictably, red is a flower colour that has prompted links with blood. The example that comes to mind most readily is that of the red Poppy worn on Armistice Day in remembrance of the fallen in the two World Wars. The association of the red

Poppy (*Papaver rhoeas*) with the fields of Flanders is explained by the opportunist nature of the plant. Its seeds can lie dormant in the soil for many years until the ground is disturbed, whereupon they germinate and flower, producing great swathes of scarlet. The intensive shelling associated with the fairly static trench warfare between 1914 and 1918 produced the ideal conditions needed for germination. It effectively ploughed up vast acres and Poppies took advantage, blooming as never before and becoming the flower of remembrance.

The soldier who first made the connection seems to have been Colonel John McCrae, who went to France as a medical officer with the first Canadian contingent. McCrae died of wounds in May 1918, but three years earlier he had been in charge of a first-aid post during the second battle of Ypres. He wrote a poem that was to become famous and symbolise the suffering and loss of life:

> In Flanders' fields the poppies blow
> Between the crosses, row on row,
> That mark our place; and in the sky
> The larks, still bravely singing, fly
> Scarce heard amid the guns below.
> We are the dead. Short days ago
> We lived, felt dawn, saw sunset glow,
> Loved and were loved, and now we lie
> In Flanders' fields.
> Take up our quarrel with the foe;
> To you from failing hands we throw
> The torch; be yours to hold it high.
> If ye break faith with us who die
> We shall not sleep, though poppies grow
> In Flanders' fields.

The Red Poppy (*Papaver rhoeas*) has become a symbol of the sacrifice made by soldiers during the First World War. They are particularly associated with the battlefields in Flanders.

An American named Moira Michael subsequently composed a moving sequel in response to McCrea's original poem:

> Oh! You who sleep in Flanders' fields
> Sleep sweet – to rise anew,
> We caught the torch you threw,
> And holding high we kept
> The faith of those who died,
> We cherish too, the Poppy red
> That grows on fields where valour led.
> It seems to signal to the skies
> That blood of heroes never dies,
> But lends a lustre to the red
> Of the flower that blooms above the dead
> In Flanders' fields.
> And now the torch and poppy red
> Wear in honour of our dead
> Fear not that ye have died for naught
> We've learned the lesson that ye taught
> In Flanders' fields.

To an extent, our burgeoning romantic interest in plants during the last two centuries, coupled with the scientific fervour for collecting species and cultivating them in ever more elaborate conservatories, is a reaction to the parlous state of affairs in the wider natural world. We have attempted to replace that lost to the growing demands of consumerism. In today's world of nature, the truth is that much of the beauty of the wild countryside has been depleted through advances in agriculture and commercial depredation. Throughout most of Europe, meadows full of flowers are largely distant memories and such places that remain survive as protected sites of scientific interest. In the absence of these pleasures of nature, we have developed our ever-increasing passion for gardening. Unfortunately, the destruction of habitat has also gained ever greater pace to meet the appetite of consumer society for material comforts.

Among the subjects that have captured attention from the media during recent years, that of global warming stands out as one of the most compelling. It is the nightmare concept that our precious earth is heading towards twilight of our own apocalyptic making. Greenhouse gases continue to accumulate in the upper atmosphere and holes are punched in the ozone layer that has stood to guard us from the worst effects of the sun's radiation. The conclusions reached by some climatologists are that, as a consequence of our own short-sightedness, we will slowly suffocate from a build-up of noxious gases or roast to a no less uncomfortable extinction.

Whether or not these predictions are realistic remains in the realms of scientific conjecture. Standing back from the headline-catching aspects and looking at the more distant view, the effect of greenhouse gases may actually be inconsequential when set beside the changes in climate that have occurred naturally in the past and that are destined, in all probability, to occur again. The small rises in temperature currently provoking so much alarm among the prognosticators of doom may also be attributable to other, long-term causes aside from the emissions of carbon dioxide from our industrial machinery. It is clear, on the other hand, that we are wreaking massive and incalculable damage on the earth's environment, the biosphere and its complex, sensitive interactions that sustain all life.

Among the prophets of our future, the French astrologer and seer Michel de Notredame, better known as Nostradamus, has captured our imaginations for almost 500 years with his prognostications of doom. Born in 1503, the obscure predictions he compiled have never been out of print and are still read avidly the world over. Whether Nostradamus was a mad crank or a gifted genius we may never know, but some of his forecasts appear to have materialised and perhaps others will do so in times to come. Among the most provocative of his forecasts is a seemingly nonsensical riddle, yet it is perhaps the awesome prediction of our children's future. In the corrupted French that Nostradamus adopted, it reads as follows:

> La voix ouye de l'insolit oyseau
> Sur le canon du respiral estage:
> Si hault viendra du froment le boisseau
> Que l'homme d'homme sera Antropophage.
>
> (*Quatrain 75. CII*)

In literal translation, this means: 'The call of the strange bird is heard on the pipe of the breathing floor; so high will become the bushels of wheat that man will cannibalise his fellow man.' Nostradamus-watchers have attempted to find obscure meanings for this rhyme, seeking metaphors while ignoring the more literal meaning. If levels of grain stocks were to rise so high in their abundance, we would hardly be faced with the extreme recourse of consuming our neighbours for sustenance. The height to which Nostradamus refers must therefore be one of scarcity, and therefore cost. The 'pipe of the breathing floor' is a chilling yet wholly apt phrase to describe the lungs of the earth, the trees that we are systematically obliterating through unceasing policies of deforestation. Starved of oxygen and water, the most precious commodities given to us by the trees, polluted by the carbon dioxide that they would otherwise cleanse from the air we breathe, Nostradamus predicted that our world will begin to perish. The strange bird, crying in the midst of desolation, can only be the bird of death.

Mutant Message Down Under, a recently published book by the American anthropologist Marlo Morgan, describes, in the form of a novel, her first-hand experience with a nomadic tribe of Aborigines in the Australian outback. If Morgan's report of their attitudes to life proves authentic, this primitive clan would appear to endorse Nostradamus' pessimistic view though they are unlikely to have heard of his medieval prognostications. The tribe, the existence of which is denied by the Australian government, represents all that is left of the pure indigenous culture of the continent, and its links with the natural world are among the closest to be found anywhere. With shocking implication, its people have adopted voluntary celibacy. The conviction of the tribe is that the world sustaining their very existence is dying. Water is becoming impossible to find in the outback and the animals and plants on which they have relied since time immemorial are disappearing so that the tribespeople can no longer find adequate nourishment. They recognise a certainty that the living earth is dying and they propose to die with it. Here, in one trenchant example, the utilitarian and the mystical strength of the green mantle is being blended inextricably into a single entity.

The 20th century will go down as an era in which the human race did more to destroy the natural environment than at any other time in history. The pace at which the materialist northern hemisphere systematically raped the Third World of its resources increased dramatically, while the burgeoning consumer society treated environmental considerations with little short of contempt. Humankind had come to believe in the empirical ability of science to resolve its problems and meet its needs. The acceleration began in the 19th century. As spiritual attitudes shifted, fleeing from day-to-day magic towards the seductive assurances of technology, nature also became subjugated to predacious demands for economic progress and consumerism. Irrespective of the consequences, exploitation of the green world replaced any remaining vestiges of reverence. Now, in the 21st century, we face the real possibility of a global catastrophe that, in spite of modern sophistication, technology is powerless to prevent, and against which science cannot formulate a solution. Already warning signs are in place. Countries the world over are experiencing unusually severe climatic conditions. Ironically (or perhaps fortuitously if we are not too late to make amends), these are precisely the circumstances in which the human psyche tends to revert away from dependence on materialism and back to an age-old reliance on mysticism and divine providence.

For the first time since the days of the Roman Empire, when the process of insulating ourselves from the land, abandoning reverence for the natural world in favour of comfort and urban chic, truly gained pace, signs are emerging of a new-found respect for our precious environment. Green political parties are now established in many European countries. Others indicate a similar trend. International organisations, including Friends of the Earth and others, have the ability to motivate governments in a way that 50 years ago would have been impossible. Eco-warriors are no longer exclusively dropouts on the fringe of society but have become a genuine force among large numbers of middle-class people.

A year 2000 survey in the United Kingdom, commissioned by the wild-plant conservation charity Plantlife, entitled 'Where have all the flowers gone?' makes for sober reading. The report, by British environmentalist Peter Marren, focuses on the situation in the UK, but it serves as a blueprint for the rest of Europe and, indeed, for global trends. It emphasises that the plight of wild plants is worse than anyone has imagined. Common species are growing scarcer and, at the same time, scarce species are dying out altogether as the countryside suffers relentless erosion of its botanical diversity. As the report points out, local extinction is accumulating with the portent of countryside gradually stripped of its ability to inspire, delight and surprise.

Until recently statistics on the extinction of wild plants have not been widely publicised, but it is revealed that at least 21 species of native flowering plant have become extinct in Britain alone during the last 150 years. Within local areas of the UK the figures are worse. The worst-hit counties are losing more than one species every year. Orchids, some of the most beautiful of all wild flowers, are disappearing at a county level at the alarming rate of one per decade. Yet here, too, conservationists are marshalling forces to redress the downward trend. Governments, industry and the public are being urged to take action. The proposals include reversal of agricultural intensification, prevention of habitat destruction and neglect, tackling environmental pollution and countering the threat posed by non-native invasive species. Organisations such as Plantlife are also stressing the need to obtain adequate data about native plants and to undertake relevant research.

Overleaf: Increasing loss of plant habitats leads to extinction of flora species.
Without more awareness of the need for protection, even the still profuse and
thriving harbinger of Spring, the Snowdrop (*Galanthus nivalis*), will begin to disappear.

The principle that 'all flesh is grass' is one the human race is becoming increasingly aware of, as ecological disaster looms. In Africa, we are already seeing more than mere hints of what may come globally as a consequence of destruction of rainforests. Of the 14.9 billion hectares (37 billion acres) of land that cover the earth's surface, a recent United Nations Environmental Programme revealed that 6.1 billion hectares (15 billion acres) constitute dry land of which 1 billion hectares (2.5 billion acres) are naturally very arid, classed as desert. There is, however, a serious problem in that the remainder of the dry land has either become desert or is currently evolving into desert. Other than isolated oases that sustain Date Palms, little can survive in these vast areas of shifting sand, high winds and searing temperatures that can reach 55°C (130°F) or more in the shade. The impact of the loss of the green mantle in these areas can be judged in the statistic that a quarter of the world's population lives within them and depends on them for livelihood.

> *The principle that 'all flesh is grass' is one the human race is becoming increasingly aware of, as ecological disaster looms.*

The sub-Sahara is now encroaching ever further southwards, year on year turning what was once fertile and life-sustaining land into desert. As a result, millions of people starve in the Horn of Africa. Among the strongest concerns of environmentalists at the turn of the 21st century is the damage that is being wrought to an area of West Africa, mainly in Mauritania, Mali, Niger and Chad, known as the Sahel. This forms a broad band of savannah separating the desert from the more tropical vegetation to the south. Its make-up is changing dramatically as a consequence of agricultural mis-use and deforestation. It is a misconception that the southern edge of the Sahara is encroaching universally on the Sahel because there is still a green belt of reasonably stable vegetation between the two. Within recent memory, however, the Sahel farming region has become noticeably drier with lighter and more erratic rains. Furthermore, parts of the green belt have been put at risk. The change is believed to have arisen because of the practice of slashing and burning, whereby natural forest and bush is cleared for agriculture. Perennial plants that used to shelter annual crops, mainly of Millet, are destroyed in the process.

A damaging progression probably began in colonial days when farmers were encouraged to cultivate peanuts in order to generate revenue for taxation. Peanut farming continued until the 1970s when crop diseases forced a reversion to Millet growing. In the Millet fields the situation is aggravated further by the practice of cutting and burning the stalks after harvest. This practice leaves little vegetation to prevent the wind from eroding the topsoil. Grain yields are now substantially reduced and it has been calculated that, in Niger alone, 2,500 square kilometres (965 square miles) are being lost each year where once-fertile land has become desert. If the green belt becomes sufficiently damaged by slash-and-burn, there will be nothing to stop the Sahara desert engulfing the whole region, and a terrible 'domino effect' will have been set in motion.

A similar story is unfolding in South America. The deforestation of the Amazon rainforest through short-sighted commercial logging exacerbated by local slash-and-burn practices is causing massive loss of soil fertility, and already having a serious effect on the lives of local populations. Off the east coast of Africa, the almost total deforestation of such unique repositories of wildlife as Madagascar, the island in the Indian Ocean once a safe haven for scores of species found nowhere else on earth, has become an environmental catastrophe. Similar destructive trends are taking place in the rest of central Africa and the jungles of southeast Asia.

There can be few more trenchant demonstrations of the growing concern about the future of the green mantle than the work of the Eden Foundation. Begun in 1985 and based in Sweden and Norway as an international, non-governmental organisation focused on arresting the ecological disaster taking place in West Africa, it operates from Zinder in the Tanout region of Niger. The policy of the Eden Foundation has been to reverse the deforestation there. It has demonstrated to farmers the importance of protecting their fields from erosion by planting perennials that will in turn, allow healthier growth of annuals and higher crop yields from smaller areas of cultivation. From 1991, local farmers have been provided with start-up material suitable for direct seeding of perennials that will encourage natural re-afforestation through seed dispersal and maturation of old rootstocks. The long-term intention is to abandon wasteful practices and allow the return of natural vegetation by introducing plants that will germinate and thrive in the present depleted conditions.

Much of the stimulus for change in our attitudes towards the green mantle was generated in 1992 at the so-called Earth Summit that took place in Rio de Janiero. More correctly known as the United Nations Conference for Environment and Development, its aim was to build a framework for the future based on sustainable growth – socially acceptable, economically viable and, no less vital, ecologically sound. Within the scope of conference agreements, Agenda 21 demanded a global consensus among governments that would produce strategies for sustainable development through widespread public participation. It resulted in the Convention on Biological Diversity, demanding national commitments to conserve the diversity of all life from genes to species and ecosystems, and to use biological resources in a sustainable manner. Another no less pertinent outcome was the Framework Convention on Climatic Change. In practice, initiatives were put in place, through individuals, local communities and commercial enterprises, to create a partnership for change and to make Agenda 21 a working reality. This, however, has suffered a recent setback in the failure of a crucial world summit during 2000 aimed at controlling emission of greenhouse gases and in the new Bush administration's rejection of the same in the USA.

One of the initiatives arising out of the Rio Conference was a visionary project with a title confusingly similar to that of the Eden Foundation. Known as the Eden Project it has been developed in England as the brainchild of Tim Smit who previously recreated the Lost Gardens of Heligan. Although still in its comparative infancy, the project is, in the words of its creators, a true symbol of humankind's desire to shift from exploitation to conservation, from fear to hope and from isolated efforts to genuine humanitarian science and engineering. Begun in 1997 as an international resource set on the Cornish Riviera of southern England, it was opened in the spring of 2001. Established in a disused china clay pit at Bodelva to the east of St Austell, the purpose is to reproduce under one roof the full range of natural plant habitats found on our planet. The Eden Project has been funded at an initial cost of £75 million, of which the Millennium Commission has contributed some £37 million with £27 million coming from the private sector and other grants. It is fast becoming a showcase of global biodiversity and human dependence on plants. The Project is open to visitors but, more importantly, this type of advanced facility is essential if botanists and ecologists are to understand the complexities of plant biodiversity and sustainable development. One of the main objectives is to improve communication and exchange of ideas about humankind's dependence on plants and to convey these basics to the widest possible audience. The Project emphasises that our dependence on the botanical kingdom is not purely materialistic but a matter of the senses. It draws attention to the links between plants and music, plants and health, plants and art, all of which constitute part of what its creators describe as our global 'garden inheritance'.

Twelve hectares (30 acres), an area roughly the size of 30 football pitches, is being covered progressively by linked and climatically controlled transparent capsules known as biomes. These provide for the conservation of entire plant populations rather than individual species. Within the Eden Project, four key climatic regions have been repro-

duced: rainforest, semi-desert, subtropics and Mediterranean. So vast is the scale of the Project that, around the south-facing wall of the pit, the Humid Tropic Biome will be able to contain fully developed trees such as Teak and Mahogany, along with some of the world's most dramatic tropical flora. More specifically, the initiatives of the Project include Atlantic rainforest conservation, biodiversity studies in the Seychelles and at Cape Fynbos in South Africa, field-based ethnobotany studies in Guyana, forest ecology in Malaysia and, closer to home, heathland restoration in conjunction with English Nature.

In medical terms, too, we are undergoing a radical shift in thinking, returning to old reliance on proven herbal therapies, as modern drugs such as antibiotics stand poised to fail us through over-dependence and misuse. The value of herbalism is being

Above: Final stages of construction work in progress on one of the massive biome capsules of the Eden Project at Bodelva, near St Austell in Cornwall. Brainchild of Tim Smit, the site was opened to the public in late 2000.

recognised increasingly to set right the internal harmony of our bodies, to rectify the 'dis-ease' manifested in sickness, as the shortcomings of modern pharmaceuticals become clear. We have seen that archaeology has revealed not only medicinal but also ritual use of plants that extends back at least 60,000 years to the time of our Neanderthal ancestors. Today, as with herbal remedies, it is not only Aborigines and the survivors of other ancient cultures who turn to sacred amber and musk, sandalwood and frangipani – people the world over are finding once more a spiritual belief in the plant world. In town apartments, suburban homes and country cottages throughout the technologically advanced world, herbs, spices and resins are being gathered for other than utilitarian needs in the kitchen, the bathroom and the make-up drawer. In echoes of times past, these same ingredients find a new purpose. In a purely spiritual sense we may associate smudge sticks of Pine, Cedar, Sage and Lavender with witches' altars but nowadays they are a scarcely less familiar sight smouldering in city offices, healing rooms and homes across North America and much of Europe.

Once upon a time, humankind believed that disregard for nature, abuse of the green mantle, would bring down the wrath of heaven.

Once upon a time, humankind believed that disregard for nature, abuse of the green mantle, would bring down the wrath of heaven. Plants were the homes of spirits. Trees were symbols of holiness. Ideas of the kind became quaint and passé. Yet today, as the consequences of our folly become clear, we are beginning a return to similar sentiments and increasingly we are giving them an underlying moral message.

From the 1950s onwards, one can detect the hint of a salutary lesson on the consequences of tampering with nature. John Wyndham's futuristic science fiction novel *The Day of the Triffids*, published in 1951 and made into a memorable British film some ten years later, envisaged an horrific situation in which man-eating plants began to take over the world of vulnerable citizens ostensibly blinded by a virulent lightning storm. The underlying theme was that of a society that was blind in a more general sense, unable to change for the better and incapable of realising external threats with any degree of effectiveness. In the 1950s a similarly nightmarish prospect formed the thrust of a popular classic made by London-based Hammer Films, *The Quatermass Experiment*. London became threatened by the mutation of an astronaut whose space voyage had suffered mishap under alien influences, turning him into a half-man, half-cactus. Albeit in more garish and humorous vein, the cult film *The Little Shop of Horrors*, made in 1960 by Roger Corman and later in the 1980s turned into a musical, indulged a similar theme. The hapless employee of a small-town grocery store was obliged to nurture a giant talking and singing plant that thrived only on a diet of blood. The animated monster vegetable was clearly modelled on a real-life carnivorous species, *Nepenthes*, the Pitcher Plant.

As I look out of my office window, deep in the heart of the Devonshire countryside in the west of England, the fields are green, and great Oaks and Ashes, though bare and spectral in the gloom and mist of winter, still stand proudly. Yet some of the trees are dead, victims of a massive summer drought a few years back. Currently we have witnessed a month of December in which storm and deluge are unparalleled in living memory. Temperatures are twice the seasonal normal for this time of year and flowers that should be deep in their winter sleep are blooming. All is not well with the green mantle of England. The television news this morning has brought images of the American Mid-West paralysed by freak and abnormally early blizzards. On a recent visit to southern Sweden, I drove for hundreds of miles through man-made forests of conifer and birch, seemingly glorious in their autumnal finery. Yet closer inspection revealed that large areas were showing the first ominous signs of sickness through acid rain. Large parts of Europe still bear the scars, only visible in part, of nuclear fallout from Chernobyl. The soil will be infected for many decades to come as radioactive caesium expends its noxious energy.

Yes, I am fearful for the green world of my children's children. On the other hand, in certain key respects, we have come a long way from 1922 when Sir James Frazer penned his formidable overview of magic and religion in nature, *The Golden Bough*. Frazer did not possess the awareness of the damage that his generation and generations to come were inflicting on the biosphere. The very word had not been invented. *The Golden Bough* is an idyll on a world that was already well on the way to being lost. It is a sentimental journey through a dying landscape. It speaks of time-honoured traditions in the green, yet nowhere among its pages does the subject of conservation emerge. We, on the other hand, have the knowledge. We know the score. It remains to be seen if we possess the wit and wisdom to use it well.

Bibliography

Allegro, John, *The Sacred Mushroom and the Cross*, Hodder (1970)

Culpeper, Nicholas, *The British Herbal and Family Physician*, Milner, London (1652)

Frazer, Sir James G., *The Golden Bough*, Macmillan (1983)

Gerard, John, *The Herball* (1597)

Graves, Robert, *The White Goddess*, Faber (1961)

Baker M., *The Folklore of Plants*, Shire, (1971)

Bentham and Hooker, *Handbook of the British Flora*, Reeve (1954)

Grimal, P., *Dictionary of Classical Mythology*, Penguin (1991)

Hollander, Lee, *The Poetic Edda*, Texas University Press (1962)

Jordan, M., *The Encyclopedia of Gods*, Kyle Cathie (1992)

Jordan, M., *Eastern Wisdom*, Carlton (1997)

Jordan, M., *Plants of Mystery and Magic*, Cassell (2001)

Keble Martin, W., *The New Concise British Flora*, Ebury Press/Michael Joseph (1982)

Skinner, C.M., *Myths and Legends of Flowers, Trees, Fruits and Plants*, Philadelphia (1911)

Thistleton-Dyer, T.E., *The Folklore of Plants*, London (1889)

Vickery, R.A.A., *Dictionary of Plant Lore*, Oxford University Press (1995)

Illustration Credits

General Index

Page numbers in *italics* refer to illustrations

Plant Species Index